The first and most profitable of all arts is agriculture.

THE COMPLETE WORKS

OF

JAMES WHITCOMB RILEY

IN SIX VOLUMES

The Old Swimmin' Hole

THE COMPLETE WORKS

OF

JAMES WHITCOMB RILEY

IN WHICH THE POEMS, INCLUDING A NUMBER HERETOFORE UNPUBLISHED,
ARE ARRANGED IN THE ORDER IN WHICH THEY WERE WRITTEN,
TOGETHER WITH PHOTOGRAPHS, BIBLIOGRAPHIC NOTES
AND A LIFE SKETCH OF THE AUTHOR

COLLECTED AND EDITED BY
EDMUND HENRY EITEL

BIOGRAPHICAL EDITION
VOLUME TWO

INDIANAPOLIS
THE BOBBS-MERRILL COMPANY
PUBLISHERS

PRESS OF
BRAUNWORTH & CO.
BOOKBINDERS AND PRINTERS
BROOKLYN, N. Y.

CONTENTS

CONTENTS

CONTENTS

CONTENTS

CONTENTS

CONTENTS

CONTENTS

CONTENTS

THE COMPLETE WORKS

OF

JAMES WHITCOMB RILEY

IN SIX VOLUMES

WHEN I DO MOCK

WHEN I do mock the blackness of the night
    With my despair—outweep the very dews
And wash my wan cheeks stark of all delight,
    Denying every counsel of dear use
In mine embittered state; with infinite
    Perversity, mine eyes drink in no sight
Of pleasance that nor moon nor stars refuse
    In silver largess and gold twinklings bright;—
I question me what mannered brain is mine
    That it doth trick me of the very food
It panteth for—the very meat and wine
    That yet should pump my starved soul with
        good
And comfortable plethora of ease,
That I might drowse away such rhymes as these.

EZRA HOUSE

[These lines was writ, in ruther high sperits, jest at the close of what's called the Anti Bellum Days, and more to be a-foolin' than anything else,—though they is more er less facts in it. But some of the boys, at the time we was all a-singin' it, fer Ezry's benefit, to the old tune of "The Oak and the Ash and the Bonny Willer Tree," got it struck off in the weekly, without leave er lisence of mine; and so sence they's allus some of 'em left to rigg me about it yit, I might as well claim the thing right here and now, so here goes. I give it jest as it appeard, fixed up and grammatisized consider'ble, as the editer told me he took the liburty of doin', in that sturling old home paper THE ADVANCE—*as sound a paper yit to-day and as stanch and abul as you'll find in a hunderd.]*

COME listen, good people, while a story I do tell,
   Of the sad fate of one which I knew so pass-
      ing well;
He enlisted at McCordsville, to battle in the South,
And protect his country's union; his name was
      Ezra House.

He was a young school-teacher, and educated high
In regards to Ray's arithmetic, and also Algebra:
He give good satisfaction, but at his country's call
He dropped his position, his Algebra and all.

2

"It's oh, I'm going to leave you, kind scholars," he
    said—
For he wrote a composition the last day and read;
And it brought many tears in the eyes of the school,
To say nothing of his sweetheart he was going to
    leave so soon.

"I have many recollections to take with me away,
Of the merry transpirations in the schoolroom so
    gay;
And of all that's past and gone I will never regret
I went to serve my country at the first of the out-
    set!"

He was a good penman, and the lines that he wrote
On that sad occasion was too fine for me to quote,—
For I was there and heard it, and I ever will recall
It brought the happy tears to the eyes of us all.

And when he left, his sweetheart she fainted away.
And said she could never forget the sad day
When her lover so noble, and galliant and gay,
Said "Fare you well, my true love!" and went
    marching away.

But he hadn't been gone for more than two months,
When the sad news come—"he was in a skirmish
    once,
And a cruel Rebel ball had wounded him full sore
In the region of the chin, through the canteen he
    wore."

But his health recruited up, and his wounds they
     got well,
But whilst he was in battle at Bull Run or Malvern
     Hill,
The news come again, so sorrowful to hear—
"A sliver from a bombshell cut off his right ear."

But he stuck to the boys, and it's often he would
     write,
That "he wasn't afraid for his country to fight."
But oh, had he returned on a furlough, I believe
He would not, to-day, have such cause to grieve.

For in another battle—the name I never heard—
He was guarding the wagons when an accident oc-
     curred,—
A comrade who was under the influence of drink,
Shot him with a musket through the right cheek, I
     think.

But his dear life was spared; but it hadn't been for
     long,
Till a cruel Rebel colonel come riding along,
And struck him with his sword, as many do sup-
     pose,
For his cap-rim was cut off, and also his nose.

But Providence, who watches o'er the noble and the
     brave,
Snatched him once more from the jaws of the
     grave;

And just a little while before the close of the war,
He sent his picture home to his girl away so far.

And she fell into decline, and she wrote in reply,
"She had seen his face again and was ready to die";
And she wanted him to promise, when she was in
    her tomb,
He would only visit that by the light of the moon.

But he never returned at the close of the war,
And the boys that got back said he hadn't the heart;
But he got a position in a powder-mill, and said
He hoped to meet the doom that his country denied.

THE VISION OF RABBI BEN ISAAC

FOR three score years my wandering feet have
    strayed
  Along a path wherein no footprint lay
Of Him, who of the cross a guide-board made
    To point me out the way.

With open eyes I dreamed that I was dead—
  Dead to all outward semblance, though I lay
With some old scrap of reason in my head
    That would not fade away.

And peering up in wonderment I saw
  My floating spirit plume its wings elate,
Yet gazing upward with a look of awe,
    It seemed to hesitate.

"Go on!" I called to it. "Leap into space,
  And sweep a way to glory with thy wings!"
"Alas!" it answered back, with troubled face,
    "They are such trembling things!"

And hovering above me, spread them wide,
　　And all their glossy plumage o'er my eyes
Shook out in downy splendor, crimson-dyed
　　With hues of Paradise.

"Nay, glorious things are they," I cried amazed,
　　And veiled my vision from their dazzling light—
"So, get thee gone—their maker must be praised"—
　　And upward through the night

It lifted like a meteor, and sailed
　　Across the gulf of darkness like a flame,
While down the smoldering wake behind it trailed
　　The ashes of my name.

It called to me—not larger than a flake
　　Of starlight did it glimmer through the gloom—
"Pray for me," fell the voice, "for Jesus' sake!
　　I see the heavens bloom."

And loathful to myself I whispered then,
　　As wholly from my gaze the glimmer went—
"O Lord, through Christ, receive my soul, Amen."
　　And like an instrument

Of music in some heavenly tumult tipped,
　　Outpouring the elixir of its voice,
Down-showering upon my senses dripped
　　The utterance, "Rejoice!

"God listens, for the angels at the door
   Are swarming out and in and out again,
And o'er and round about me evermore
   They sing 'Good will to men!' "

Then suddenly the voice in quaverings
   Fell wailingly—"Alas! for I alone
Of all the glorious throng have tarnished wings
   That Heaven will not own.

"The angel Truth has pityingly said
   That every plume impure Christ will condemn,
And that the stain self-righteousness is red
   As blood on all of them."

Then to my soul I cried aloud: "Return
   That I may bow my head in holier prayer,
And all the recompense of good I earn
   Shall blossom everywhere."

"Not so." It answered, as in some surprise—
   "The angel Faith has whispered 'Look above,'
And shading with her wings my dazzled eyes,
   Points out the angel Love,

"Who, weeping, bends above me, and her tears
   Baptize me, and her sister Mercy trips
Along the golden clouds, and Christ appears
   With sorrow on His lips"—

Then silence, and as one who vainly wars
  With inner strife: "Come back to me!" I cried,
And pealing down a pathway of the stars
  A ringing voice replied—

"Now is thy soul's probation so complete
  It may but answer thee with one farewell;"
And, filtered through the gloom, lo! at my feet
  A snow-white feather fell.

DAN PAINE

OLD friend of mine, whose chiming name
   Has been the burthen of a rhyme
Within my heart since first I came
   To know thee in thy mellow prime:
     With warm emotions in my breast
     That can but coldly be expressed,
     And hopes and wishes wild and vain,
     I reach my hand to thee, Dan Paine.

In fancy, as I sit alone
   In gloomy fellowship with care,
I hear again thy cheery tone,
   And wheel for thee an easy chair;
     And from my hand the pencil falls—
     My book upon the carpet sprawls,
     As eager soul and heart and brain
     Leap up to welcome thee, Dan Paine.

A something gentle in thy mien,
   A something tender in thy voice,
Has made my trouble so serene,
   I can but weep, from very choice.

And even then my tears, I guess,
Hold more of sweet than bitterness,
And more of gleaming shine than rain,
Because of thy bright smile, Dan Paine.

The wrinkles that the years have spun
  And tangled round thy tawny face,
Are kinked with laughter, every one,
  And fashioned in a mirthful grace.
    And though the twinkle of thine eyes
    Is keen as frost when Summer dies,
    It can not long as frost remain
    While thy warm soul shines out, Dan Paine.

And so I drain a health to thee:—
  May merry Joy and jolly Mirth
Like children clamber on thy knee,
  And ride thee round the happy earth!
    And when, at last, the hand of Fate
    Shall lift the latch of Canaan's gate,
    And usher me in thy domain,
    Smile on me just as now, Dan Paine.

OLD HEC'S IDOLATRY

HEIGH-O! our jolly tilts at New World
    song!—
What was the poem indeed! and where the bard—
"Stabbing his ink-pot ever, not his heart,"
As Hector phrased it contumeliously,
Mouthing and munching, at the orchard-stile,
A water-cored rambo whose spirted juice
Glanced, sprayed and flecked the sunlight as he
    mouth'd
And muncht, and muncht and mouth'd. All loved
    the man!
"Our Hector" as his *Alma Mater* oozed
It into utterance—"Old Hec" said we
Who knew him, hide-and-tallow, hoof-and-horn!
So he: "O ay! my soul! our New World song—
The tweedle-deedles of our modern school—
A school of minnows,—not one gamy bass—
To hook the angler, not the angler him.
Here! all ye little fishes: tweedle-dee!
Soh! one—along the vasty stream of time—
Glints to the surface with a gasp,—and, lo,
A bubble! and he thinks, 'My eye!—see there,
Ye little fishes,—there's a song I've sung!'

Another gapes: another bubble; then
He thinks: 'Well, is it not a wondrous art
To breathe a great immortal poem like that!'
And then another—and another still—
And yet another,—till from brim to brim
The tide is postuled over with a pest
Of bubbles—bursting bubbles! Ay! O ay!"
So, bluff old Hec. And we, who knew his mood
Had ramped its worst—unless we roused it yet
To ire's horiffickest insanity
By some inane, unguarded reference
To "verse beragged in Hoosier dialect"—
(A strangely unforgotten coinage of
Old Hec's, long years agone)—we, so, forbore
A word, each glimpsing each, as down we sank,
Couched limply in the orchard's selvage, where—
The rambo finished and the soggy core
Zippt at a sapphire wasp with waist more slim
Than any slender lady's, of old wars,
Pent fasting for long sennights in tall towers
That overtop the undercringing seas—
With one accordant voice, the while he creased
His scroll of manuscript, we said, "Go on."
Then Hector thus:

AN IDYL OF THE KING

Erewhile, as Autumn, to King Arthur's court
Came Raelus, clamoring: "Lo, has our house
Been sacked and pillaged by a lawless band

Of robber knaves, led on by Alstanés,
The Night-Flower named, because of her fair face,
All like a lily gleaming in the dusk
Of her dark hair—and like a lily brimmed
With dewy eyes that drip their limpid smiles
Like poison out, for by them has been wro't
My elder brother's doom, as much I fear.
While three days gone was holden harvest-feast
At Lynion Castle—clinging like a gull
High up the gray cliffs of Caerleon—
Came, leaf-like lifted from the plain below
As by a twisted wind, a rustling pack
Of bandit pillagers, with Alstanés
Bright-fluttering like a red leaf in the front.
And ere we were aware of fell intent—
Not knowing whether it was friend or foe—
We found us in their toils, and all the house
In place of guests held only prisoners—
Save that the host, my brother, wro't upon
By the strange beauty of the robber queen,
Was left unfettered, but by silken threads
Of fine-spun flatteries and wanton smiles
Of the enchantress, till her villain thieves
Had rifled as they willed and signal given
To get to horse again. And so they went—
Their leader flinging backward, as she rode,
A kiss to my mad brother—mad since then,—
For from that sorry hour he but talked
Of Alstanés, and her rare beauty, and
Her purity—ay, even that he said

Was star-white, and should light his life with love
Or leave him groping blindly in its quest
Thro' all eternity. So, sighing, he
Went wandering about till set of sun,
Then got to horse, and bade us all farewell;
And with his glamoured eyes bent trancedly
Upon the tumbled sands that marked the way
The robber-woman went, he turned and chased
His long black shadow o'er the edge of night."

—So Raelus, all seemingly befret
With such concern as nipped his utterance
In scraps of speech: at which Sir Lancelot,
Lifting a slow smile to the King, and then
Turning his cool eye on the youth—"And you
Would track this siren-robber to her hold
And rout her rascal followers, and free
Your brother from the meshes of this queen
Of hearts—for there you doubtless think him?"
     "Ay!"
Foamed Raelus, cheek flushed and eye aflame,—
"So even have I tracked, and found them, too,
And know their burrow, shrouded in a copse,
Where, faring in my brother's quest, I heard
The nicker of his horse, and followed on,
And found him tethered in a thicket wild,
As tangled in its tress of leaf and limb
As is a madman's hair; and down the path
That parted it and ran across a knoll
And dipped again, all suddenly I came

Upon a cave, wide-yawning 'neath a beard
Of tangled moss and vine, whence issuing
I heard, blown o'er my senses faint and clear
As whiffs of summer wind, my brother's voice
Lilting a love-song, with the burden tricked
With dainty warblings of a woman's tongue:
And even as I listening bent, I heard
Such peals of wanton merriment as made
My own heart flutter as a bird that beats
For freedom at the bars that prison it.
So turned I then and fled as one who flies
To save himself alone—forgetful all
Of that my dearer self—my brother.—O!"—
Breaking as sharply as the icy blade
That loosens from the eave to slice the air
And splinter into scales of flying frost—
"Thy help! Thy help! A dozen goodly knights—
Ay, even that, if so it be their hearts
Are hungry as my own to right the wrong!"

So Raelus. And Arthur graciously
Gave ear to him, and, patient, heard him thro',
And pitied him, and granted all he asked;
Then took his hand and held it, saying, "Strong
And ever stronger may its grasp be knit
About the sword that flashes in the cause
Of good."
          Thus Raelus, on the morrow's front,
Trapped like a knight and shining like a star,
Pranced from the archway of the court, and led

His glittering lances down the gleaming road
That river-like ran winding till it slipped
Out of the palace view and spilled their shields
Like twinkling bubbles o'er the mountain brim.

Then happed it that as Raelus rode, his tongue
Kept even pace and cantered ever on
Right merrily.   His brother, as he said,
Had such an idle soul within his breast—
Such shallowness of fancy for his heart
To drift about in—that he well believed
Its anchor would lay hold on any smile
The lees of womanhood might offer him.
As for himself, he loved his brother well,
Yet had far liefer see him stark and white
In marble death than that his veins should burn
With such vitality as spent its flame
So garishly it knew no steady blaze,
But ever wavered round as veered the wind
Of his conceit; for he had made his boast—
Tho' to his own shame did he speak of it—
That with a wink he could buy every smile
That virtue owned.   So tattled Raelus
Till, heated with his theme, he lifted voice
And sang the song, "The Light of Woman's Eyes!"

"O bright is gleaming morn on mountain height;
And bright the moon, slipt from its sheath of
        night,—
    But brighter is the light of woman's eyes.

"And bright the dewdrop, trembling on the lip
Of some red rose, or lily petal-tip,
  Or lash of pink,—but brighter woman's eyes.

"Bright is the firefly's ever-drifting spark
That throbs its pulse of light out in the dark;
  And bright the stars,—but brighter woman's eyes.

"Bright morn or even; bright or moon or star,
And all the many twinkling lights that are,—
  O brighter than ye all are woman's eyes."

So Raelus sang.—And they who rode with him
Bewildered were, and even as he sang
Went straggling, twos and threes, and fell behind
To whisper wonderingly, "Is he a fool?"
And "Does he waver in his mind?" and "Does
The newness of adventure dazzle him?"
So spake they each to each, till far beyond,
With but one loathful knight in company,
They saw him quit the beaten track, and turn
Into the grassy margin of a wood.
And loitering, they fell in mocking jest
Of their strange leader! "See! why, see!" said
    one,—
"He needs no help to fight his hornets' nest,
But one brave knight to squire him!"—pointing on
To where fared on the two and disappeared.
"O ay!" said one, "belike he is some old
War-battered knight of long-forgotten age,
That, bursting from his chrysalis, the grave,

Comes back to show us tricks we never dreamed!"
"Or haply," said another, with a laugh,—
"He rides ahead to tell them that he comes
And shrive them ere his courage catches up."
And merry made they all, and each in turn
Filliped a witty pellet at his head:
Until, at last, their shadows shrunk away
And shortened 'neath them and the hour was noon,
They flung them from their horses listlessly
Within the grassy margin of the wood
Where had passed Raelus an hour agone:
And, hungered, spied a rustic; and they sent
To have them such refreshment as might be
Found at the nearest farm,—where, as it chanced,
Was had most wholesome meat, and milk, and
    bread;
And honey, too, celled in its fretted vase
Of gummy gold and dripping nectar-sweet
As dreamed-of kisses from the lips of love;
Wine, too, was broughten, rosy as the dawn
That ushers in the morning of the heart;
And tawny, mellow pear, whose golden ore
Fell molten on the tongue and oozed away
In creamy and delicious nothingness;
And netted melon, musky as the breath
Of breezes blown from out the Orient;
And purple clusterings of plum and grape,
Blurred with a dust dissolving at the touch
Like flakes the fairies had snowed over them.
And as the idlers basked, with toast and song
And graceful dalliance and wanton jest,

A sound of trampling hooves and jingling reins
Brake sudden, stilled them; and from out a dim
Path leading from the bosky wood there came
A troop of mounted damsels, nigh a score,
Led by a queenly girl, in crimson clad,
With lissome figure lithe and willowy,
And face as fair and sweet and pure withal
As might a maiden lily-blossom be
Ere it has learned the sin of perfect bloom:
Her hair, blown backward like a silken scarf
And fondled by the sun, was glossier
And bluer black than any raven's wing.
"And O!" she laughed, not knowing she was heard
By any but her fellows: "Men are fools!"
Then drawing rein, and wheeling suddenly,
Her charger mincing backward,—"Raelus—
My Raelus is greater than ye all,
Since he is such a fool that he forgets
He is a man, and lets his tongue of love
Run babbling like a silly child's; and, pah!
I puff him to the winds like thistle-down!"
And, wheeling as she spake, found staring up,
Wide-eyed and wondering, a group of knights,
Half lifted, as their elbows propped their heads,
Half lying; and one, smirker than the rest,
Stood bowing very low, with upturned eyes
Lit with a twinkling smile: "Fair lady—and
Most gracious gentlewomen"—seeing that
The others drew them back as tho' abashed
And veiled their faces with all modesty,
Tho' she, their leader, showed not any qualm,—

"Since all unwittingly we overheard
Your latest speech, and since we know at last
'All men are fools,' right glad indeed am I
That such a nest of us remains for you
To vanquish with those eyes." Then, serious,
That she nor smiled nor winced, nor anything—
"Your pardon will be to me as a shower
Of gracious rain unto a panting drouth."
So bowed in humblest reverence; at which
The damsel, turning to her followers,
Laughed musically,—"See! he proves my words!"
Whereat the others joined with inward glee
Her pealing mirth; and in the merriment
The knights chimed, too, and he, the vanquished one,
Till all the wood rang as at hunting-tide
When bugle-rumors float about the air
And echoes leap and revel in delight.
Then spake the vanquished knight, with mental eye
Sweeping the vantage-ground that chance had
        gained,—
"Your further pardon, lady: Since the name
Of Raelus fell from those lips of thine,
We fain would know of him. He led us here,
And as he went the way wherefrom your path
Emerges, haply you may tell us where
He may be found?"

                    "What! Raelus?" she cried,—
"He comes with you?—The brave Sir Raelus?—
That mighty champion?—that gallant knight?—
That peerless wonder of all nobleness?
Then proud am I to greet ye, knowing that;

And, certes, had I known of it ere now,
Then had I proffered you more courtesy
And told you, ere the asking, that he bides
The coming of his friends a league from this,
Hard by a reedy mere, where in high tune
We left him singing, nigh an hour agone."
Then, as she lightly wheeled her horse about
And signal gave to her companions
To follow, gaily cried: "Tell Raelus
His cousin sends to him her sad farewells
And fond regrets, and kisses many as
His valorous deeds are numbered in her heart."
And with "Fair morrow to ye, gentle knights!"
Her steed's hooves struck the highway at a bound;
And dimly thro' the dust they saw her lead
Her fluttering cavalcade as recklessly
As might a queen of Araby, fleet-horsed,
Skim o'er the level sands of Syria.
So vanished. And the knights with one accord
Put foot in stirrup, and, with puzzled minds
And many-channeled marvelings, filed in
The woody path, and fared them on and on
Thro' denser glooms, and ways more intricate;
Till, mystified at last and wholly lost,
They made full halt, and would have turned them
    back
But that a sudden voice brake on their ears
All piteous and wailing, as distressed:
And, following these cries, they sharply came
Upon an open road that circled round
A reedy flat and sodden tract of sedge,

Moated with stagnant water, crusted thick
With slimy moss, wherein were wriggling things
Entangled, and blind bubbles bulging up
And bursting where from middle way upshot
A tree-trunk, with its knarled and warty hands
As tho' upheld to clutch at sliding snakes
Or nip the wet wings of the dragon-fly.
Here gazing, lo! they saw their comrade, he
That had gone on with Raelus; and he
Was tugging to fling back into its place
A heavy log that once had spanned the pool
And made a footway to the sedgy flat
Whence came the bitter wailing cries they heard.
Then hastened they to join him in his task;
But, panting, as they asked of Raelus,
All winded with his work, yet jollier
Than meadow-lark at morn, he sent his voice
In such a twittering of merriment,
The wail of sorrow died and laughter strewed
Its grave with melody.
                    "O Raelus!
Rare Raelus!" he cried and clapped his hands,
And even in the weeds that edged the pool
Fell wrestling with his mirth.—"Why, Raelus,"
He said, when he at last could speak again,
"Drew magnet-like—you know that talk of his,—
And so, adhesive, did I cling and cling
Until I found us in your far advance,
And, hidden in the wood, I stayed to say
'Twas better we should bide your coming. 'No.'
Then on again; and still a second time—

'Shall we not bide their coming?' 'No!' he said;
And on again, until the third; and 'No—
We'll push a little further.' As we did;
And, sudden, came upon an open glade—
There to the northward,—by a thicket bound:
Then he dismounted, giving me his rein,
And, charging me to keep myself concealed,
And if he were not back a certain time
To ride for you and search where he had gone,
He crossed the opening and passed from sight
Within the thicket. I was curious:
And so, dismounting, tethered our two steeds
And followed him; and, creeping warily,
Came on him where—unseen of him—I saw
Him pause before the cave himself described
Before us yesternoon. And here he put
His fingers to his lips and gave a call
Bird-like and quavering: at which a face,
As radiant as summer sun at morn,
Parted the viny curtains of the cave;
And then, a moment later, came in view
A woman even fairer than my sight
Might understand. 'What! dare you come again?'
As, lifting up her eyes all flashingly,
She scorched him with a look of hate.—'Begone!
Or have you—traitor, villain, knave, and cur,—
Bro't minions of the law to carry out
The vengeance of your whimpering jealousy?'
Then Raelus, all cowering before
Her queenly anger, faltered: 'Hear me yet;
I do not threaten. But your love—your love!—

O give me that. I know you pure as dew:
Your love! Your love!—The smile that has gone
    out
And left my soul a midnight of despair!—
Your love or life! For I have even now
Your stronghold girt about with certain doom
If you but waver in your choice.—Your love!'
At which, as quick as tho't, leapt on him there
A strong man from the covert of the gloom;
And others, like to him, from here and there
Came skurrying. I, turning, would have fled,
But found myself as suddenly beset
And tied and tumbled there with Raelus.
And him they haltered by his squirming heels
Until he did confess such villainy
As made me wonder if his wits were sound—
Confessed himself a renegade—a thief—
Ay, even one of them, save that he knew
Not that nice honor even thieves may claim
Among themselves.—And so ran on thro' such
A catalogue of littlenesses, I
For deafest shame had even stopped my ears
But that my wrists were lockt. And when he came
To his confession of his lie at court,
By which was gained our knightly sympathy
And valiant service on this fools' crusade,
I seemed to feel the redness of my blush
Soak thro' my very soul. There I brake in:
'Fair lady and most gallant,—to my shame
Do I admit we have been duped by such
An ingrate as this bundled lump of flesh

That I am helpless to rise up and spurn:
Unbind me, and I promise such amends
As knightly hands may deign to wreak upon
A thing so vile as he.' Then, laughing, she:
'First tell me, by your honor, where await
Your knightly brothers and my enemies.'
To which I answered, truthfully, I knew
Not where you lingered, but not close at hand
I was assured. Then all abrupt, she turned:
'Get every one within! We ride at once!'
And scarce a dozen minutes ere they came
Outpouring from the cave in such a guise
As made me smile from very wonderment.—
From head to heel in woman's dress they came,
Clad richly, too, and trapped and tricked withal
As maidenly, but in the face and hand,
As ever damsels flock at holiday.
Then were their chargers bro't, caparisoned
In keeping; and they mounted, lifting us,
Still bounden, with much jest and mockery
Of soft caress and wanton blandishments,
As tho' they were of sex their dress declared.
And so they carried us until they came
Upon the road there as it nicks the copse;
And so drew rein, dismounted, leaving some
To guard their horses; hurried us across
This footway to the middle of the flat.
Here Raelus was bounden to a tree,
Stript to the waist; my fetters cut, and then
A long, keen switch put in my hand, and 'Strike!
Strike as all duty bids you!' said the queen.

And so I did, with right good will at first;
Till, softened as I heard the wretch's prayers
Of anguish, I at last withheld my hand.
'What! tiring?' chirpt the queen: 'Give me the
     stick!'
And swish, and swish, and mercy how it rained!
Then all the others, forming circlewise,
Danced round and round the howling wretch,
     and jeered
And japed at him, and mocked and scoffed at him,
And spat upon him. And I turned away
And hid my face; then raised it pleadingly:
Nor would they listen my appeal for him;
But left him so, and thonged and took me back
Across the mere, and drew the bridge, that none
Might go to him, and carried me with them
Far on their way, and freed me once again;
And back I turned, tho' loath, to succor him."
And even as he ceased they heard the wail
Break out anew, and crossed without a word,
And Raelus they found, and without word
They loosed him. And he brake away and ran
As runs a lie the truth is hard upon.

Thus did it fare with Raelus. And they
Who knew of it said naught at court of it,
Nor from that day spake ever of him once,
Nor heard of him again, nor cared to hear.

A MOTHER-SONG

MOTHER, O mother! forever I cry for you,
  Sing the old song I may never forget;
Even in slumber I murmur and sigh for you.—
    Mother, O mother,
        Sing low, "Little brother,
Sleep, for thy mother bends over thee yet!"

Mother, O mother! the years are so lonely,
  Filled but with weariness, doubt and regret!
Can't you come back to me—for to-night only,
    Mother, my mother,
        And sing, "Little brother,
Sleep, for thy mother bends over thee yet!"

Mother, O mother! of old I had never
  One wish denied me, nor trouble to fret;
Now—must I cry out all vainly forever,—
    Mother, sweet mother,
        O sing, "Little brother,
Sleep, for thy mother bends over thee yet!"

Mother, O mother! must longing and sorrow
  Leave me in darkness, with eyes ever wet,
And never the hope of a meeting to-morrow?
    Answer me, mother,
        And sing, "Little brother,
Sleep, for thy mother bends over thee yet!"

THE LOST PATH

ALONE they walked—their fingers knit together,
  And swaying listlessly as might a swing
Wherein Dan Cupid dangled in the weather
  Of some sun-flooded afternoon of Spring.

Within the clover-fields the tickled cricket
  Laughed lightly as they loitered down the lane,
And from the covert of the hazel-thicket
  The squirrel peeped and laughed at them again.

The bumblebee that tipped the lily-vases
  Along the roadside in the shadows dim,
Went following the blossoms of their faces
  As though their sweets must needs be shared with
    him.

Between the pasture bars the wondering cattle
  Stared wistfully, and from their mellow bells
Shook out a welcoming whose dreamy rattle
  Fell swooningly away in faint farewells.

And though at last the gloom of night fell o'er them,
  And folded all the landscape from their eyes,
They only knew the dusky path before them
  Was leading safely on to Paradise.

MY BRIDE THAT IS TO BE

O SOUL of mine, look out and see
  My bride, my bride that is to be!—
  Reach out with mad, impatient hands,
And draw aside futurity
As one might draw a veil aside—
  And so unveil her where she stands
Madonna-like and glorified—
  The queen of undiscovered lands
Of love, to where she beckons me—
My bride, my bride that is to be.

The shadow of a willow-tree
  That wavers on a garden-wall
  In summer-time may never fall
In attitude as gracefully
As my fair bride that is to be;—
  Nor ever Autumn's leaves of brown
As lightly flutter to the lawn
As fall her fairy-feet upon

30

The path of love she loiters down.—
O'er drops of dew she walks, and yet
Not one may stain her sandal wet—
Ay, she might *dance* upon the way
Nor crush a single drop to spray,
So airy-like she seems to me,—
My bride, my bride that is to be.

I know not if her eyes are light
As summer skies or dark as night,—
I only know that they are dim
    With mystery: In vain I peer
    To make their hidden meaning clear,
    While o'er their surface, like a tear
That ripples to the silken brim,
A look of longing seems to swim
    All worn and weary-like to me;
And then, as suddenly, my sight
Is blinded with a smile so bright,
    Through folded lids I still may see
    My bride, my bride that is to be.

Her face is like a night of June
Upon whose brow the crescent-moon
Hangs pendent in a diadem
Of stars, with envy lighting them.—
    And, like a wild cascade, her hair
Floods neck and shoulder, arm and wrist,
Till only through a gleaming mist
    I seem to see a Siren there,

With lips of love and melody
  And open arms and heaving breast
  Wherein I fling myself to rest,
The while my heart cries hopelessly
For my fair bride that is to be.

   .   .   .   .

Nay, foolish heart and blinded eyes!
My bride hath need of no disguise.—
  But, rather, let her come to me
In such a form as bent above
  My pillow when, in infancy,
I knew not anything but love.—
O let her come from out the lands
  Of Womanhood—not fairy isles,—
And let her come with Woman's hands
  And Woman's eyes of tears and smiles,—
With Woman's hopefulness and grace
Of patience lighting up her face:
And let her diadem be wrought
Of kindly deed and prayerful thought,
That ever over all distress
May beam the light of cheerfulness.—
And let her feet be brave to fare
The labyrinths of doubt and care,
That, following, my own may find
The path to Heaven God designed.—
O let her come like this to me—
My bride—my bride that is to be.

LULLABY

THE maple strews the embers of its leaves
  O'er the laggard swallows nestled 'neath the
      eaves;
And the moody cricket falters in his cry—Baby-
      bye!—
And the lid of night is falling o'er the sky—Baby-
      bye!—
    The lid of night is falling o'er the sky!

The rose is lying pallid, and the cup
Of the frosted calla-lily folded up;
And the breezes through the garden sob and sigh—
      Baby-bye!—
O'er the sleeping blooms of Summer where they
      lie—Baby-bye!—
    O'er the sleeping blooms of summer where they
      lie!

Yet, Baby—O my Baby, for your sake
This heart of mine is ever wide awake,
And my love may never droop a drowsy eye—
      Baby-bye!—
Till your own are wet above me when I die—
      Baby-bye!—
    Till your own are wet above me when I die.

THE ROMAUNT OF KING MORDAMEER

HO! did ye hear of Mordameer,
The King of Slumberland!
A lotus-crown upon his brow—
A poppy in his hand,
And all the elves that people dreams
To bow at his command.

His throne is wrought of blackest night,
Enriched with rare designs
Wherein the blazing comet runs
And writhes and wreaths and twines
About a crescent angel-face
That ever smiling shines.

The dais is of woven rays
Of starlight fringed with shade,
And jeweled o'er with gems of dew,
And dyed and interlaid
With every gleaming tint and hue
Of which the flowers are made.

And when the day has died away
In darkness o'er the land,
The King bends down his dusky face
And takes the sleeper's hand,
And lightly o'er his folded eyes
He waves his magic wand.

And lo! within his princely home,
Upon his downy bed,
With soft and silken coverlets
And curtains round him spread,
The rich man rolls in troubled sleep,
And moans in restless dread:

His eyes are closed, yet Mordameer
May see their stony stare
As plainly fixed in agony
As though the orbs were bare
And glaring at the wizard throng
That fills the empty air:—

A thousand shapes, with phantom japes,
Dance o'er the sleeper's sight,—
With fingers bony-like and lean,
And faces pinched and white,
And withered cheeks, and sunken eyes
With ever-ravening sight.

And such the dreams that Mordameer
Brings to the child of Pride,—
The worn and wasted forms that he

Hath stinted and denied—
Of those who filled his coffers up
    And empty-handed died.

And then again he waves his wand:
    And from his lair of straw
The felon, with his fettered limbs,
    Starts up with fear and awe,
And stares with starting eyes upon
    A vision of the law:

A grim procession passes by,
    The while he glares in fear—
With faces, from a wanton's smile
    Down to a demon's leer,—
The woman marching at the front,
    The hangman at the rear.

All ways are clear to Mordameer:
    The ocean knows his tread;
His feet are free on land or sea:—
    Above the sailor's head
He hangs a dream of home, and bends
    Above his cottage-bed:

And, nestled in the mother's arms,
    A child, surpassing fair,
In slumber lies, its tiny hands
    Entangled in her hair,
And round its face a smile that moves
    Its lips as though in prayer.

And lo! the good king feasts its eyes
 With fruits from foreign shores,
And pink-lipped shells that ever mock
 The ocean as it roars;
And in the mother's arms he folds
 The form that she adores.

Through all the hovels of the poor
 He steals with noiseless tread,
And presses kisses o'er and o'er
 Where sorrow's tears are shed,
Till old caresses live once more
 That are forever dead.

Above the soldier in his tent
 Are glorious battles fought;
And o'er the prince's velvet couch,
 And o'er the peasant's cot,
And o'er the pallet of disease
 His wondrous spells are wrought.

He bends him o'er the artist's cot,
 And fills his dazzled mind
With airy forms that float about
 Like clouds in summer wind,
O'er landscapes that the angels wrought
 And God Himself designed.

And drifting through the poet's dreams
 The seraph trails her wings,
And fills the chancels of his soul

With heavenly whisperings,
Till, swooning with delight, he hears
    The song he never sings.

He walks the wide world's every way,
    This monarch grand and grim;
All paths that reach the human heart,
    However faint and dim,
He journeys, for the darkest night
    Is light as day to him.

And thus the lordly Mordameer
    Rules o'er his mystic realm,
With gems from out the star's red core
    To light his diadem,
And kings and emperors to kneel
    And kiss his garment's hem.

For once, upon a night of dreams,
    Adown the aisles of space
I strayed so far that I forgot
    Mine own abiding-place,
And wandered into Slumberland,
    And met him face to face.

DEARTH

I HOLD your trembling hand to-night—and
   yet
  I may not know what wealth of bliss is mine,
  My heart is such a curious design
Of trust and jealousy! Your eyes are wet—
So must I think they jewel some regret,—
   And lo, the loving arms that round me twine
   Cling only as the tendrils of a vine
Whose fruit has long been gathered: I forget,
   While crimson clusters of your kisses press
     Their wine out on my lips, my royal fare
   Of rapture, since blind fancy needs must guess
     They once poured out their sweetness other-
       where,
   With fuller flavoring of happiness
     Than e'en your broken sobs may now
       declare.

THE SONG I NEVER SING

AS when in dreams we sometimes hear
   A melody so faint and fine
And musically sweet and clear,
It flavors all the atmosphere
   With harmony divine,—
      So, often in my waking dreams,
      I hear a melody that seems
      Like fairy voices whispering
      To me the song I never sing.

Sometimes when brooding o'er the years
   My lavish youth has thrown away—
When all the glowing past appears
But as a mirage that my tears
   Have crumbled to decay,—
      I thrill to find the ache and pain
      Of my remorse is stilled again,
      As, forward bent and listening,
      I hear the song I never sing.

40

A murmuring of rhythmic words,
  Adrift on tunes whose currents flow
Melodious with the trill of birds,
And far-off lowing of the herds
  In lands of long ago;
    And every sound the truant loves
    Comes to me like the coo of doves
    When first in blooming fields of Spring
    I heard the song I never sing.

The echoes of old voices, wound
  In limpid streams of laughter where
The river Time runs bubble-crowned,
And giddy eddies ripple round
  The lilies growing there;
    Where roses, bending o'er the brink,
    Drain their own kisses as they drink,
    And ivies climb and twine and cling
    About the song I never sing.

An ocean-surge of sound that falls
  As though a tide of heavenly art
Had tempested the gleaming halls
And crested o'er the golden walls
  In showers on my heart. . . .
    Thus—thus, with open arms and eyes
    Uplifted toward the alien skies,
    Forgetting every earthly thing,
    I hear the song I never sing.

O nameless lay, sing clear and strong,
  Pour down thy melody divine
Till purifying floods of song
Have washed away the stains of wrong
    That dim this soul of mine!
      O woo me near and nearer thee,
      Till my glad lips may catch the key,
      And, with a voice unwavering,
      Join in the song I never sing.

UNSPOKEN

O HE can hold her hand, and full and fair
, Look in her face and fling her smile for
  smile,
And loosen from his lips such words the while
As make him wonder how his tongue may dare
Such dalliance. And when in wordless prayer
  His heart lies gasping, he can reconcile
  His talk to that glib, recitative style
The silly gossip chatters everywhere.
But O, one utterance—one stormy word
  Is fastened down in silence pitiless;
No struggling murmur of it ever heard—
  No echo welling out of his distress
To plead aloud its mission long deferred,
  And leap up fountain-like in thankfulness.

Yet he is bold enough in dreams—last night
  He held her in his arms, and in the strands
  Of her down-streaming hair he bathed his
    hands,
And fretted it in golden foam, as bright
And billowy it floated o'er his sight.
  Her breath was like a breeze of fairy-lands
  That reels above a bed of bloom, and fans

43

Its fragrant life away in sheer delight.
So even did he whisper through the sighs
   That quavered as his spirit stayed to drain
The mad intoxication of her eyes;
   Then felt a pang of pleasure keen as pain—
A barb of ecstasy, shot arrow-wise,
   In such a kiss as cleft his heart in twain.

But waking, when the morning of her face
   Shines full upon him, voiceless has he grown
   Save that inanimately mirthful tone
That ripples ever on its foolish race
And finds nor rest nor joyance in the chase;
   And so it is a never-ending moan
   Wails on unheard, unheeded and unknown
But by the echoes of its hiding-place.
What poverty like this?—to laugh, and sing,
   And babble like a brook in summer-time;
To circle o'er the world on airy wing,
      Or clamber into Heaven on rounds of rhyme,
When in the soul, forever lingering,
      There lives a love unspeakably sublime.

THANKSGIVING DAY AT HUNCHLEY'S

I F you never heard of Hunchley, I would say in
  his behalf,
He's as jovial a bachelor as ever raised a laugh,
And as fond of boon companions, yet withal as tried
  and true
A gentleman of honor as the writer ever knew.

And if he has a weakness, as a weakness it depends
On a certain strength of kindness he bestows upon
  his friends;
Being simple, undesigning, and of courteous
  address,
All hearts are open to him and his friends are
  numberless.

And this is how it happened some discrepancies
  befell
At the late Thanksgiving dinner which began at his
  hotel,
Where, it seems, the guests invited were selected
  more to be
In keeping with his bounty than the laws of
  harmony.

45

For there among the number were two rivals of the
    press,
Who had paragraphed each other with prolonged
    maliciousness,
And in their respective columns had a thousand
    times declared
That the other fellow "daresn't," and the other
    fellow dared.

And cheek by jowl together were two members of
    the bar,
Politically, legally, and socially at war,
Who denounced each other daily, and in every
    local phrase
That could make the matter binding all the balance
    of their days.

Of the medical fraternity ("fraternity" is good)
There were four or five disciples of the healing
    brotherhood—
Botanic and eclectic, and some others that persist
In orthographic wranglings, such as "homeopo-
    thist";

And an ordinary actor, and an actor of renown,
Whose cue, it seemed, for smiling was the other
    actor's frown;
And the most loquacious author my remembrance
    can recall,
And a little bench-leg poet that couldn't talk at all.

In fact the guests assembled, as they gathered round
    the feast
Wore expressions such as savored not of thankful-
    ness the least,
And to a close observer were suggestive of the
    dread
And shadowy disaster that was hanging overhead.

Now the simple Mr. Hunchley had invited, with the
    rest,
A melancholy pastor, and, in honor of the guest
And the notable occasion, he desired a special
    "grace,"
Which the thankful pastor offered with a very
    thankless face.

And at this unhappy juncture came a journalistic
    pun,
Which the rival designated as a most atrocious one,
At which the grim projector, with a covert look of
    hate,
Shook a little dust of "fine-cut" in the other fellow's
    plate.

And the viands circulated, with a sudden gust of wit
From a lawyer—instituted for the other's benefit,—
Then the victim spun a story with exasperating
    mirth
That reflected his opponent as of small judicial
    worth.

Then a medical discussion on the stomach swelled
    the gale
And the literary appetite began to droop and fail;
While a sportive reminiscence from the absented-
    minded host
Blanched the features of the pastor to the pallor of
    a ghost.

And a deep sonorous murmur slowly grew, and
    grew, and grew
Till the similes that suited it were singularly few,—
For even now at leisure, and with nothing else to do,
A task of lesser promise I can say I never knew.

I have heard the tread of armies as they marched
    upon the foe,
And, among the Alps, have listened to the avalanche
    of snow;
I have leaned upon Niagara, and have heard the
    wailing tide
Where it leaps its awful chasm in unending suicide.

I have heard the trampling footsteps of the roaring
    hurricane
As he lashed his tail of lightning, and tossed his
    shaggy mane;
I have heard the cannonading of the devastating
    storm,
And the falling politician howling loudly for
    reform.

But no mystic voice of terror ever bred of Nature's
    law
Could awake the sense of wonder and dismay, and
    doubt and awe
That thrilled my inmost being as the conversation
    swelled
To a mad, chaotic focus in which everybody yelled.

There's a vision in my fancy, misty-like and
    undefined,
Of an actor with his collar loose and sticking up
    behind,
And another (though I hesitate to chronicle the
    fact)
Writhing underneath the table in a wild contortion
    act.

There's a shadowy remembrance of a group of three
    or four
Who were seemingly dissecting another on the
    floor;
And the form of Mr. Hunchley dancing round a
    couple more,
And a phantom with a chicken-leg a-breaking for
    the door.

And here my memory wavers—I recall the heated
    breath
Of the gentleman who held me with the very grip
    of death,

And as my reeling pencil scrawls the scene of my
 release
I'm as full of glad thanksgiving as my soul is full of
 peace.

But this is how it happened these discrepancies
 befell
At the late Thanksgiving dinner Hunchley gave at
 his hotel,
Where, it seems, the guests invited were selected
 more to be
In keeping with his bounty than the laws of
 harmony.

APART

I

THEY stood on either side the gate—
Though fastened with the hands of fate
A touch might lift the latch's weight.

The moonlight, with a faded grace,
Fell o'er the whiteness of her face
Like some soiled veil of bridal lace.

The fan she held went fluttering
About her mouth on restless wing
As though it were a wounded thing.

And in her breast an ache of dread
Held back the word she would have said,
And sent a weary sigh instead.

II

He waited, with his eager eyes
Half muffled in a weak disguise
Of carelessness and cold surprise.

Within his breast he heard the moan:
"How desolate and all alone,
And pitiless my heart has grown!"

And yet a nameless ache of dread
Held back the word he would have said,
And sent a weary sigh instead.

The long, black shadows of the trees
Whose branches wavered in the breeze,
Fell o'er them like their destinies.

They parted. Yet the wild wind saith
That two fair ghosts with failing breath
Walk hand in hand the path of death.

TOIL

HE had toiled away for a weary while,
  Through day's dull glare and night's deep
    gloom;
And many a long and lonesome mile
He had paced in the round of his dismal room;
He had fared on hunger—had drunk of pain
As the drouthy earth might drink of rain;
And the brow he leaned in his trembling palm
Throbbed with a misery so intense
That never again did it seem that calm
Might come to him with the gracious balm
Of old-time languor and indolence.
And he said, "I will leave the tale half told,
And leave the song for the winds to sing;
And the pen—that pitiless blade of gold
That stabs my heart like a dagger-sting—
I will drive to the hilt through the inkstand's
    top
And spill its blood to the last black drop!"
Then he masked his voice with a laugh, and
    went

Out in the world with a lawless grace—
With a brazen lie in his eyes and face
Told in a smile of glad content:
He roved the round of pleasures through,
And tasted each as it pleased him to;
He joined old songs, and the clink and din
Of the revelers at the banquet hall;
And he tripped his feet where the violin
Spun its waltz for the carnival;
He looked, bedazed, on the luring wile
And the siren-light of a woman's smile,
And peered in her eyes as a diver might
Peer in the sea ere he leaps outright,—
Caught his breath, with a glance above,
And dropped full-length in the depths of love.

.   .   .   .

'Tis well if ever the false lights die
On the alien coasts where our wreck'd hopes
    lie!
'Tis well to feel, through the blinding rain,
Our outflung hands touch earth again!
So the castaway came, safe from doom,
Back at last to his lonely room,
Filled with its treasure of work to do
And radiant with the light and bloom
Of the summer sun and his glad soul, too!
And sweet as ever the song of birds,
Over his work he sang these words:—

"O friends are good, with their princely ways,
And royal hearts they are goodly things;
And fellowship, in the long dark days
When the drear soul cowers with drooping
    wings,
Is a thing to yearn for.—*Mirth* is good,—
For a ringing laugh is a rhythmic cry
Blown like a hail from the Angelhood
To the barque of the lone soul drifting by.—
Goodly, too, is a mute caress
Of woman's hands and their tenderness—
The warm breath wet with the dews of love—
The vine-like arms, and the fruit thereof—
The touch that thrills, and the kiss that melts,—
But Toil is sweeter than all things else."

HIS ROOM

I'M home again, my dear old Room,
I'm home again, and happy, too,
As, peering through the brightening gloom,
  I find myself alone with you:
    Though brief my stay, nor far away,
    I missed you—missed you night and day—
    As wildly yearned for you as now.—
    Old Room, how are you, anyhow?

My easy chair, with open arms,
  Awaits me just within the door;
The littered carpet's woven charms
  Have never seemed so bright before,—
    The old rosettes and mignonettes
    And ivy-leaves and violets,
    Look up as pure and fresh of hue
    As though baptized in morning-dew.

Old Room, to me your homely walls
  Fold round me like the arms of love,
And over all my being falls
  A blessing pure as from above—

56

Even as a nestling child caressed
And lulled upon a loving breast,
With folded eyes, too glad to weep
And yet too sad for dreams or sleep.

You've been so kind to me, old Room—
    So patient in your tender care,
My drooping heart in fullest bloom
    Has blossomed for you unaware;
        And who but you had cared to woo
        A heart so dark, and heavy too,
        As in the past you lifted mine
        From out the shadow to the shine?

For I was but a wayward boy
    When first you gladly welcomed me
And taught me work was truer joy
    Than rioting incessantly:
        And thus the din that stormed within
        The old guitar and violin
        Has fallen in a fainter tone
        And sweeter, for your sake alone.

Though in my absence I have stood
    In festal halls a favored guest,
I missed, in this old quietude,
    My worthy work and worthy rest—
        By *this* I know that long ago
        You loved me first, and told me so
        In art's mute eloquence of speech
        The voice of praise may never reach.

For lips and eyes in truth's disguise
　Confuse the faces of my friends,
Till old affection's fondest ties
　　I find unraveling at the ends;
　　　But, as I turn to you, and learn
　　　To meet my griefs with less concern,
　　　Your love seems all I have to keep
　　　Me smiling lest I needs must weep.

Yet I am happy, and would fain
　Forget the world and all its woes;
So set me to my tasks again,
　　Old Room, and lull me to repose:
　　　And as we glide adown the tide
　　　Of dreams, forever side by side,
　　　I'll hold your hands as lovers do
　　　Their sweethearts' and talk love to you.

TO LEONAINIE

*In memory of Leonainie, infant daughter of W. B.
and Lotta Titus, these lines are tenderly inscribed.*

"LEONAINIE!" angels missed her—
    Baby angels—they
Who behind the stars had kissed her
  · E'er she came away;
And their little, wandering faces
Drooped o'er Heaven's hiding-places
Whiter than the lily-vases
    On the Sabbath day.

"Leonainie!" crying, crying,
    Crying through the night,
Till her lisping lips replying,
    Laughing with delight,
Drew us nearer yet, and nearer
That we might the better hear her
Baby-words, and love her dearer
    Hearing not aright.

Only spake the little lisper
   In the Angel-tongue,
Fainter than a fairy-whisper
   Murmured in among
Dewy blossoms covered over
With the fragrant tufts of clover,
Where the minstrel honey-rover
   Twanged his wings and sung.

"Leonainie!"—And the glimmer
   Of her starry eyes
Faded, and the world grew dimmer
   E'en as Paradise
Blossomed with a glory brighter
Than the waning stars, and whiter
Than the dying moon, and lighter
   Than the morning skies.

THE SHOWER

THE landscape, like the awed face of a child
   Grew curiously blurred; a hush of death
Fell on the fields, and in the darkened wild
   The zephyr held its breath.

No wavering glamour-work of light and shade
   Dappled the shivering surface of the brook;
The frightened ripples in their ambuscade
   Of willows trilled and shook.

The sullen day grew darker, and anon
   Dim flashes of pent anger lit the sky;
With rumbling wheels of wrath came rolling on
   The storm's artillery.

The cloud above put on its blackest frown,
   And then, as with a vengeful cry of pain,
The lightning snatched it, ripped and flung it
      down
   In raveled shreds of rain:

While I, transfigured by some wondrous art,
   Bowed with the thirsty lilies to the sod,
My empty soul brimmed over, and my heart
   Drenched with the love of God.

YE SCHOLAR

H O! ho! Ye Scholar recketh not how lean
His lank frame waxeth in ye hectic
gloom
That smeareth o'er ye dim walls of his room
His wavering shadow! Shut is he, I ween,
Like as a withered nosegay, in between
Ye musty, mildewed leaves of some volume
Of ancient lore ye moth and he consume
In jointure. Yet a something in his mien
Forbids all mockery, though quaint is he,
And eke fantastical in form and face
As that Old Knight ye Tale of Chivalry
Made mad immortally, yet spared ye grace
Of some rare virtue which we sigh to see,
And pour our laughter out most tenderly.

DEATH IS DEAD

AND did you know our old friend Death is
dead?
　　Ah me! he died last night; my ghost was
　　　there,
And all his phantom-friends from everywhere
Were sorrowfully grouped about his bed.
"I die; God help the living now!" he said
　　With such a ghastly pathos, I declare
　　The tears oozed from the blind eyes of the air
And spattered on his face in gouts of red.
And then he smiled—the dear old bony smile
　　That glittered on us in that crazy whim
When first our daring feet leapt the defile
　　Of life and ran so eagerly to him:
And so he smiled upon us, even while
　　The kind old sockets grew forever dim.

TOM JOHNSON'S QUIT

A PASSEL o' the boys last night—
    An' me amongst 'em—kind o' got
To talkin' Temper'nce left an' right,
    An' workin' up "blue-ribbon," *hot;*
An' while we was a-countin' jes'
    How many hed gone into hit
An' signed the pledge, some feller says,—
      "Tom Johnson's quit!"

We laughed, of course—'cause Tom, you know,
    Has spiled more whisky, boy an' man,
And seed more trouble, high an' low,
    Than any chap but Tom could stand:
And so, says I, *"He's* too nigh dead
    Fer Temper'nce to benefit!"
The feller sighed ag'in, and said—
      "Tom Johnson's quit!"

We all *liked* Tom, an' that was why
    We sort o' simmered down ag'in,
And ast the feller ser'ously
    Ef he wa'n't tryin' to draw us in:

He shuck his head—tuck off his hat—
   Helt up his hand an' opened hit,
An' says, says he, "I'll *swear* to that—
     Tom Johnson's quit!"

Well, we was stumpt, an' tickled, too,—
   Because we knowed ef Tom *hed* signed
There wa'n't no man 'at wore the "blue"
   'At was more honester inclined:
An' then and there we kind o' riz,—
   The hull dern gang of us 'at bit—
An' th'owed our hats and let 'er whiz,—
     "Tom Johnson's quit!"

I've heerd 'em holler when the balls
   Was buzzin' 'round us wus'n bees,
An' when the ole flag on the walls
   Was flappin' o'er the enemy's,
I've heerd a-many a wild "hooray"
   'At made my heart git up an' git—
But Lord!—to hear 'em shout that way!—
     "Tom Johnson's quit!"

But when we saw the chap 'at fetched
   The news wa'n't jinin' in the cheer,
But stood there solemn-like, an' reched
   An' kind o' wiped away a tear,
We someway sort o' stilled ag'in,
   And listened—I kin hear him yit,
His voice a-wobblin' with his chin,—
     "Tom Johnson's quit—

"I hain't a-givin' you no game—
  I wisht I was! . . . An hour ago,
This operator—what's his name—
  The one 'at works at night, you know?—
Went out to flag that Ten Express,
  And sees a man in front of hit
Th'ow up his hands an' stagger—yes,—
  Tom Johnson's quit!"

THE LITTLE DEAD MAN

YET NOT SO DEAD AS ANOTHER

I

O IT was a little dead man,
      At peace with all the earth;
His eyes were veiled to sorrow,
    And his lips were stilled to mirth.

His ears were closed to laughter,
  · And to mockery and strife,
And I never saw a dead man
    So happy in my life.

His hands were meekly hidden
    At his very last request—
The right in his hip pocket,
    And the other in his vest.

His collar was thrown open,
    And he wore his easy clothes—
Had his ordinary boots on,
    With rosin on the toes.

And he bade his trusty barber,
  With the latest breath he drew,
To shave and shave him closely,
  And *very* closely too.

II

And then the little dead man
  Lay coffined for the tomb.
The hearse was at the doorway—
  The mourners in the room—

When suddenly a stranger,
  Who had called the day before
With a book beneath his elbow,
  Entered softly at the door.

And he turned him to the mourners
  With a business air, and said:
"I must really beg your pardon,
  But the gentleman that's dead

"Was kind enough to tell me,
  If I'd call around to-day
He'd be prepared to listen
  To all I had to say.

"And in view of that engagement,
  I would gently intimate
(As it may pitch the funeral
  Some dozen hours late),

"That you have my indulgence,"
  And with eyelids downward thrown,
They left the little dead man
  And the agent all alone.

As only stars may lighten
  Up the grandeur of the plains,
And the mountains where the midnight
  In her mystic beauty reigns,

So the stars must shed their glory
  O'er imagination's vales,
And illuminate the story
  Where the poet's pencil fails.

*　　*　　*　　*　　*　　*

But there was a little dead man—
  Ah! so very dead indeed,
They fastened down his coffin lid
  With most judicious speed.

For they whose latest office
  Was to shroud his form from sight,
Saw a note-book in the left hand,
  And a pencil in the right.

OLD-FASHIONED ROSES

THEY ain't no style about 'em,
  And they're sort o' pale and faded
Yit the doorway here, without 'em,
  Would be lonesomer, and shaded
    With a good 'eal blacker shadder
      Than the morning-glories makes,
    And the sunshine would look sadder
      Fer their good old-fashion' sakes.

I like 'em 'cause they kind o'
  Sort o' *make* a feller like 'em!
And I tell you, when I find a
  Bunch out whur the sun kin strike 'em,
    It allus sets me thinkin'
      O' the ones 'at used to grow
    And peek in through the chinkin'
      O' the cabin, don't you know!

And then I think o' mother,
  And how she ust to love 'em—
When they wuzn't any other,
  'Less she found 'em up above 'em!

And her eyes, afore she shut 'em,
    Whispered with a smile and said
We must pick a bunch and putt 'em
    In her hand when she wuz dead.

But, as I wuz a-sayin',
    They ain't no style about 'em
Very gaudy er displayin',
    But I wouldn't be without 'em,—
        'Cause I'm happier in these posies,
          And hollyhawks and sich,
        Than the hummin'-bird 'at noses
          In the roses of the rich.

THE EMPTY SONG

"WHAT have we but an empty song?"
    Said the minstrel, as he bent
To stay the fingers that trailed along
    The strings of her instrument.

"The clasp of your hand is warm in mine,
    And your breath on my brow is wet—
I have drunk of your lips as men drink wine,
    But my heart is thirsty yet."

The starlight shivered a little space,
    And the sigh of the wind uprose
And blew a cloud o'er the moon's wan face,
    And swooned back in repose.

.   .   .   .

The years ooze on in a stagnant flood:
    One drifts as the winds allow;
And one writes rhymes with his heart's own
        blood,
    But his soul is thirsty now.

Youthful portrait

A ROSE IN OCTOBER

I

I STRAYED, all alone, where the Autumn
   Had swept, in her petulant wrath:
All the flowers, that had bloomed in the garden,
   She had gathered, and flung in her path.
And I saw the dead face of the lily,
   Struck down, by the rain, and the sleet,
And the pink, with her lashes yet weeping,
   Drooped low in the dust, at my feet.

II

The leaves on the branches still swinging,
   Were blanched with the crimson of death;
And the vines that still clung to the trellis,
   Were palsied, and shook at a breath.
And I sighed: "So hath fate, like the Autumn,
   Swept over my path, till I see,
As I walk through life's desolate garden
   Not a rose is left blooming for me!"

III

"Heigho!" said a voice of low laughter—
    "How blind are you poets!" And there,
At the gate, just in front of me, leaning,
    Stood Rosalind May, I declare!
I stammered, confused, for the moment;
    But was blest for the rest of my life,
For my Rose of October there promised
    She'd bloom for me aye, as—my wife.

ROMANCIN'

I 'B'EN a-kindo' *"musin',"* as the feller says, and
　　I'm
About o' the conclusion that they hain't no better
　　time,
When you come to cipher on it, than the times we
　　ust to know
When we swore our first *"dog-gone-it"* sorto'
　　solum-like and low!

You git my idy, do you?—*Little* tads, you under-
　　stand—
Jest a-wishin' thue and thue you that you on'y wuz
　　a *man.*—
Yit here I am, this minit, even sixty, to a day,
And fergittin' all that's in it, wishin' jest the other
　　way!

I hain't no hand to lectur' on the times, er *dim-*
　　onstrate
Whare the trouble is, er hector and domineer with
　　Fate,—

But when I git so flurried, and so pestered-like and
    blue,
And so rail owdacious worried, let me tell you what
    I do!—

I jest gee-haw the hosses, and onhook the swingle-
    tree,
Whare the hazel-bushes tosses down theyr shadders
    over me;
And I draw my plug o' navy, and I climb the fence,
    and set
Jest a-thinkin' here, i gravy! tel my eyes is wringin'-
    wet!

Tho' I still kin see the trouble o' the *presunt,* I kin
    see—
Kindo' like my sight wuz double—all the things
    that *ust* to be;
And the flutter o' the robin and the teeter o' the
    wren
Sets the willer-branches bobbin' "howdy-do" thum
    Now to *Then!*

The deadnin' and the thicket's jest a-bilin' full of
    June,
Thum the rattle o' the cricket, to the yallar-
    hammer's tune;
And the catbird in the bottom, and the sapsuck on
    the snag,
Seems ef they can't—od-rot 'em!— jest do nothin'
    else but brag!

They's music in the twitter of the bluebird and the
    jay,
And that sassy little critter jest a-*peckin'* all the
    day;
They's music in the "flicker," and they's music in
    the thrush,
And they's music in the snicker o' the chipmunk in
    the brush!

They's music *all around* me!—And I go back, in a
    dream
Sweeter yit than ever found me fast asleep,—and in
    the stream
That ust to split the medder whare the dandylions
    growed,
I stand knee-deep, and redder than the sunset down
    the road.

Then's when I' b'en a-fishin'!—And they's other
    fellers, too,
With theyr hick'ry-poles a-swishin' out behind 'em;
    and a few
Little "shiners" on our stringers, with theyr tails
    tiptoein' bloom,
As we dance 'em in our fingers all the happy jurney
    home.

I kin see us, true to Natur', thum the time we
    started out,
With a biscuit and a 'tater in our little "round-
    about"!—

I kin see our lines a-tanglin', and our elbows in a
    jam,
And our naked legs a-danglin' thum the apern o'
    the dam.

I kin see the honeysuckle climbin' up around the
    mill,
And kin hear the worter chuckle, and the wheel
    a-growlin' still;
And thum the bank below it I kin steal the old
    canoe,
And jest git in and row it like the miller ust to do.

W'y, I git my fancy focused on the past so mortul
    plane
I kin even smell the locus'-blossoms bloomin' in the
    lane;
And I hear the cow-bells clinkin' sweeter tunes 'n
    "Money-musk"
Fer the lightnin'-bugs a-blinkin' and a-dancin' in the
    dusk.

And when I've kep' on "musin'," as the feller says,
    tel I'm
Firm-fixed in the conclusion that they hain't no
    better time,
When you come to cipher on it, than the *old*
    times,—I de-clare
I kin wake and say "dog-gone-it!" jest as soft as
    any prayer!

THE LITTLE OLD POEM THAT NOBODY
READS

THE little old poem that nobody reads
  Blooms in a crowded space,
Like a ground-vine blossom, so low in the weeds
  That nobody sees its face—
    Unless, perchance, the reader's eye
    Stares through a yawn, and hurries by,
    For no one wants, or loves, or heeds
    The little old poem that nobody reads.

The little old poem that nobody reads
  Was written—where?—and when?
Maybe a hand of goodly deeds
  Thrilled as it held the pen:
    Maybe the fountain whence it came
    Was a heart brimmed o'er with tears of shame,
    And maybe its creed is the worst of creeds—
    The little old poem that nobody reads.

But, little old poem that nobody reads,
  Holding you here above
The wound of a heart that warmly bleeds
  For all that knows not love,
    I well believe if the old World knew
    As dear a friend as I find in you,
    That friend would tell it that all it needs
    Is the little old poem that nobody reads.

A SLEEPING BEAUTY

I

AN alien wind that blew and blew
Over the fields where the ripe grain grew,

Sending ripples of shine and shade
That crept and crouched at her feet and played.

The sea-like summer washed the moss
Till the sun-drenched lilies hung like floss,

Draping the throne of green and gold
That lulled her there like a queen of old.

II

Was it the hum of a bumblebee,
Or the long-hushed bugle eerily

Winding a call to the daring Prince
Lost in the wood long ages since?—

A dim old wood, with a palace rare
Hidden away in its depths somewhere!

Was it the Princess, tranced in sleep,
Awaiting her lover's touch to leap

Into the arms that bent above?—
To thaw his heart with the breath of love—

And cloy his lips, through her waking tears,
With the dead-ripe kiss of a hundred years!

III

An alien wind that blew and blew.—
I had blurred my eyes as the artists do,

Coaxing life to a half-sketched face,
Or dreaming bloom for a grassy place.

The bee droned on in an undertone;
And a shadow-bird trailed all alone

Across the wheat, while a liquid cry
Dripped from above, as it went by.

What to her was the far-off whir
Of the quail's quick wing or the chipmunk's
      chirr?—

What to her was the shade that slid
Over the hill where the reapers hid?—

Or what the hunter, with one foot raised,
As he turned to go—yet, pausing, gazed?

LEEDLE DUTCH BABY

LEEDLE Dutch baby haff come ter town!
Jabber und jump till der day gone down—
Jabber und sphlutter und sphlit hees jaws—
Vot a Dutch baby dees Londsmon vas!
I dink dose mout' vas leedle too vide
Ober he laugh fon dot also-side!
Haff got blenty off deemple und vrown?—
Hey! leedle Dutchman come ter town!

Leedle Dutch baby, I dink me proud
Ober your fader can schquall dot loud
Ven he vas leedle Dutch baby like you
Und yoost don't gare, like he alvays do!—
Guess ven dey vean him on beer, you bet
Dot's der because dot he aind veaned yet!—
Vot you said off he dringk you down?—
Hey! leedle Dutchman come ter town!

Leedle Dutch baby, yoost schquall avay—
Schquall fon preakfast till gisterday!
Better you all time gry und shout
Dan shmile me vonce fon der coffin out!
Vot I gare off you keek my nose
Downside-up mit your heels und toes—
Downside, oder der oopside-down?—
Hey! leedle Dutchman come ter town!

82

LINES

ON HEARING A COW BAWL IN A DEEP FIT OF
DEJECTION ON THE EVENING OF JULY 3,
A. D. 1879.

PORTENTOUS sound! mysteriously vast
 And awful in the grandeur of refrain
That lifts the listener's hair as it swells past,
 And pours in turbid currents down the lane.

The small boy at the wood-pile, in a dream
 Slow trails the meat-rind o'er the listless
  saw;
The chickens roosting o'er him on the beam
 Uplift their drowsy heads with cootered
  awe.

The "gung-oigh!" of the pump is strangely
  stilled:
 The smoke-house door bangs once em-
  phatic'ly,
Then bangs no more, but leaves the silence
 filled
 With one lorn plaint's despotic minstrelsy.

Yet I would join thy sorrowing madrigal,
 Most melancholy cow, and sing of thee
Full-hearted through my tears, for, after all,
 'Tis very kine in you to sing for me.

FRIEND OF A WAYWARD HOUR

FRIEND of a wayward hour, you came
    Like some good ghost, and went the same;
And I within the haunted place
Sit smiling on your vanished face,
    And talking with—your name.

But thrice the pressure of your hand—
First hail—congratulations—and
Your last "God bless you!" as the train
That brought you snatched you back again
    Into the unknown land.

"God bless me?" Why, your very prayer
Was answered ere you asked it there,
I know—for when you came to lend
Me your kind hand, and call me friend,
    God blessed me unaware.

LINES

THOU little naked statuette,
　　With fairy head a-tip,
And eyelids ever downward let,
　　And silence on thy lip,
　　　　Thou comest from a friend unknown,
　　　　　　Nor wilt confess,
　　　　E'en in mute syllables of stone,
　　　　　　That friend's address.

And so, still pools of gratitude
　　I pour out at thy feet;
And could it mirror back thy nude
　　Perfection half as sweet
　　　　As rests within this heart of mine
　　　　　　That friend unknown,
　　　　Why, smiles would light that face of thine
　　　　　　And warm the stone.

PAN

THIS Pan is but an idle god, I guess,
    Since all the fair midsummer of my dreams
  He loiters listlessly by woody streams,
Soaking the lush glooms up with laziness;
Or drowsing while the maiden-winds caress
  Him prankishly, and powder him with gleams
  Of sifted sunshine. And he ever seems
Drugged with a joy unutterable—unless
  His low pipes whistle hints of it far out
Across the ripples to the dragon-fly
  That, like a wind-born blossom blown about,
Drops quiveringly down, as though to die—
  Then lifts and wavers on, as if in doubt
  Whether to fan his wings or fly without.

WHEN OUR BABY DIED

WHEN our baby died—
   My Ma she ist cried an' cried!
Yes 'n' my Pa *he* cried, too—
An' *I* cried—An' me an' you.—
An' I 'tended like my doll
She cried too—An' ever'—all—
O ist *ever'body* cried
   When our baby died!

   When our baby died—
Nen I got to took a ride!
An' we all ist rode an' rode
Clean to Heav'n where baby goed—
Mighty nigh!—An' nen Ma she
Cried ag'in—an' Pa—an' me.—
All but ist the *Angels* cried
   When our baby died!

A FULL HARVEST

SEEMS like a feller'd ort'o jes' to-day
   Git down and roll and waller, don't you
     know,
In that-air stubble, and flop up and crow,
Seein' sich crops! I'll undertake to say
There're no wheat's ever turned out thataway
   Afore this season!—Folks is keerless, though,
   And too fergitful—'caze we'd ort'o show
More thankfulness!—Jes' looky hyonder, hey?—
   And watch that little reaper wadin' thue
That last old yaller hunk o' harvest-ground—
   Jes natchur'ly a-slicin' it in two
Like honeycomb, and gaumin' it around
   The field—like it had nothin' else to do
   On'y jes' waste it all on me and you!

MY BACHELOR CHUM

A CORPULENT man is my bachelor chum,
    With a neck apoplectic and thick—
An abdomen on him as big as a drum,
    And a fist big enough for the stick;
With a walk that for grace is clear out of the case,
    And a wobble uncertain—as though
His little bow-legs had forgotten the pace
    That in youth used to favor him so.

He is forty, at least; and the top of his head
    Is a bald and a glittering thing;
And his nose and his two chubby cheeks are as red
    As three rival roses in spring.
His mouth is a grin with the corners tucked in,
    And his laugh is so breezy and bright
That it ripples his features and dimples his chin
    With a billowy look of delight.

He is fond of declaring he "don't care a straw"—
    That "the ills of a bachelor's life
Are blisses compared with a mother-in-law,
    And a boarding-school miss for a wife!"

So he smokes and he drinks, and he jokes and he
    winks,
  And he dines and he wines, all alone,
With a thumb ever ready to snap as he thinks
  Of the comforts he never has known.

But up in his den—(Ah, my bachelor chum!)—
  I have sat with him there in the gloom,
When the laugh of his lips died away to become
  But a phantom of mirth in the room.
And to look on him there you would love him,
    for all
  His ridiculous ways, and be dumb
As the little girl-face that smiles down from the
    wall
  On the tears of my bachelor chum.

TOMMY SMITH

DIMPLE-CHEEKED and rosy-lipped,
    With his cap-rim backward tipped,
Still in fancy I can see
Little Tommy smile on me—
        Little Tommy Smith.

Little unsung Tommy Smith—
Scarce a name to rhyme it with;
Yet most tenderly to me
Something sings unceasingly—
        Little Tommy Smith.

On the verge of some far land
Still forever does he stand,
With his cap-rim rakishly
Tilted; so he smiles on me—
        Little Tommy Smith.

Elder-blooms contrast the grace
Of the rover's radiant face—
Whistling back, in mimicry,
"Old—Bob—White!" all liquidly—
        Little Tommy Smith.

O my jaunty statuette
Of first love, I see you yet,
Though you smile so mistily,
It is but through tears I see,
      Little Tommy Smith.

But, with crown tipped back behind,
And the glad hand of the wind
Smoothing back your hair, I see
Heaven's best angel smile on me,—
      Little Tommy Smith.

THE LAUGHTER OF THE RAIN

The rain sounds like a laugh to me—
A low laugh poured out limpidly.

MY very soul smiles as I listen to
    The low, mysterious laughter of the rain,
  Poured musically over heart and brain
Till sodden care, soaked with it through and
        through,
Sinks; and, with wings wet with it as with dew,
  My spirit flutters up, with every stain
  Rinsed from its plumage, and as white again
As when the old laugh of the rain was new.
  Then laugh on, happy Rain! laugh louder yet!—
Laugh out in torrent-bursts of watery mirth;
  Unlock thy lips of purple cloud, and let
Thy liquid merriment baptize the earth,
  And wash the sad face of the world, and set
  The universe to music dripping-wet!

ETERNITY

O WHAT a weary while it is to stand,
　　Telling the countless ages o'er and o'er,
　Till all the finger-tips held out before
Our dazzled eyes by heaven's starry hand
Drop one by one, yet at some dread command
　Are held again, and counted evermore!
　How feverish the music seems to pour
Along the throbbing veins of anthems grand!
　And how the cherubim sing on and on—
The seraphim and angels—still in white—
　Still harping—still enraptured—far withdrawn
In hovering armies tranced in endless flight!
　. . . God's mercy! is there never dusk or dawn,
　Or any crumb of gloom to feed upon?

LAST WORDS

HE left me for a foreign land:
  I could not even free
One little tear to gem the hand
  That God had given me;
For "I will follow soon, my dear,"
  I laughed with girlish air,—
"The sun that cheers our pathway here
  Shall beam upon us there!"

And so we parted. . . . Listen, God!—
  I may not even free
One little tear to dew the sod
  Where, sleeping peacefully,
He waits in foreign lands—my dear!
  But prophecy and prayer,—
"The sun that cheers our pathway here
  Shall beam upon us—*there!*"

AT BAY

DESPERATE, at last I stand
    Ready, Fate, with open hand
To grasp yours, or to strike
Blow for blow—just as you like.

You have dogged me day by day—
Chased me when a child at play:
Even from the mother-nest
Pushed me when I needed rest.

You have crouched along my track
Like a hound, and hurled me back,
While your dog's-tongue lapped the blood
Of my murdered babyhood.

Pitilessly, year by year,
From the farthest past to here,
You have fallen like a blight
On each blossom of delight.

You have risen up between
Me and every hope serene
That has promised rest at last
From the trials of the past.

96

You have shut the light of day
From my present—stolen away
All my faith in better things
Than sheer desperation brings.

But as now I come to know
That I may no farther go,
I have turned—not to resist,
But to greet you hand or fist.

A WORN-OUT PENCIL

WELLADAY!
  Here I lay
You at rest—all worn away,
    O my pencil, to the tip
    Of our old companionship!

Memory
Sighs to see
What you are, and used to be,
    Looking backward to the time
    When you wrote your earliest rhyme!—

When I sat
Filing at
Your first point, and dreaming that
    Your initial song should be
    Worthy of posterity.

With regret
I forget
If the song be living yet,
    Yet remember, vaguely now,
    It was honest, anyhow.

You have brought
Me a thought—
Truer yet was never taught,—
    That the silent song is best,
    And the unsung worthiest.

So if I,
When I die,
May as uncomplainingly
    Drop aside as now you do,
    Write of me, as I of you:—

Here lies one
Who begun
Life a-singing, heard of none;
    And he died, satisfied,
    With his dead songs by his side.

GOD BLESS US EVERY ONE

"GOD bless us every one!" prayed Tiny Tim,
   Crippled, and dwarfed of body, yet so tall
Of soul, we tiptoe earth to look on him,
     High towering over all.

He loved the loveless world, nor dreamed indeed
   That it, at best, could give to him, the while,
But pitying glances, when his only need
     Was but a cheery smile.

And thus he prayed, "God bless us every one!"—
   Enfolding all the creeds within the span
Of his child-heart; and so, despising none,
     Was nearer saint than man.

I like to fancy God, in Paradise,
   Lifting a finger o'er the rhythmic swing
Of chiming harp and song, with eager eyes
     Turned earthward, listening—

The Anthem stilled—the Angels leaning there
   Above the golden walls—the morning sun
Of Christmas bursting flower-like with the prayer,
     "God bless us every one!"

THE TREE-TOAD

" 'S CUR'OUS-LIKE," said the tree-toad,
        "I've twittered fer rain all day;
    And I got up soon,
    And hollered tel noon—
  But the sun, hit blazed away,
      Tel I jest clumb down in a crawfish-hole,
      Weary at hart, and sick at soul!

"Dozed away fer an hour,
    And I tackled the thing ag'in:
    And I sung, and sung,
    Tel I knowed my lung
  Was jest about give in;
      And *then,* thinks I, ef hit don't rain *now,*
      They's nothin' in singin', anyhow!

"Onc't in a while some farmer
    Would come a-drivin' past;
    And he'd hear my cry,
    And stop and sigh—
  Tel I jest laid back, at last,
      And I hollered rain tel I thought my
          th'oat
      Would bust wide open at ever' note!

"But I *fetched* her!—O *I fetched* her!—
  'Cause a little while ago,
    As I kindo' set,
    With one eye shet,
  And a-singin' soft and low,
    A voice drapped down on my fevered
        brain,
    A-sayin',—'*Ef you'll jest hush I'll
        rain!*' "

LAUGHING SONG

SING us something full of laughter;
  Tune your harp, and twang the strings
Till your glad voice, chirping after,
  Mates the song the robin sings:
Loose your lips and let them flutter
  Like the wings of wanton birds,—
Though they naught but laughter utter,
  Laugh, and we'll not miss the words.

Sing in ringing tones that mingle
  In a melody that flings
Joyous echoes in a jingle
  Sweeter than the minstrel sings:
Sing of Winter, Spring or Summer,
  Clang of war, or low of herds;
Trill of cricket, roll of drummer—
  Laugh, and we'll not miss the words.

Like the lisping laughter glancing
  From the meadow brooks and springs,
Or the river's ripples dancing
  To the tune the current sings—
Sing of Now, and the Hereafter;
  Let your glad song, like the birds',
Overflow with limpid laughter—
  Laugh, and we'll not miss the words.

THE WITCH OF ERKMURDEN

I

WHO cantereth forth in the night so late—
  So late in the night, and so nigh the dawn?
'Tis The Witch of Erkmurden who leapeth the gate
Of the old churchyard where the three Sprites wait
  Till the whir of her broom is gone.

And who peereth down from the belfry tall,
  With the ghost-white face and the ghastly stare,
With lean hands clinched in the grated wall
Where the red vine rasps and the rank leaves fall,
  And the clock-stroke drowns his prayer?

II

The wee babe wails, and the storm grows loud,
  Nor deeper the dark of the night may be,
For the lightning's claw, with a great wet cloud,
Hath wiped the moon and the wild-eyed crowd
  Of the stars out wrathfully.

Knuckled and kinked as the hunchback shade
  Of a thorn-tree bendeth the bedlam old
Over the couch where the mother-maid,
With her prayerful eyes, and the babe are laid,
  Waiting the doom untold.

"Mother, O Mother, I only crave
  Mercy for him and the babe—not me!"
"Hush! for it maketh my brain to rave
Of my two white shrouds, and my one wide grave,
  And a mound for my children three."

"Mother, O Mother, I only pray
  Pity for him who is son to thee
And more than my brother.—" "Wilt hush, I say!
Though I meet thee not at the Judgment Day,
  I will bury my children three!"

"Then hark! O Mother, I hear his cry—
  Hear his curse from the church-tower now,—
'Ride thou witch till thy hate shall die,
Yet hell as Heaven eternally
  Be sealed to such as thou!'"

An infant's wail—then a laugh, god wot,
  That strangled the echoes of deepest hell;
And a thousand shuttles of lightning shot,
And the moon bulged out like a great red blot,
  And a shower of blood-stars fell.

III

There is one wide grave scooped under the eaves—
  Under the eaves as they weep and weep;
And, veiled by the mist that the dead storm weaves,
The hag bends low, and the earth receives
  Mother and child asleep.

There's the print of the hand at either throat,
   And the frothy ooze at the lips of each,
But both smile up where the new stars float,
And the moon sails out like a silver boat
   Unloosed from a stormy beach.

IV

Bright was the morn when the sexton gray
   Twirled the rope of the old church-bell,—
But it answered not, and he tugged away—
And lo, at his feet a dead man lay—
   Dropped down with a single knell.

And the scared wight found, in the lean hand
      gripped,
   A scrip which read: "O the grave is wide,
But it empty waits, for the low eaves dripped
Their prayerful tears, and the three Sprites slipped
   Away with my babe and bride."

THE BALLAD OF SMILES AND TEARS

BY LEE O. HARRIS AND JAMES WHITCOMB RILEY

I

WHEN the gleeful Spring on dancing feet
  Pranks the sward of the forest aisles,
And the bluebird pipes from his old retreat
  O then may the glad face bloom with smiles:
  But whenever the wind of winter piles
    The drifting snow on the frozen meres,
  And the feet are worn with the weary miles,
    Then hearts that are heavy may melt in tears.

II

When the soul is brimmed with a joy too sweet
  To waste like that of a laughing child's,
When the lips of love for the first time meet,
  O then may the glad face bloom with smiles:
  But whenever the kiss of love defiles,
    And friendship wanes with the waning years,
  When faith has perished, and hope beguiles,
    Then hearts that are heavy may melt in tears.

III

When the brow is crowned and the song complete,
   And the minstrel's guerdon reconciles
The victor-soul to the heart's defeat,
   O then may the glad face bloom with smiles:
   But whenever the world in scorn compiles
      Its ready pages of scoffs and jeers,
   And the brain is weary of envy's wiles,
      Then hearts that are heavy may melt in tears.

L'ENVOY

When the eyelids droop like a drowsy child's,
O then may the glad face bloom with smiles:
But whenever the waking is fraught with fears,
Then hearts that are heavy may melt in tears.

THIS MAN JONES

THIS man Jones was what you'd call
  A feller 'at had no sand at all;
Kind o' consumpted, and undersize,
And sallor-complected, with big sad eyes,
And a kind-of-a sort-of-a hang-dog style,
And a sneakin' sort-of-a half-way smile
'At kind o' give him away to us
As a preacher, maybe, er somepin' wuss.

Didn't take with the gang—well, no—
But still we managed to use him, though,—
Coddin' the gilly along the rout',
And drivin' the stakes 'at he pulled out—
Fer I was one of the bosses then,
And of course stood in with the canvasmen;
And the way we put up jobs, you know,
On this man Jones jes' beat the show!

Ust to rattle him scandalous,
And keep the feller a-dodgin' us,
And a-shyin' round half skeered to death,
And afeerd to whimper above his breath;

Give him a cussin', and then a kick,
And then a kind-of-a backhand lick—
Jes' fer the fun of seein' him climb
Around with a head on most the time.

But what was the curioust thing to me,
Was along o' the party—let me see,—
Who was our "Lion Queen" last year?—
Mamzelle Zanty, or De La Pierre?—
Well, no matter—a stunnin' mash,
With a red-ripe lip, and a long eyelash,
And a figger sich as the angels owns—
And one too many fer this man Jones.

He'd allus wake in the afternoon,
As the band waltzed in on the lion-tune,
And there, from the time 'at she'd go in
Till she'd back out of the cage ag'in,
He'd stand, shaky and limber-kneed—
'Specially when she come to "feed
The beasts raw meat with her naked hand"—
And all that business, you understand.

And it *was* resky in that den—
Fer I think she juggled three cubs then,
And a big "green" lion 'at used to smash
Collar-bones fer old Frank Nash;
And I reckon now she hain't fergot
The afternoon old "Nero" sot
His paws on *her!*—but as fer me,
It's a sort-of-a mixed-up mystery :—

Kind o' remember an awful roar,
And see her back fer the bolted door—
See the cage rock—heerd her call
"God have mercy!" and that was all—
Fer they ain't no livin' man can tell
What it's like when a thousand yell
In female tones, and a thousand more
Howl in bass till their throats is sore!

But the keeper said 'at dragged her out,
They heerd some feller laugh and shout—
"Save her! Quick! I've got the cuss!"
And yit she waked and smiled on *us!*
And we daren't flinch, fer the doctor said,
Seein' as this man Jones was dead,
Better to jes' not let her know
Nothin' o' that fer a week er so.

WAIT

WE know, O faltering heart,
 Thy need is great:
But weary is the way that leads to art,
And all who journey there must bear their part—
 Must bear their part, and—wait.

The way is wild and steep,
 And desolate:
No flowers blossom there, nor lilies peep
Above the walls to warn you, as you weep,
 With one white whisper—"Wait."

You will find thorns, alas!
 And keen as fate:
And, reaching from rank fens of withered grass,
Briers will clutch your feet, nor let you pass—
 And you must wait—must wait.

And though with failing sight
 You see the gate
Of Promise locked and barred, with swarthy
 Night
Guarding the golden keys of morning-light,—
 Press bravely on—and wait.

LELLOINE

I

TINY queen,
  Lelloine!
Little eyes laugh out between
  Dimpled fingers that were busy
But a weary moment since
  Mischief-making—for she is a
Match for Puck the fairy prince!
She must ever be advancing
Some new prank; and laughing, dancing,
  Disappearing at the door,
Like a sunbeam leaving shaded
  All that was so bright before—
Like a sunbeam leaving faded
  Flowers on the floor.
O, you joking, dear provoking,
  Little laughing Lelloine!

II

Calm, serene,
Lelloine!
Lying lily-like between
The blurred leaves of life and love

That our wet eyes bend above,
Lisp nor laughter on the lips:
Two white rose-leaves now eclipse
Such of glances as the chance
Dimple dances in advance.
Darling! Darling! tell us why
You do neither laugh nor cry;
Even though you moaned in pain,
We could be so glad again!
What unchanging smile is this
That we shudder so to kiss?

    Hearts are leaning low to glean
    All your meaning, Lelloine.

A DREAM OF AUTUMN

MELLOW hazes, lowly trailing
    Over wood and meadow, veiling
Somber skies, with wild fowl sailing
    Sailor-like to foreign lands;
And the north wind overleaping
Summer's brink, and flood-like sweeping
Wrecks of roses where the weeping-
    Willows wring their helpless hands.

Flared, like Titan torches flinging
Flakes of flame and embers, springing
From the vale, the trees stand swinging
    In the moaning atmosphere;
While in dead'ning lands the lowing
Of the cattle, sadder growing,
Fills the sense to overflowing
    With the sorrow of the year.

Sorrowfully, yet the sweeter
Sings the brook in rippled meter
Under boughs that lithely teeter
    Lorn birds, answering from the shores

Through the viny, shady-shiny
Interspaces, shot with tiny
Flying motes that fleck the winy
   Wave-engraven sycamores.

Fields of ragged stubble, wrangled
With rank weeds, and shocks of tangled
Corn, with crests like rent plumes dangled
   Over Harvest's battle-plain;
And the sudden whir and whistle
Of the quail that, like a missile,
Whizzes over thorn and thistle,
   And, a missile, drops again.

Muffled voices, hid in thickets
Where the redbird stops to stick its
Ruddy beak betwixt the pickets
   Of the truant's rustic trap;
And the sound of laughter ringing
Where, within the wild vine swinging,
Climb Bacchante's schoolmates, flinging
   Purple clusters in her lap.

Rich as wine, the sunset flashes
Round the tilted world, and dashes
Up the sloping West, and splashes
   Red foam over sky and sea—
Till my dream of Autumn, paling
In the splendor all-prevailing,
Like a sallow leaf goes sailing
   Down the silence solemnly.

SINCE MY MOTHER DIED

SINCE my mother died, the tone
Of my voice has fainter grown,
And my words, so strangely few,
Are as strange to me as you.
Something like a lens is drawn
Over all I look upon,
And the world is O so wide,
    Since my mother died.

Since my mother died, my face
Knows not any resting-place,
Save in visions, lightly pressed
In its old accustomed rest
On her shoulder. But I wake
With a never-ending ache
In my heart, and naught beside,
    Since my mother died.

Since my mother died, the years
Have been drooping like my tears,
Till the bloom is washed away
From my cheeks, and slow decay

Seams the corners of my eyes,
Where my childish laughter lies
Drowned in tears that never dried
     Since my mother died.

Since my mother died, my feet
Falter in the crowded street,
With bewildered steps that seem
Tangled in some grassy dream,
And, in busy haunts of men,
Slowly down the past again
Do I wander weary-eyed
     Since my mother died.

Since my mother died, O friends!
No one leads me now, or lends
Me a kindly word, or touch
Of the hands I need so much;
No one counsels me, or cares
For my trials, doubts, despairs,
And the world is O so wide,
     Since my mother died.

BELLS JANGLED

I LIE low-coiled in a nest of dreams;
  The lamp gleams dim i' the odorous gloom,
And the stars at the casement leak long gleams
  Of misty light through the haunted room
Where I lie low-coiled in dreams.

The night winds ooze o'er my dusk-drowned face
  In a dewy flood that ebbs and flows,
Washing a surf of dim white lace
  Under my throat and the dark red rose
In the shade of my dusk-drowned face.

There's a silken strand of some strange sound
  Slipping out of a skein of song:
Eerily as a call unwound
  From a fairy bugle, it slides along
In a silken strand of sound.

There's the tinkling drip of a faint guitar;
  There's a gurgling flute, and a blaring horn
Blowing bubbles of tune afar
  O'er the misty heights of the hills of morn,
To the drip of a faint guitar.

119

And I dream that I neither sleep nor wake—
　　Careless am I if I wake or sleep,
For my soul floats out on the waves that break
　　In crests of song on the shoreless deep
Where I neither sleep nor wake.

DUSK SONG—THE BEETLE

THE shrilling locust slowly sheathes
  His dagger-voice, and creeps away
Beneath the brooding leaves where breathes
  The zephyr of the dying day:
One naked star has waded through
  The purple shallows of the night,
And faltering as falls the dew
  It drips its misty light.

    O'er garden blooms,
      On tides of musk,
    The beetle booms adown the glooms
    And bumps along the dusk.

The katydid is rasping at
  The silence from the tangled broom:
On drunken wings the flitting bat
  Goes staggering athwart the gloom;
The toadstool bulges through the weeds,
  And lavishly to left and right
The fireflies, like golden seeds,
  Are sown about the night.

O'er slumbrous blooms,
On floods of musk,
The beetle booms adown the glooms
And bumps along the dusk.

The primrose flares its baby-hands
    Wide open, as the empty moon,
Slow lifted from the underlands,
    Drifts up the azure-arched lagoon;
The shadows on the garden walk
    Are frayed with rifts of silver light;
And, trickling down the poppy-stalk,
    The dewdrop streaks the night.

O'er folded blooms,
On swirls of musk,
The beetle booms adown the glooms
And bumps along the dusk.

SLEEP

THOU drowsy god, whose blurred eyes, half
      awink,
  Muse on me,—drifting out upon thy dreams,
  I lave my soul as in enchanted streams
Where reveling satyrs pipe along the brink,
And, tipsy with the melody they drink,
  Uplift their dangling hooves and down the beams
  Of sunshine dance like motes. Thy languor seems
An ocean-depth of love wherein I sink
  Like some fond Argonaut, right willingly,—
Because of wooing eyes upturned to mine,
  And siren-arms that coil their sorcery
About my neck, with kisses so divine,
  The heavens reel above me, and the sea
  Swallows and licks its wet lips over me.

MARTHY ELLEN

THEY'S nothin' in the name to strike
A feller more'n common like!
'Taint liable to git no praise
Ner nothin' like it nowadays;
An' yit that name o' her'n is jest
As purty as the purtiest—
And more'n that, I'm here to say
I'll live a-thinkin' thataway
      And die fer Marthy Ellen!

It may be I was prejudust
In favor of it from the fust—
'Cause I kin ricollect jest how
We met, and hear her mother now
A-callin' of her down the road—
And, aggervatin' little toad!—
I see her now, jest sort o' half-
Way disapp'inted, turn and laugh
      And mock her—"Marthy Ellen!"

Our people never had no fuss,
And yit they never tuck to us;
We neighbered back and foreds some;
Until they see she liked to come
To our house—and me and her
Was jest together ever'whur
And all the time—and when they'd see
That I liked her and she liked me,
      They'd holler "Marthy Ellen!"

When we growed up, and they shet down
On me and her a-runnin' roun'
Together, and her father said
He'd never leave her nary red,
So he'p him, ef she married me,
And so on—and her mother she
Jest agged the gyrl, and said she 'lowed
She'd ruther see her in her shroud,
    I *writ* to Marthy Ellen—

That is, I kind o' tuck my pen
In hand, and stated whur and when
The undersigned would be that night,
With two good hosses, saddled right
Fer lively travelin', in case
Her folks 'ud like to jine the race.
She sent the same note back, and writ
"The rose is red!" right under it—
      "Your'n allus, Marthy Ellen."

That's all, I reckon—Nothin' more
To tell but what you've heerd afore—
The same old story, sweeter though
Fer all the trouble, don't you know.
Old-fashioned name! and yit it's jest
As purty as the purtiest;
And more'n that, I'm here to say
I'll live a-thinkin' thataway,
    And die fer Marthy Ellen!

THE LITTLE TOWN O' TAILHOLT

YOU kin boast about yer cities, and their stiddy
     growth and size,
And brag about yer County-seats, and business en-
     terprise,
And railroads, and factories, and all sich foolery—
But the little Town o' Tailholt is big enough fer me!

You kin harp about yer churches, with their steeples
     in the clouds,
And gas about yer graded streets, and blow about
     yer crowds;
You kin talk about yer *"the*aters," and all you've got
     to see—
But the little Town o' Tailholt is *show* enough
     fer me!

They hain't no *style* in our town—hit's little-like
     and small—
They hain't no *"churches,"* nuther,—jes' the meet-
     in'-house is all;
They's no sidewalks, to speak of—but the highway's
     allus free,
And the little Town o' Tailholt is wide enough
     fer me!

Some finds it discommodin'-like, I'm willing to
    admit
To hev but one post-office, and a womern keepin'
    hit,
And the drug-store, and shoe-shop, and grocery, all
    three—
But the little Town o' Tailholt is handy 'nough
    fer me!

You kin smile and turn yer nose up, and joke and
    hev yer fun,
And laugh and holler "Tail-holts is better holts'n
    none!"
Ef the city suits you better, w'y, hit's where you'd
    ort'o be—
But the little Town o' Tailholt's good enough
    fer me!

WHERE SHALL WE LAND

Where shall we land you, sweet?
—Swinburne

ALL listlessly we float
  Out seaward in the boat
    That beareth Love.
Our sails of purest snow
Bend to the blue below
    And to the blue above.
        Where shall we land?

We drift upon a tide
Shoreless on every side,
    Save where the eye
Of Fancy sweeps far lands
Shelved slopingly with sands
    Of gold and porphyry.
        Where shall we land?

The fairy isles we see,
Loom up so mistily—
    So vaguely fair,

128

We do not care to break
Fresh bubbles in our wake
　　To bend our course for there.
　　　Where shall we land?

The warm winds of the deep
Have lulled our sails to sleep,
　　And so we glide
Careless of wave or wind,
Or change of any kind,
　　Or turn of any tide.
　　　Where shall we land?

We droop our dreamy eyes
Where our reflection lies
　　Steeped in the sea,
And, in an endless fit
Of languor, smile on it
　　And its sweet mimicry.
　　　Where shall we land?

"Where shall we land?"　God's grace!
I know not any place
　　So fair as this—
Swung here between the blue
Of sea and sky, with you
　　To ask me, with a kiss,
　　　"Where shall we land?"

HOPE

HOPE, bending o'er me one time, snowed the
      flakes
  Of her white touches on my folded sight,
And whispered, half rebukingly, "What makes
  My little girl so sorrowful to-night?"

O, scarce did I unclasp my lids, or lift
  Their tear-glued fringes, as with blind embrace
I caught within my arms the mother-gift,
  And with wild kisses dappled all her face.

That was a baby dream of long ago:
  My fate is fanged with frost, and tongued with
      flame:
My woman-soul, chased naked through the snow,
  Stumbles and staggers on without an aim.

And yet, here in my agony, sometimes
  A faint voice reaches down from some far height,
And whispers through a glamouring of rhymes,—
  "What makes my little girl so sad to-night?"

THE LITTLE TINY KICKSHAW

—And any little tiny kickshaw.
—SHAKESPEARE.

O THE little tiny kickshaw that Mither sent tae
    me,
'Tis sweeter than the sugar-plum that reepens on the
    tree,
Wi' denty flavorin's o' spice an' musky rosemarie,
The little tiny kickshaw that Mither sent tae me.

'Tis luscious wi' the stalen tang o' fruits frae ower
    the sea,
An' e'en its fragrance gars me laugh wi' langin' lip
    an' ee,
Till a' its frazen scheen o' white maun melten hinnie
    be—
Sae weel I luve the kickshaw that Mither sent tae
    me.

O I luve the tiny kickshaw, an' I smack my lips wi'
    glee,
Aye mickle do I luve the taste o' sic a luxourie,
But maist I luve the luvein' han's that could the
    giftie gie
O' the little tiny kickshaw that Mither sent tae me.

131

DEATH

LO, I am dying! And to feel the King
  Of Terrors fasten on me, steeps all sense
Of life, and love, and loss, and everything,
In such deep calms of restful indolence,
His keenest fangs of pain are sweet to me
As fusèd kisses of mad lovers' lips
When, flung shut-eyed in spasmed ecstasy,
They feel the world spin past them in eclipse,
And so thank God with ever-tightening lids!
But what I see, the soul of me forbids
All utterance of; and what I hear and feel,
The rattle in my throat could ill reveal
Though it were music to your ears as to
Mine own.—Press closer—closer—I have grown
So great, your puny arms about me thrown
Seem powerless to hold me here with you;—
I slip away—I waver—and—I fall—
Christ! What a plunge! Where am I dropping? All
My breath bursts into dust—I can not cry—
I whirl—I reel and veer up overhead,
And drop flat-faced against—against—the sky—
Soh, bless me! I am dead!

TO THE WINE-GOD MERLUS

A Toast of Jucklet's

HO! ho! thou jolly god, with kinkèd lips
  And laughter-streaming eyes, thou liftest
    up
The heart of me like any wassail-cup,
And from its teeming brim, in foaming drips,
Thou blowest all my cares. I cry to thee,
Between the sips:—Drink long and lustily;
Drink thou my ripest joys, my richest mirth,
My maddest staves of wanton minstrelsy;
Drink every song I've tinkered here on earth
With any patch of music; drink! and be
Thou drainer of my soul, and to the lees
Drink all my lover-thrills and ecstasies;
And with a final gulp—ho! ho!—drink me,
And roll me o'er thy tongue eternally.

THE GINOINE AR-TICKLE

TALKIN' o' poetry,—There're few men yit
   'At's got the stuff boiled down so's it'll pour
Out sorgum-like, and keeps a year and more
   Jes' sweeter ever' time you tackle it!
Why, all the jinglin' truck 'at hes been writ
   Fer twenty year and better is so pore
   You cain't find no sap in it any more
'N you'd find juice in puff-balls!—AND I'D
      QUIT!
What people wants is facts, I apperhend;
  And naked Natur is the thing to give
Your writin' bottom, eh? And I contend
  'At honest work is allus bound to live.
Now them's my views; 'cause you kin recommend
Sich poetry as that from end to end.

A BRIDE

"O I AM weary!" she sighed, as her billowy
    Hair she unloosed in a torrent of gold
That rippled and fell o'er a figure as willowy,
    Graceful and fair as a goddess of old:
Over her jewels she flung herself drearily,
    Crumpled the laces that snowed on her breast,
Crushed with her fingers the lily that wearily
    Clung in her hair like a dove in its nest.
      —And naught but her shadowy form in the
        mirror
        To kneel in dumb agony down and weep near
        her!

"Weary?"—of what? Could we fathom the
      mystery?—
Lift up the lashes weighed down by her tears
And wash with their dews one white face from her
      history,
    Set like a gem in the red rust of years?
Nothing will rest her—unless he who died of her
    Strayed from his grave, and, in place of the
      groom,
Tipping her face, kneeling there by the side of her,
    Drained the old kiss to the dregs of his doom.
      —And naught but that shadowy form in the
        mirror
        To kneel in dumb agony down and weep near
        her!

STANZAS FOR A NEW SONG

WHISTLE us something old, you know!
  Pucker your lips with the old-time twist,
And whistle the jigs of the long ago,
  Or the old hornpipes that you used to whist.
    Some old, old tune that we oft averred
    Was a little the oldest thing we'd heard
    Since "the bob-tailed nag" was a frisky colt,
    In the babbling days of old "Ben Bolt."

Whistle us something old and gray—
  Some toothless tune of the bygone years—
Some bald old song that limps to-day
  With a walking-stick this vale of tears.
    Whistle a stave of the good old days,
    E'er the fur stood up in a thousand ways
    On the listener's pelt as he ripped and tore,
    And diddle-dee-blank-blanked Pinafore.

CHORUS

Whistle us something old, you know!
  Pucker your lips with the old-time twist,
And whistle the jigs of the long ago,
  Or the old hornpipes that you used to whist.

LINES TO AN ONSETTLED YOUNG MAN

"O WHAT is Life at last," says you,
  , "'At woman-folks and man-folks
          too,
Cain't oncomplainin', worry through?

"An' what is Love, 'at no one yit
'At's monkeyed with it kin forgit,
Er gits fat on remembern hit?

"An' what is Death?"—W'y, looky hyur—
Ef Life an' Love don't suit you, sir,
Hit's jes' the thing yer lookin' fer!

PLANTATION HYMN

H EAR dat rum'lin' in de sky!
Hol' fas', brudders, till you git dah!
O, dat's de good Lord walkin' by,
Hol' fas', brudders, till you git dah!

CHORUS

Mahster! Jesus!
You done come down to please us,
And dahs de good Lord sees us,
As he goes walkin' by!

See dat lightnin' lick his tongue?
Hol' fas', brudders, till you git dah!
'Spec he taste de song 'ut de angels sung—
Hol' fas', brudders, till you git dah!

De big black clouds is bust in two,
Hol' fas', brudders, till you git dah!
And dahs de 'postles peekin' frue,
Hol' fas', brudders, till you git dah!

138

Know dem angels ev'ry one,
　Hol' fas', brudders, till you git dah!
Kase dey's got wings and we'se got none,
　Hol' fas', brudders, till you git dah!

CHORUS

Mahster!　Jesus!
You done come down to please us,
And dahs de good Lord sees us,
　As he goes walkin' by!

LAWYER AND CHILD

HOW large was Alexander, father,
  That parties designate
The historic gentleman as rather
  Inordinately great?

Why, son, to speak with conscientious
  Regard for history,
Waiving all claims, of course, to heights
    pretentious,—
  About the size of me.

To Mr. and Mrs. Hugh B. Wilson
→ On Their ←
Golden Wedding

I

Your Golden Wedding! — Fifty years
Of comradeship, through smiles and tears! —
Through summer sun, and winter sleet —
You walked the ways with willing feet;
For, journeying together thus,
Each path held something glorious.
No winter wind could blow so chill
But found you even warmer still
In fervor of affection — blest
In knowing all was for the best;
And so, content, you faced the storm,
And fared on, smiling, arm in arm.

II

But why this moralizing strain
Beside a hearth that glows again
As on your Wooden Wedding-day;
When butter-prints and paddles lay
Around in dough-boxes for you there,
And all such "woodnish" concerns.

And "woodmush" they are,— for now
Who can afford to keep a cow,
And pestle some old churn, when you
Can buy good butter—"Goldsu", too—
Far cheaper than you can afford
To make it and neglect the Lord!

III

And round your hearth the faces gleam
That may recall, as in a dream,
The brightness of a time when Tin
(Came clattering) and flashing in,
And raising noise enough to "siege
And settle any swarm of bees!
But those were darling times, no doubt,
To see the mother pouring out
The "tins" of milk, and tilting up
The coffee-pot above your cup;
Or, with ~~with~~ the ladle from the wall,
Dipping and serving mush for all.

IV

And all the "Weddings", as they came, —
The "Glass"— the "China",— still the same
You see them, till the last ere this,—
The "Silver",— and your wedded bliss
Abated not,— for love appears
Just silvered over with the years:
Silver the grandchild's laughter you hear,
Silver his hopes; and silver-clear
Your silent prayer for him,— and still
Silver your faith through good or ill —
Silver and silver everywhere
Bright as the silver of your hair.

V

But on your Golden Wedding!
What can I give to you to-day
Who am too very poor indeed
To offer that I so much need —
If gold I gave, I fear, alack!
I'd have to make you give it back.

And so, in lieu — and little worse —
I proffer you this dross of verse —
The merest tinsel, I admit
But take it — I have more of it,
And with it take the fond regard
Of one that loves — and loves you hard!

J. W. Riley.

Greenfield, Dec. 23.
— 1884

THE LOST KISS

I PUT by the half-written poem,
 While the pen, idly trailed in my hand,
Writes on,—"Had I words to complete it,
 Who'd read it, or who'd understand?"
But the little bare feet on the stairway,
 And the faint, smothered laugh in the hall,
And the eery-low lisp on the silence,
 Cry up to me over it all.

So I gather it up—where was broken
 The tear-faded thread of my theme,
Telling how, as one night I sat writing,
 A fairy broke in on my dream,
A little inquisitive fairy—
 My own little girl, with the gold
Of the sun in her hair, and the dewy
 Blue eyes of the fairies of old.

'Twas the dear little girl that I scolded—
 "For was it a moment like this,"
I said, "when she knew I was busy,
 To come romping in for a kiss?—

141

Come rowdying up from her mother,
  And clamoring there at my knee
For 'One 'ittle kiss for my dolly,
  And one 'ittle uzzer for me!' "

God, pity the heart that repelled her,
  And the cold hand that turned her away,
And take, from the lips that denied her,
  This answerless prayer of to-day!
Take, Lord, from my mem'ry forever
  That pitiful sob of despair,
And the patter and trip of the little bare feet,
  And the one piercing cry on the stair!

I put by the half-written poem,
  While the pen, idly trailed in my hand,
Writes on,—"Had I words to complete it,
  Who'd read it, or who'd understand?"
But the little bare feet on the stairway,
  And the faint, smothered laugh in the hall,
And the eery-low lisp on the silence,
  Cry up to me over it all.

MICHAEL FLYNN AND THE BABY

LUK at 'ere, ould baby,—who
　　Shak's the fist av 'im at you?
Who's the spalpeen wid the stim
Av his poipe a pokin' 'im?
Who's the divil grinnin' 'ere
In the eyes av yez, me dear?
Arrah! darlint, spake and soy
Don't yez know yer feyther—boy?

Wheer's the gab yer mither had
Whin she blarneyed yer ould dad
Wid her tricks and 'ily words
Loike the liltin' av the birds?
Wheer's the tongue av Michael Flynn,
And the capers av the chin
He's a-waggin' at yez?—Hoy?
Don't yez know yer feyther—boy?

Arrah! baby, wid the eyes
Av the saints in Paradise,
And Saint Patrick's own bald pate,
Is it yer too howly swate
To be changin' words because
It's the hod, and not the cross,
Ornamints me showlder?—soy?
Don't yez know yer feyther—boy?

ON A SPLENDUD MATCH

*[On the night of the marraige of the foregoin'
couple, which shall be nameless here, these lines was
ca'mly dashed off in the albun of the happy bride
whilse the shivver-ree was goin' on outside the resi-
dence.]*

H E was warned aginst the *womern*—
  She was warned aginst the *man*.—
And ef *that* won't make a weddin',
  W'y, they's nothin' else that can!

THE SINGER

WHILE with Ambition's hectic flame
   He wastes the midnight oil,
And dreams, high-throned on heights of
     fame,
   To rest him from his toil,—

Death's Angel, like a vast eclipse,
   Above him spreads her wings,
And fans the embers of his lips
   To ashes as he sings.

GUINEVERE

WHAT is it I am waiting for?
My footfall in the corridor
Jars upward through the night, and swings
The brazen silence till it rings
Like any bell. My weak knees faint
Before the sad face of my saint,
And, 'twixt my lifted eyes and tears,
Dim lists of mounted cavaliers
Swim past. . . . A nodding plume that dips
To brush the dead prayers from my lips
Like dust—. God's mercy! rid my sight
Of Launcelot, or blind me quite!
I know what duty is! Ah, Christ!
The memory of our latest tryst
Is fanged within my very soul! . . .
I swear to you, in all control
I held myself! . . . 'Twas love, I wis,
That sprang upon that kiss of his,
And drank and drained it to the lees
Of three God-shaken destinies.
'Twas love, I tell you, wild, insane,
Stark mad and babbling, wanton, vain—
But tell me, Where is Arthur?—or,
What is it I am waiting for?

THE WEREWIFE

SHE came to me in a dazzling guise
  Of gleaming tresses and glimmering eyes,
With long, limp lashes that drooped and made
For their baleful glances bowers of shade;
And a face so white—so white and sleek
That the roses blooming in either cheek
Flamed and burned with a crimson glow
Redder than ruddiest roses blow—
Redder than blood of the roses know
That Autumn spills in the drifted snow.
And what could my fluttering, moth-winged soul
Do but hover in her control?—
With its little, bewildered bead-eyes fixed
Where the gold and the white and the crimson
    mixed?
And when the tune of her low laugh went
Up from that ivory instrument
That you would have called her throat, I swear
The notes built nests in her gilded hair,
And nestled and whistled and twittered there,
And wooed me and won me to my despair.
And thus it was that she lured me on,
Till the latest gasp of my love was gone,

147

And my soul lay dead, with a loathing face
Turned in vain from her dread embrace,—
For even its poor dead eyes could see
Her sharp teeth sheathed in the flesh of me,
And her dripping lips, as she turned to shake
The red froth off that her greed did make,
As my heart gripped hold of a deathless ache,
And the kiss of her stung like the fang of a snake.

THE BAN

I

STRANGE dreams of what I used to be,
And what I dreamed I *would* be, swim
Before my vision, faint and dim
As misty distances we see
In pictured scenes of fairy lands;
And ever on, with empty hands,
And eyes that ever lie to me,
And smiles that no one understands,
I grope adown my destiny.

II

Some say I waver as I walk
Along the crowded thoroughfares;
And some leer in my eyes, and talk
Of dulness, while I see in theirs—
Like fishes' eyes, alive or dead—
But surfaces of vacancy—
Blank disks that never seem to see,
But glint and glow and glare instead.

149

III

The ragged shawl I wear is wet
With driving, dripping rains, and yet
It seems a royal raiment, where,
Through twisted torrents of my hair,
I see rare gems that gleam and shine
Like jewels in a stream of wine;
The gaping shoes that clothe my feet
Are golden sandals, and the shrine
Where courtiers grovel and repeat
Vain prayers, and where, in joy thereat,
A fair Prince doffs his plumèd hat,
And kneels, and names me all things sweet.

IV

Sometimes the sun shines, and the lull
Of winter noon is like a tune
The stars might twinkle to the moon
If night were white and beautiful—
For when the clangor of the town
And strife of traffic softens down,
The wakeful hunger that I nurse,
In listening, forgets to curse,
Until—ah, joy! with drooping head
I drowse, and dream that I am dead
And buried safe beyond their eyes
Who either pity or despise.

AN IDIOT

I'M on'y thist a' idiot—
   That's what folks calls a feller what
     Ain't got no mind
      Of any kind,
Ner don't know nothin' he's forgot.—
     I'm one o' *them*—But I know why
     The bees buzz *this* way when they fly,—
     'Cause honey it gits on their wings.
     Ain't thumbs and fingers funny things?

   What's money? Hooh! it's thist a hole
   Punched in a round thing 'at won't roll
     'Cause they's a string
      Poked through the thing
And fastened round your neck—that's all!
     Ef I could git my money off,
     I'd buy whole lots o' whoopin'-cough
     And give it to the boy next door
     Who died 'cause he ain't got no more.

   What is it when you die? *I* know,—
   You can't wake up ag'in, ner go
     To sleep no more—
      Ner kick, ner snore,

Ner lay and look and watch it snow;
　　And when folks slaps and pinches you—
　　You don't keer nothin' *what* they do.
　　No honey on the *angels'* wings!
　　Ain't thumbs and fingers funny things?

AN ORDER FOR A SONG

MAKE me a song of all good things,
    And fill it full of murmurings,
Of merry voices, such as we
Remember in our infancy;
But make it tender, for the sake
Of hearts that brood and tears that break,
And tune it with the harmony,
    The sighs of sorrow make.

Make me a song of summer-time,
And pour such music down the rhyme
As ripples over gleaming sands
And grassy brinks of meadow-lands;
But make it very sweet and low,
For need of them that sorrow so,
Because they reap with empty hands
    The dreams of long ago.

Make me a song of such a tone,
That when we croon it all alone,
The tears of longing as they drip,
Will break in laughter on the lip;
And make it, oh, so pure and clear
And jubilant that every ear
Shall drink its rapture sip by sip,
    And Heaven lean to hear.

THE CONQUEROR

HE hears the whir of the battle-drum,
   And the shrill-voiced fife, and the
      bugle-call,
With a thirsty spirit that drinks it all
   As men might drink the wine poured from
Old wicker flagons raimented
   With the rust and dust of ages dead.

He plunges into the crimson sea
   Of carnage, and with a dauntless pride,
He swims, with his good star, side by side,
   To the blood-sprayed heights of Victory,
Where never his glory waxes dim,
   Though a woman's weak hand conquers
      him.

And high and alone—as the sculptor makes
   Him set in stone that the world may see—
He sits there, crowned eternally,
   And sheltered under a flag that shakes
Her silken stripes and her silver stars
   Into a tangle of endless wars.

AFTER DEATH

A FANCY

AH! this delights me more than words could
    tell,—
  To just lie stark and still, with folded hands
That tremble not at greeting or farewell,
    Nor fumble foolishly in loosened strands
      Of woman's hair, nor grip with jealousy
      To find her face turned elsewhere smilingly.

With slumbrous lids, and mouth in mute repose,
  And lips that yearn no more for any kiss—
Though it might drip, as from the red-lipped rose
    The dewdrop drips, 'twere not so sweet as this
      Unutterable density of rest
      That reigns in every vein of brain and breast!

And thus—soaked with still laughter through and
    through—
  I lie here dreaming of the forms that pass
Above my grave, to drop, with tears, a few
    White flowers that but curdle the green grass;—
      And if they read such sermons, they could see
      How I do pity them that pity me.

THE MAD LOVER

MY eyes are feverish and dull;
    I'm tired, and my throat hurts so!
And life has grown so pitiful—
    So very pitiful I know
Not any hope of rest or peace,
    But just to live on ache by ache,
Feeling my heart click on, nor cease,
    Nor ever wholly break.

You smiled so sweetly, Miriam Wayne,
    I could not help but love your smile,
And fair as sunshine after rain
    It glimmered on me all the while.
Why, it did soak as summer light
    Through all my life, until, indeed,
I ripened as an apple might
    From golden rind to seed.

Fate never wrought so pitiless
    An evil, as when first your eyes
Poured back in mine the tenderness
    That made the world a Paradise—

For Miriam, remembering
  The warm white hands that lay in mine
Like wisps of sunshine vanishing,
  Your kisses, spilled like wine

Down over forehead, face and lips,
  Till I lay drunken with delight
From crown of soul to finger-tips—
  . . . Shriek, Memory, in mad affright!—
Howl at the moon like any hound!
  Yelp "love" and "liar" every breath,
And "Heaven is lost and hell is found!"
  So moan yourself to death!

TO ROBERT BURNS

SWEET Singer that I loe the maist
O' ony, sin' wi' eager haste
I smacket bairn-lips ower the taste
      O' hinnied sang,
I hail thee, though a blessed ghaist
      In Heaven lang!

For, weel I ken, nae cantie phrase,
Nor courtly airs, nor lairdly ways,
Could gar me freer blame, or praise,
      Or proffer hand,
Where "Rantin' Robbie" and his lays
      Thegither stand.

And sae these hamely lines I send,
Wi' jinglin' words at ilka end,
In echo o' the sangs that wend
      Frae thee to me
Like simmer-brooks, wi' mony a bend
      O' wimplin' glee.

In fancy, as, wi' dewy een,
I part the clouds aboon the scene
Where thou wast born, and peer atween,

I see nae spot
In a' the Hielands half sae green
And unforgot!

I see nae storied castle-hall,
Wi' banners flauntin' ower the wall
And serf and page in ready call,
Sae grand to me
As ane puir cotter's hut, wi' all
Its poverty.

There where the simple daisy grew
Sae bonnie sweet, and modest, too,
Thy liltin' filled its wee head fu'
O' sic a grace,
It aye is weepin' tears o' dew
Wi' droopit face.

Frae where the heather bluebells fling
Their sangs o' fragrance to the Spring,
To where the lavrock soars to sing,
Still lives thy strain,
For a' the birds are twittering
Sangs like thine ain.

And aye, by light o' sun or moon,
By banks o' Ayr, or Bonnie Doon,
The waters lilt nae tender tune
But sweeter seems
Because they poured their limpid rune
Through a' thy dreams.

Wi' brimmin' lip, and laughin' ee,
Thou shookest even Grief wi' glee,
Yet had nae niggart sympathy
      Where Sorrow bowed,
But gavest a' thy tears as free
      As a' thy gowd.

And sae it is we loe thy name
To see bleeze up wi' sic a flame,
That a' pretentious stars o' fame
      Maun blink asklent,
To see how simple worth may shame
      Their brightest glent.

HER VALENTINE

SOMEBODY'S sent a funny little valentine to
    me.
It's a bunch of baby-roses in a vase of filigree,
And hovering above them—just as cute as he can
    be—
Is a fairy cupid tangled in a scarf of poetry.

And the prankish little fellow looks so knowing in
    his glee,
With his golden bow and arrow, aiming most
    unerringly
At a pair of hearts so labeled that I may read and
    see
That one is meant for "One Who Loves," and one
    is meant for me.

But I know the lad who sent it! It's as plain as
    A-B-C!—
For the roses they are *blushing,* and the vase stands
    awkwardly,
And the little god above it—though as cute as he
    can be—
Can not breathe the lightest whisper of his burning
    love for me.

SONGS TUNELESS

I

HE kisses me! Ah, now, at last,
   He says good night as it should be,
His great warm eyes bent yearningly
Above my face—his arms locked fast
   About me, and mine own eyes dim
   With happy tears for love of him.

He kisses me! Last night, beneath
   A swarm of stars, he said I stood
   His one fair form of womanhood,
And springing, shut me in the sheath
   Of a caress that almost hid
   Me from the good his kisses did.

He kisses me! He kisses me!
   This is the sweetest song I know,
   And so I sing it very low
And faint, and O so tenderly
   That, though you listen, none but he
   May hear it as he kisses me.

II

"How can I make you love me more?"—
  A thousand times she asks me this,
  Her lips uplifted with the kiss
That I have tasted o'er and o'er,
  Till now I drain it with no sense
  Other than utter indolence.

"How can I make you love me more?"—
  A thousand times her questioning face
  Has nestled in its resting-place
Unanswered, till, though I adore
  This thing of being loved, I doubt
  Not I could get along without.

"How can she make me love her more?"—
  Ah! little woman, if, indeed,
  I might be frank as is the need
Of frankness, I would fall before
  Her very feet, and there confess
  My love were more if hers were less.

III

Since I am old I have no care
  To babble silly tales of when
  I loved, and lied, as other men
Have done, who boasted here and there,
  They would have died for the fair thing
  They after murdered, marrying.

Since I am old I reason thus—
   No thing survives, of all the past,
   But just regret enough to last
Us till the clods have smothered us;—
   Then, with our dead loves, side by side,
   We may, perhaps, be satisfied.

Since I am old, and strive to blow
   Alive the embers of my youth
   And early loves, I find, in sooth,
An old man's heart may burn so low,
   'Tis better just to calmly sit
   And rake the ashes over it.

SISTER JONES'S CONFESSION

I THOUGHT the deacon liked me, yit
    I warn't adzackly shore of it—
Fer, mind ye, time and time ag'in,
When jiners 'ud be comin' in,
I'd seed him shakin' hands as free
With all the sistern as with me!
But jurin' last Revival, where
He called on *me* to lead in prayer
An' kneeled there with me, side by side,
A-whisper'n' "he felt sanctified
Jes' tetchin' of my gyarment's hem,"—
That settled things as fur as them—
Thare *other* wimmin was concerned!—
And—well!—I know I must 'a' turned
A dozen colors!—*Flurried?—la!*—
No mortal sinner never saw
A gladder widder than the one
A-kneelin' there and wonderun'
Who'd pray!—So glad, upon my word,
I railly couldn't thank the Lord!

THE DEAD JOKE AND THE FUNNY MAN

LONG years ago, a funny man,
   Flushed with a strange delight,
Sat down and wrote a funny thing
   All in the solemn night;
And as he wrote he clapped his hands
   And laughed with all his might.
     For it was such a funny thing,
     O, such a very funny thing,
     This wonderfully funny thing,
He
       Laughed
         Outright.

And so it was this funny man
   Printed this funny thing—
Forgot it, too, nor ever thought
   It worth remembering,
Till but a day or two ago.
   (Ah! what may changes bring!)
     He found this selfsame funny thing
     In an exchange—"O, funny thing!"
     He cried, "You dear old funny thing!"
And
       Sobbed
         Outright.

SLEEP

ORPHANED, I cry to thee:
Sweet Sleep! O kneel and be
A mother unto me!
Calm thou my childish fears;
Fold—fold mine eyelids to, all tenderly,
And dry my tears.

Come, Sleep, all drowsy-eyed
And faint with languor,—slide
Thy dim face down beside
Mine own, and let me rest
And nestle in thy heart, and there abide,
A favored guest.

Good night to every care,
And shadow of despair!
Good night to all things where
Within is no delight!—
Sleep opens her dark arms, and, swooning
there,
I sob: Good night—good night!

ONE ANGEL

"A HOMELY little woman with big hands":
'Twas thus she named herself, and shook
her head
All solemnly, the day that we were wed,
While I—well, I laughed lightly as I said,—
"No prince am I astray from fairy lands,
O, 'homely little woman with big hands'!"

"My homely little woman with big hands"
I called her ever after,—first, intent
On irony and admonition blent;
Then out of—since she smiled—pure merriment;
And lastly, from sheer lack of reprimands.
Brave, homely little woman with big hands!

My homely little woman with big hands,
Somehow, grew almost beautiful to me
As time went by; Her features I could see
Grow ever fairer; and so tenderly
The strong hands clung, their touches were
commands,
Dear homely little woman with big hands!

* * * * * * *

A homely little woman, with big hands
  Folded all patiently across her breast—
  The plain face fair and beautiful in rest—
  But O, the lips that answer not when pressed!
"Make me," I cry to God, who understands,
"A homely little angel with big hands!"

LAUGHTER

WITHIN the coziest corner of my dreams
He sits, high-throned above all gods that
be
Portrayed in marble-cold mythology,
Since from his joyous eyes a twinkle gleams
So warm with life and light it ever seems
Spraying in mists of sunshine over me,
And mingled with such rippling ecstasy
As overleaps his lips in laughing streams.
Ho! look on him, and say if he be old
Or youthful! Hand in hand with gray old
Time
He toddled when an infant; and, behold!—
He hath not aged, but to the lusty prime
Of babyhood—his brow a trifle bold—
His hair a raveled nimbus of gray gold.

AN INVOCATION

SWEET Sleep, with mellow palms trailed
      listlessly
  Above mine eyelids, folding out the light
  Of coming day, and shutting in the night
That gave but now such wondrous dreams to me—
Bide with me yet with thy dear sorcery,
  Until once more I grow forgetful quite
  Of all the cares that blur my waking sight
With dim, regretful tears! I beg of thee
To lift again thy wand with magic filled,
  And filter through my faith the words: Behold,
Aladdin, as thou badest me, I build
  A new dream o'er the ruins of the old—
Thine all eternal palace, silver-silled,
  And walled with harps, and roofed with crowns
      of gold!

FROM BELOW

IN the dim summer night they were leaning alone
  From the balcony over the walk;
He, careless enough, one had guessed by the tone
  Of his voice and his murmurous talk;
And she—well, her laugh flowed as sweet to the
     breeze
  As the voice of the faint violin
That ran, with a ripple of ivory keys,
  Through the opera warbled within.

    .   .   .   .

In the odorous locust-boughs trailed o'er the eaves,
  The nightingale paused in his tune,
And the mute katydid hid away in the leaves
  That were turned from the smile of the moon:
And the man sat alone, with his fingers clenched
     tight
  O'er a heart that had failed in its beat,
While the passers-by saw but a spatter of light
  Where he dropped his cigar in the street.

GLAMOUR

W AS it in the misty twilight, or the midnight,
        or the morning,
   Or was it in the glare of noon, or dazzle of the
        day,
That, half asleep and half awake, and without word
     or warning,
   My fancy, slowly slipping earthly anchor, sailed
        away?

O leave me and my lazy dream a little while
        together,
   Blending each within the other as we waken in
        the dawn,
With languid lids anointed by the balmy summer
        weather
   As it wells above the casement that our vision
        swoons upon!

Linger with me yet a little, O my lazy dream! nor
     leave me;
   Though we hear the swallows twitter, it is only in
        their sleep:

And I want you just to cling to me and love me and
    deceive me
  A little ere the morning when I waken but to
    weep.

Ah! dream of mine, I see you growing clearer yet
    and clearer;
  Your fairy face comes back again from out the
    misty past,
And your smile shines on before you till, approach-
    ing ever nearer,
  It gilds your grave into a glorious trysting-place
    at last.

And you lean there—waiting for me—here's the
    dainty rose-leaf letter
  That you sent me, saying, "Meet me here, and
    share my deep delight
For my love by this long silence is so truer, purer,
    better,
  That you will taste of Heaven when you touch
    my lips to-night."

Was it in the misty twilight, or the midnight, or the
    morning,
  Or was it in the glare of noon, or dazzle of the
    day,
That, half asleep and half awake, and without word
    or warning,
  My fancy, slowly slipping earthly anchor, sailed
    away?

SILENCE

THOUSANDS and thousands of hushed
      years ago,
  Out on the edge of Chaos, all alone
  I stood on peaks of vapor, high upthrown
Above a sea that knew nor ebb nor flow,
Nor any motion won of winds that blow,
  Nor any sound of watery wail or moan,
  Nor lisp of wave, nor wandering undertone
Of any tide lost in the night below.
So still it was, I mind me, as I laid
  My thirsty ear against mine own faint sigh
To drink of that, I sipped it, half afraid
  'Twas but the ghost of a dead voice spilled by
The one starved star that tottered through the
      shade
  And came tiptoeing toward me down the sky.

PUCK

O IT was Puck! I saw him yesternight
    Swung up betwixt a phlox-top and the rim
Of a low crescent moon that cradled him,
Whirring his rakish wings with all his might,
And pursing his wee mouth, that dimpled white
    And red, as though some dagger keen and slim
    Had stung him there, while ever faint and dim
His eery warblings piped his high delight,
Till I, grown jubilant, shrill answer made,
    At which all suddenly he dropped from view;
And peering after, 'neath the everglade,
    What was it, do you think, I saw him do?
I saw him peeling dewdrops with a blade
    Of starshine sharpened on his hat-wing shoe.

A MORTUL PRAYER

OH! Thou that veileth from all eyes
   The glory of Thy face,
And setteth throned behind the skies
   In Thy abiding-place:
Though I but dimly reco'nize
   Thy purposes of grace;
And though with weak and wavering
   Deserts, and vex'd with fears,
I lift the hands I can not wring
   All dry of sorrow's tears,
Make puore my prayers that daily wing
   Theyr way unto Thy ears!

Oh! with the hand that tames the flood
   And smooths the storm to rest,
Make ba'mmy dews of all the blood
   That stormeth in my brest,
And so refresh my hart to bud
   And bloom the loveliest.
Lull all the clammer of my soul
   To silunce; bring release

Unto the brane still in controle
  Of doubts; bid sin to cease,
And let the waves of pashun roll
  And kiss the shores of peace.

Make me to love my feller man—
  Yea, though his bitterness
Doth bite as only adders can—
  Let *me* the fault confess,
And go to him and clasp his hand
  And love him none the less.
So keep me, Lord, ferever free
  From vane concete er whim;
And he whose pius eyes can see
  My faults, however dim,—
Oh! let him pray the least fer me,
  And me the most fer him.

A ROUGH SKETCH

I CAUGHT, for a second, across the crowd—
  Just for a second, and barely that—
A face, pox-pitted and evil-browed,
   Hid in the shade of a slouch-rim'd hat—
     With small gray eyes, of a look as keen
     As the long, sharp nose that grew between.

And I said: 'Tis a sketch of Nature's own,
  Drawn i' the dark o' the moon, I swear,
On a tatter of Fate that the winds have blown
   Hither and thither and everywhere—
     With its keen little sinister eyes of gray,
     And nose like the beak of a bird of prey!

GRANDFATHER SQUEERS

"MY grandfather Squeers," said The Raggedy
Man,
As he solemnly lighted his pipe and began—

"The most indestructible man, for his years,
And the grandest on earth, was my grandfather
Squeers!

"He said, when he rounded his threescore-and-ten,
'I've the hang of it now and can do it again!'

"He had frozen his heels so repeatedly, he
Could tell by them just what the weather would be;

"And would laugh and declare, 'while *the Almanac*
would
Most falsely prognosticate, *he* never could!'

"Such a hale constitution had grandfather Squeers
That, though he'd used *'navy'* for sixty-odd years,

180

"He still chewed a dime's worth six days of the
    week,
While the seventh he passed with a chew in each
    cheek.

"Then my grandfather Squeers had a singular
    knack
Of sitting around on the small of his back,

"With his legs like a letter Y stretched o'er the
    grate
Wherein 'twas his custom to ex-pec-tor-ate.

"He was fond of tobacco in *manifold* ways,
And would sit on the door-step, of sunshiny days,

"And smoke leaf-tobacco he'd raised strictly for
The pipe he'd used all through the Mexican War."

And The Raggedy Man said, refilling the bowl
Of his *own* pipe and leisurely picking a coal

From the stove with his finger and thumb, "You
    can see
What a tee-nacious habit he's fastened on me!

"And my grandfather Squeers took a special delight
In pruning his corns every Saturday night

"With a horn-handled razor, whose edge he excused
By saying 'twas one that his grandfather used;

"And, though deeply etched in the haft of the same
Was the ever-euphonious Wostenholm's name,

" 'Twas my grandfather's custom to boast of the
    blade
As 'a Seth Thomas razor—the best ever made!'

"No Old Settlers' Meeting, or Pioneers' Fair,
Was complete without grandfather Squeers in the
    chair,

"To lead off the program by telling folks how
'He used to shoot deer where the Court-house
    stands now'—

"How 'he felt, of a truth, to live over the past,
When the country was wild and unbroken and vast,

" 'That the little log cabin was just plenty fine
For himself, his companion, and fambly of nine!—

" 'When they didn't have even a pump, or a tin,
But drunk surface-water, year out and year in,

" 'From the old-fashioned gourd that was sweeter,
    by odds,
Than the goblets of gold at the lips of the gods!' "

Then The Raggedy Man paused to plaintively say
It was clockin' along to'rds the close of the day—

And he'd *ought* to get back to his work on the
    lawn,—
Then dreamily blubbered his pipe and went on:

"His teeth were imperfect—my grandfather owned
That he couldn't eat oysters unless they were
    'boned';

"And his eyes were so weak, and so feeble of sight,
He couldn't sleep with them unless, every night,

"He put on his spectacles—all he possessed,—
Three pairs—with his goggles on top of the rest.

"And my grandfather always, retiring at night,
Blew down the lamp-chimney to put out the light;

"Then he'd curl up on edge like a shaving, in bed,
And puff and smoke pipes in his sleep, it is said:

"And would snore oftentimes, as the legends relate,
Till his folks were wrought up to a terrible state,—

"Then he'd snort, and rear up, and roll over; and
    there
In the subsequent hush they could hear him chew
    air.

"And so glaringly bald was the top of his head
That many's the time he has musingly said,

"As his eyes journeyed o'er its reflex in the glass,—
'I must set out a few signs of *Keep Off the Grass!*'

"So remarkably deaf was my grandfather Squeers
That he had to wear lightning-rods over his ears

"To even hear thunder—and oftentimes then
He was forced to request it to thunder again."

MY LADDIE WI' THE BASHFU' GRACE

MY laddie wi' the bashfu' grace,
   That darena spak the tender loe
That glints o'er a' thy bonny face
   Like winter sunset on the snow,—
Gin ye wad only tak my hand,
   And ask, wi' pressure fond and true,
My heart—my heart wad understand,
      And gie its loe to you.

But sin' ye winna spak me free,
   Or darena tak the langin' tip
O' ain puir finger,—come to me
   In mirk o' nicht and touch my lip—
Then a' the glowin' universe
   Will bloom wi' stars, and flow'rs, and a',
And God's ain sel' abide wi' us,
      Nor ever gang awa'.

A TRESS OF HAIR

THIS tress of hair my sweetheart sent to me,
  And so I bent above it tenderly
    And kissed the dainty bow
That bound the wisp of sunshine, thrilled forsooth,
Because her lips had nestled there—in truth,
    She told me so.

And I remember, reading that, the flush
That fevered all my face, and the heart's hush
    And hurry in my ears;
And how the letter trembled and grew blurred
Until my eyes could read no other word—
    For happy tears.

This tress of hair! Why, I did hug and hold
It here against my heart, and call it gold
    With Heaven's own luster lit;
And I did stroke and smooth its gleaming strands,
And pet and fondle it with foolish hands,
    And talk to it!

186

And now I pray God's blessing may alight
Upon the orange flowers she wears to-night.
    Her features—keep them fair,
Dear Lord, but let her lips not quite forget
The love they kindled once is gilding yet
    This tress of hair.

IN A BOX

I SAW them last night in a box at the play—
   Old age and young youth side by side.—
You might know by the glasses that pointed that
      way
   That they were—a groom and a bride;
And you might have known, too, by the face of the
      groom,
   And the tilt of his head, and the grim
Little smile of his lip, he was proud to presume
   That we men were all envying him.

Well, she was superb—an Elaine in the face—
   A Godiva in figure and mien,
With the arm and the wrist of a Parian "Grace,"
   And the high-lifted brow of a queen;
But I thought, in the splendor of wealth and of
      pride,
   And her beauty's ostensible prize,
I should hardly be glad if she sat by my side
   With that far-away look in her eyes.

THE PASSING OF A HEART

O TOUCH me with your hands—
                    For pity's sake!
My brow throbs ever on with such an ache
As only your cool touch may take away;
And so, I pray
            You, touch me with your hands!

Touch—touch me with your hands.—
                    Smooth back the hair
You once caressed, and kissed, and called so fair
That I did dream its gold would wear alway,
And lo, to-day—
            O touch me with your hands!

Just touch me with your hands,
                    And let them press
My weary eyelids with the old caress,
And lull me till I sleep. Then go your way,
That Death may say:
            He touched her with his hands.

AN OLD-TIMER

HERE where the wayward stream
   Is restful as a dream,
  And where the banks o'erlook
A pool from out whose deeps
My pleased face upward peeps,
     I cast my hook.

Silence and sunshine blent!—
A Sabbath-like content
  Of wood and wave;—a free-
Hand landscape grandly wrought
Of Summer's brightest thought
     And mastery.—

For here form, light and shade,
And color—all are laid
  With skill so rarely fine,
The eye may even see
The ripple tremblingly
     Lip at the line.

I mark the dragon-fly
Flit waveringly by
  In ever-veering flight,

190

Till, in a hush profound,
I see him eddy round
    The "cork," and—'light!

Ho! with the boy's faith then
Brimming my heart again,
  And knowing, soon or late,
The "nibble" yet shall roll
Its thrills along the pole,
    I—breathless—wait.

ERE I WENT MAD

ERE I went mad—
O you may never guess what dreams I had!
Such hosts of happy things did come to me.
One time, it seemed, I knelt at some one's knee,
My wee lips threaded with a strand of prayer,
With kinks of kisses in it here and there
To stay and tangle it the while I knit
A mother's long-forgotten name in it.
Be sure, I dreamed it all, but I was glad
—Ere I went mad!

Ere I went mad,
I dreamed there came to me a fair-faced lad,
Who led me by the wrist where blossoms grew
In grassy lands, and where the skies were blue
As his own eyes. And he did lisp and sing,
And weave me wreaths where I sat marveling
What little prince it was that crowned me queen
And caught my face so cunningly between
His dimple-dinted hands, and kept me glad
—Ere I went mad!

Ere I went mad,
Not even winter weather made me sad·
I dreamed, indeed, the skies were ne'er so dull
That *his* smile might not make them beautiful.
And now, it seemed, he had grown O so fair
And straight and strong that, when he smoothed
        my hair,
I felt as any lily with drooped head
That leans, in fields of grain unharvested,
By some lithe stalk of barley—pure and glad
—Ere I went mad!

Ere I went mad,
The last of all the happy dreams I had
Was of a peerless king—a conqueror—
Who crowned me with a kiss, and throned me for
One hour!   Ah, God of Mercy! what a dream
To tincture life with!   Yet I made no scream
As I awakened—with these eyes you see,
That may not smile till love comes back to me,
And lulls me back to those old dreams I had
—Ere I went mad!

O HER BEAUTY

O HER beauty was such that it dazzled my
        eyes
Like a dreamer's, who, gazing in day-dying skies,
Sees the snow of the clouds and the gold of the sun
And the blue of the heavens all blended in one
Indescribable luster of glorious light,
Swooning into the moon of a midsummer night.

O her beauty was such that I fancied her hair
Was a cloud of the tempest, tied up with a glare
Of pale purple lightning, that darted and ran
Through the coils like the blood in the veins of a
        man:
And from dark silken billows that girdled her
        free,
Her shoulder welled up like the moon from the sea.

O her beauty was such, as I knelt, with the tips
Of the fingers uplifted she snatched from my lips,
And saw the white flood of her wrath as it dashed
O'er the features, that one moment later had flashed
From my vision forever, I raised not a knee
Till I had thanked God for so rescuing me.

THE SUMMER-TIME

O THE Summer-time to-day
    Makes my words
  Jes' flip up and fly away
    Like the birds!
        —'Tain't no use to try to sing,
        With yer language on the wing,
        Jes' too glad fer anything
            But to stray
            Where it may
Thue the sunny summer weather of the day!

    Lordy! what a Summer-time
        Fer to sing!
    But my words flops out o' rhyme,
        And they wing
            Furder yit beyent the view
            Than the swallers ever flew,
            Er a mortal wanted to—
                'Less his eye
                Struck the sky
Ez he kind o' sort o' thought he'd like to fly!

195

Ef I *could* sing—sweet and low—
And my tongue
Could *twitter,* don't you know,—
Ez I sung
Of the Summer-time, 'y Jings!
All the words and birds and things
That kin warble, and hes wings,
Would jes' swear
And declare
That they never heerd sich singin' anywhere!

SONG OF PARTING

SAY farewell, and let me go:
   Shatter every vow!
All the future can bestow
  Will be welcome now!
    And if this fair hand I touch
    I have worshiped overmuch,
    It was my mistake—and so,
    Say farewell, and let me go.

Say farewell, and let me go:
  Murmur no regret,
Stay your tear-drops ere they flow—
  Do not waste them yet!
    They might pour as pours the rain,
    And not wash away the pain:—
    I have tried them and I know.—
    Say farewell, and let me go.

Say farewell, and let me go:
  Think me not untrue—
True as truth is, even so
  I am true to you!
    If the ghost of love may stay
    Where my fond heart dies to-day,
    I am with you alway—so,
    Say farewell, and let me go.

THE WANDERING JEW

THE stars are failing, and the sky
  Is like a field of faded flowers
The winds on weary wings go by;
  The moon hides, and the tempest lowers;
    And still through every clime and age
    I wander on a pilgrimage
    That all men know an idle quest,
    For that the goal I seek is—REST!

I hear the voice of summer streams,
  And, following, I find the brink
Of cooling springs, with childish dreams
  Returning as I bend to drink—
    But suddenly, with startled eyes,
    My face looks on its grim disguise
    Of long gray beard; and so, distressed,
    I hasten on, nor taste of rest.

I come upon a merry group
  Of children in the dusky wood,
Who answer back the owlet's whoop,
  That laughs as it had understood;
    And I would pause a little space,
    But that each happy blossom-face
    Is like to one *His* hands have blessed
    Who sent me forth in search of rest.

Sometimes I fain would stay my feet
  In shady lanes, where huddled kine
Couch in the grasses cool and sweet,
  And lift their patient eyes to mine;
      But I, for thoughts that ever then
      Go back to Bethlehem again,
      Must needs fare on my weary quest,
      And weep for very need of rest.

Is there no end? I plead in vain:
  Lost worlds nor living answer me.
Since Pontius Pilate's awful reign
  Have I not passed eternity?
      Have I not drunk the fetid breath
      Of every fevered phase of death,
      And come unscathed through every pest
      And scourge and plague that promised
        rest?

Have I not seen the stars go out
  That shed their light o'er Galilee,
And mighty kingdoms tossed about
  And crumbled clod-like in the sea?
      Dead ashes of dead ages blow
      And cover me like drifting snow,
      And time laughs on as 'twere a jest
      That I have any need of rest.

THE USED-TO-BE

BEYOND the purple, hazy trees
Of summer's utmost boundaries;
Beyond the sands—beyond the seas—
Beyond the range of eyes like these,
　And only in the reach of the
　Enraptured gaze of Memory,
　There lies a land, long lost to me,—
　　The land of Used-to-be!

A land enchanted—such as swung
In golden seas when sirens clung
Along their dripping brinks, and sung
To Jason in that mystic tongue
　That dazed men with its melody—
　O such a land, with such a sea
　Kissing its shores eternally,
　　Is the fair Used-to-be.

A land where music ever girds
The air with belts of singing-birds,
And sows all sounds with such sweet
　　words,

That even in the low of herds
  A meaning lives so sweet to me,
  Lost laughter ripples limpidly
  From lips brimmed over with the glee
    Of rare old Used-to-be.

Lost laughter, and the whistled tunes
Of boyhood's mouth of crescent runes,
That rounded, through long afternoons,
To serenading plenilunes—
  When starlight fell so mistily
  That, peering up from bended knee,
  I dreamed 'twas bridal drapery
    Snowed over Used-to-be.

O land of love and dreamy thoughts,
And shining fields, and shady spots
Of coolest, greenest grassy plots,
Embossed with wild forget-me-nots!—
  And all ye blooms that longingly
  Lift your fair faces up to me
  Out of the past, I kiss in ye
    The lips of Used-to-be.

AT UTTER LOAF

I

AN afternoon as ripe with heat
    As might the golden pippin be
With mellowness if at my feet
    It dropped now from the apple-tree
    My hammock swings in lazily.

II

The boughs about me spread a shade
    That shields me from the sun, but weaves
    With breezy shuttles through the leaves
Blue rifts of skies, to gleam and fade
    Upon the eyes that only see
    Just of themselves, all drowsily.

III

Above me drifts the fallen skein
    Of some tired spider, looped and blown,
As fragile as a strand of rain,
    Across the air, and upward thrown
    By breaths of hay-fields newly mown—
So glimmering it is and fine,
I doubt these drowsy eyes of mine.

IV

Far-off and faint as voices pent
   In mines, and heard from underground,
Come murmurs as of discontent,
   And clamorings of sullen sound
The city sends me, as, I guess,
To vex me, though they do but bless
Me in my drowsy fastnesses.

V

I have no care.   I only know
   My hammock hides and holds me here
   In lands of shade a prisoner:
While lazily the breezes blow
   Light leaves of sunshine over me,
And back and forth and to and fro
   I swing, enwrapped in some hushed glee,
   Smiling at all things drowsily.

MY OLD FRIEND

YOU'VE a manner all so mellow,
    My old friend,
That it cheers and warms a fellow,
    My old friend,
Just to meet and greet you, and
Feel the pressure of a hand
That one may understand,
    My old friend.

Though dimmed in youthful splendor,
    My old friend,
Your smiles are still as tender,
    My old friend,
And your eyes as true a blue
As your childhood ever knew,
And your laugh as merry, too,
    My old friend.

For though your hair is faded,
    My old friend,
And your step a trifle jaded,
    My old friend,

Old Time, with all his lures
In the trophies he secures,
Leaves young that heart of yours,
    My old friend.

And so it is you cheer me,
    My old friend,
For to know you and be near you,
    My old friend,
Makes my hopes of clearer light,
And my faith of surer sight,
And my soul a purer white,
    My old friend.

KISSING THE ROD

O HEART of mine, we shouldn't
    Worry so!
What we've missed of calm we couldn't
    Have, you know!
What we've met of stormy pain,
And of sorrow's driving rain,
We can better meet again,
    If it blow!

We have erred in that dark hour
    We have known,
When our tears fell with the shower,
    All alone!—
Were not shine and shower blent
As the gracious Master meant?—
Let us temper our content
    With His own.

For, we know, not every morrow
    Can be sad;
So, forgetting all the sorrow
    We have had,
Let us fold away our fears,
And put by our foolish tears,
And through all the coming years
    Just be glad.

From a photograph taken when twenty-eight years old

THE RIVAL

I SO loved once, when Death came by I hid
    Away my face,
And all my sweetheart's tresses she undid
    To make my hiding-place.

The dread shade passed me thus unheeding; and
    I turned me then
To calm my love—kiss down her shielding hand
    And comfort her again.

And lo! she answered not: And she did sit
    All fixedly,
With her fair face and the sweet smile of it,
    In love with Death, not me.

THE LIGHT OF LOVE

SONG

THE clouds have deepened o'er the night
   Till, through the dark profound,
The moon is but a stain of light,
   And all the stars are drowned;
And all the stars are drowned, my love,
   And all the skies are drear;
But what care we for light above,
   If light of love is here?

The wind is like a wounded thing
   That beats about the gloom
With baffled breast and drooping wing,
   And wail of deepest doom;
And wail of deepest doom, my love;
   But what have we to fear
From night, or rain, or winds above,
   With love and laughter here?

LET SOMETHING GOOD BE SAID

WHEN over the fair fame of friend or foe
    The shadow of disgrace shall fall, instead
Of words of blame, or proof of thus and so,
    Let something good be said.

Forget not that no fellow-being yet
    May fall so low but love may lift his head:
Even the cheek of shame with tears is wet,
    If something good be said.

No generous heart may vainly turn aside
    In ways of sympathy; no soul so dead
But may awaken strong and glorified,
    If something good be said.

And so I charge ye, by the thorny crown,
    And by the cross on which the Saviour bled,
And by your own soul's hope of fair renown,
    Let something good be said!

THE OLD HAND-ORGAN

HARSH-VOICED it was, and shrill and high,
With hesitating stops and stutters,
As though the vagrant melody,
Playing so long about the gutters,
Had been infected with some low
Malignant type of vertigo.

A stark-eyed man that stared the sun
Square in the face, and without winking;
His soldier cap pushed back, and one
Scarred hand that grasped the crank,
unshrinking
But from the jingling discord made
By shamefaced pennies as he played.

HOME AT NIGHT

WHEN chirping crickets fainter cry,
   And pale stars blossom in the sky,
And twilight's gloom has dimmed the bloom
And blurred the butterfly:

When locust-blossoms fleck the walk,
And up the tiger-lily stalk
The glowworm crawls and clings and falls
And glimmers down the garden-walls:

When buzzing things, with double wings
Of crisp and raspish flutterings,
Go whizzing by so very nigh
One thinks of fangs and stings:—

O then, within, is stilled the din
Of crib she rocks the baby in,
And heart and gate and latch's weight
Are lifted—and the lips of Kate.

A DREAM OF INSPIRATION

TO loll back, in a misty hammock, swung
From tip to tip of a slim crescent moon
That gems some royal-purple night of June—
To dream of songs that never have been sung
Since the first stars were stilled and God was young
And Heaven as lonesome as a lonesome tune:
To lie thus, lost to earth, with lids aswoon;
By curious, cool winds back and forward flung,
With fluttering hair, blurred eyes, and utter ease
Adrift like lazy blood through every vein;
And then,—the pulse of unvoiced melodies
Timing the raptured sense to some refrain
That knows nor words, nor rhymes, nor
euphonies,
Save Fancy's hinted chime of unknown seas.

THE PIPER'S SON

IN olden days there dwelt a piper's son,
  Hight Thomas, who, belike from indigence,
    Or utter lack of virtuous preference
Of honorable means of thrift, did, one
Weak hour of temptation—(weaker none!)—
    Put by ye promptings of his better sense,
    And rashly gat him o'er a neighbor's fence
Wherein ye corner was a paling run
About a goodly pig; and thence he lured,
    All surreptitiously, ye hapless beast,
And had it slaughtered, salted down, and cured—
    Yea, even tricked and garnished for ye feast,
Ere yet ye red-eyed Law had him immured,
    And round and soundly justice-of-ye-peaced.

HIS LAST PICTURE

THE skies have grown troubled and dreary;
   The clouds gather fold upon fold;
The hand of the painter is weary
   And the pencil has dropped from its hold:
The easel still leans in the grasses,
   And the palette beside on the lawn,
But the rain o'er the sketch as it passes
   Weeps low—for the artist is gone.

The flowers whose fairy-like features
   Smiled up in his own as he wrought,
And the leaves and the ferns were his teachers,
   And the tints of the sun what they taught;
The low-swinging vines, and the mosses—
   The shadow-filled boughs of the trees,
And the blossomy spray as it tosses
   The song of the bird to the breeze.

The silent white laugh of the lily
   He learned; and the smile of the rose
Glowed back on his spirit until he
   Had mastered the blush as it glows;

And his pencil has touched and caressed them,
   And kissed them, through breaths of perfume,
To the canvas that yet shall have blessed them
   With years of unwithering bloom.

Then come!—Leave his palette and brushes
   And easel there, just as his hand
Has left them, ere through the dark hushes
   Of death, to the shadowy land,
He wended his way, happy-hearted
   As when, in his youth, his rapt eyes
Swept the pathway of Fame where it started,
   To where it wound into the skies.

A VARIATION

I AM tired of this!
   Nothing else but loving!
Nothing else but kiss and kiss,
   Coo, and turtle-doving!
     Can't you change the order some?
     Hate me just a little—come!

Lay aside your "dears,"
   "Darlings," "kings," and "princes!"
Call me knave, and dry your tears—
   Nothing in me winces,—
     Call me something low and base—
     Something that will suit the case!

Wish I had your eyes
   And their drooping lashes!
I would dry their teary lies
   Up with lightning-flashes—
     Make your sobbing lips unsheathe
     All the glitter of your teeth!

Can't you lift one word—
   With some pang of laughter—
Louder than the drowsy bird

Crooning 'neath the rafter?
  Just one bitter word, to shriek
  Madly at me as I speak!

How I hate the fair
  Beauty of your forehead!
How I hate your fragrant hair!
  How I hate the torrid
    Touches of your splendid lips,
    And the kiss that drips and drips!

Ah, you pale at last!
  And your face is lifted
Like a white sail to the blast,
  And your hands are shifted
    Into fists: and, towering thus,
    You are simply glorious!

Now before me looms
  Something more than human;
Something more than beauty blooms
  In the wrath of Woman—
    Something to bow down before
    Reverently and adore.

THERE IS A NEED

THERE is a need for every ache of pain
   That falls unto our lot. No heart may bleed
That resignation may not heal again,
        And teach us—there's a need.

There is a need for every tear that drips
   Adown the face of sorrow. None may heed,
But weeping washes whiter on the lips
        Our prayers—and there's a need.

There is a need for weariness and dearth
   Of all that brings delight. At topmost speed
Of pleasure sobs may break amid our mirth
        Unheard—and there's a need.

There is a need for all the growing load
   Of agony we bear as years succeed;
For lo, the Master's footprints in the road
        Before us—There's a need.

TO A SKULL

TURN your face this way;
   I'm not weary of it—
Every hour of every day
   More and more I love it—
Grinning in that jolly guise
Of bare bones and empty eyes!

Was this hollow dome,
   Where I tap my finger,
Once the spirit's narrow home—
   Where you loved to linger,
Hiding, as to-day are we,
From the selfsame destiny?

O'er and o'er again
   Have I put the query—
Was existence so in vain
   That you look so cheery?—
Death of such a benefit
That you smile, possessing it?

Did your throbbing brow
   Tire of all the flutter
Of such fancyings as now

You, at last, may utter
In that grin so grimly bland
Only death can understand?

Has the shallow glee
    Of old dreams of pleasure
Left you ever wholly free
    To float out, at leisure,
O'er the shoreless, trackless trance
Of unsounded circumstance?

Only this I read
    In your changeless features,—
You, at least, have gained a meed
    Held from living creatures:
You have naught to ask.—Beside,
You do grin so satisfied!

THE VOICES

DOWN in the night I hear them:
  The Voices—unknown—unguessed,—
That whisper, and lisp, and murmur,
  And will not let me rest.—

Voices that seem to question,
  In unknown words, of me,
Of fabulous ventures, and hopes and dreams
  Of this and the World to be.

Voices of mirth and music,
  As in sumptuous homes; and sounds
Of mourning, as of gathering friends
  In country burial-grounds.

Cadence of maiden voices—
  Their lovers' blent with these;
And of little children singing,
  As under orchard trees.

And often, up from the chaos
  Of my deepest dreams, I hear
Sounds of their phantom laughter
  Filling the atmosphere:

They call to me from the darkness;
　They cry to me from the gloom,
Till I start sometimes from my pillow
　And peer through the haunted room;

When the face of the moon at the window
　Wears a pallor like my own,
And seems to be listening with me
　To the low, mysterious tone,—

The low, mysterious clamor
　Of voices that seem to be
Striving in vain to whisper
　Of secret things to me;—

Of a something dread to be warned of;
　Of a rapture yet withheld;
Or hints of the marvelous beauty
　Of songs unsyllabled.

But ever and ever the meaning
　Falters and fails and dies,
And only the silence quavers
　With the sorrow of my sighs.

And I answer:—O Voices, ye may not
　Make me to understand
Till my own voice, mingling with you,
　Laughs in the Shadow-land.

MY HENRY

HE'S jes' a great, big, awk'ard, hulkin'
        Feller,—humped, and sort o' sulkin'-
Like, and ruther still-appearin'—
Kind-as-ef he wuzn't keerin'
        Whether school helt out er not—
        That's my Henry, to a dot!

Allus kind o' liked him—whether
Childern, er growed-up together!
Fifteen year' ago and better,
'Fore he ever knowed a letter,
        Run acrosst the little fool
        In my Primer-class at school.

When the Teacher wuzn't lookin',
He'd be th'owin' wads; er crookin'
Pins; er sprinklin' pepper, more'n
Likely, on the stove; er borin'
        Gimlet-holes up thue his desk—
        Nothin' *that* boy wouldn't resk!

But, somehow, as I was goin'
On to say, he seemed so knowin',
Other ways, and cute and cunnin'—

Allus wuz a notion runnin'
　　Thue my giddy, fool-head he
　　Jes' had be'n cut out fer me!

Don't go much on *prophesyin'*,
But last night whilse I wuz fryin'
Supper, with that man a-pitchin'
Little Marthy round the kitchen,
　　Think-says-I, "Them baby's eyes
　　Is my Henry's, jes' p'cise!"

LOVE'S AS BROAD AS LONG

LOOKY here!—you fellers—you
   Poets I'm a talkin' to,—
Allus rhymin', right er wrong,
'Bout your "little" love, and "long"—
'Pears to me 'at nary one
Of you fellers gits much fun
Out o' lovin'—tryin' to fit
Out some fool-receet fer it!—
      Love's as broad as long!

Now, I 'low 'at love's a thing
You cain't jes' set down and sing
Out your order fer, and say
You'll hev yourn a certain way;
And how "long" a slice you'll take,
Er how short—'cause love don't make
No distinctions, and you'll find,
When it comes, it's all one kind—
      Jes' as broad as long!

Fust, one of you'll p'tend
"Love's no idle song," and send
Up his voice in jes' the song
He's th'owed up on—"Love me long!"

Now, they hain't no womern needs
No sich talk as that!—er heeds
Sich advice as would infer
You hed any doubts o' her!
    Love's as broad as long.

Ner I don't see any use,
Er occasion, er excuse
Fer some other chap to say,
In his passioneter way,
"Love me madly, as of yore!"—
'Cause I've seed sich love afore,
'At got fellers down, and jes'
Wooled 'em round till they confessed
    Love was broad as long.

No; I'll tell you: You jes' let
Love alone, and you kin bet,
When the time comes, Love'll be
Right on hands as punctchully
As he was the day Eve sot
Waitin', in the gyarden-spot,
Fer ole Adam jes' to go
On ahead and tell her so!
    Love's as broad as long!

LOCKERBIE STREET

SUCH a dear little street it is, nestled away
From the noise of the city and heat of the day,
In cool shady coverts of whispering trees,
With their leaves lifted up to shake hands with the
    breeze
Which in all its wide wanderings never may meet
With a resting-place fairer than Lockerbie Street!

There is such a relief, from the clangor and din
Of the heart of the town, to go loitering in
Through the dim, narrow walks, with the sheltering
    shade
Of the trees waving over the long promenade,
And littering lightly the ways of our feet
With the gold of the sunshine of Lockerbie Street.

And the nights that come down the dark pathways
    of dusk,
With the stars in their tresses, and odors of musk
In their moon-woven raiments, bespangled with
    dews,
And looped up with lilies for lovers to use

In the songs that they sing to the tinkle and beat
Of their sweet serenadings through Lockerbie
    Street.

O my Lockerbie Street! You are fair to be seen—
Be it noon of the day, or the rare and serene
Afternoon of the night—you are one to my heart,
And I love you above all the phrases of art,
For no language could frame and no lips could
    repeat
My rhyme-haunted raptures of Lockerbie Street.

THE OLD, OLD WISH

LAST night, in some lost mood of meditation,
The while my dreamy vision ranged the far
Unfathomable arches of creation,
I saw a falling star:

And as my eyes swept round the path it embered
With the swift-dying glory of its glow,
With sudden intuition I remembered
A wish of long ago—

A wish that, were it made—so ran the fancy
Of credulous young lover and of lass—
As fell a star, by some strange necromancy,
Would surely come to pass.

And, of itself, the wish, reiterated
A thousand times in youth, flashed o'er my
brain,
And, like the star, as soon obliterated,
Dropped into night again.

For my old heart had wished for the unending
    Devotion of a little maid of nine—
And that the girl-heart, with the woman's
      blending,
        Might be forever mine.

And so it was, with eyelids raised, and weighty
    With ripest clusterings of sorrow's dew,
I cried aloud through Heaven: "O little Katie!
      When will my wish come true?"

A LIFE-LESSON

THERE! little girl; don't cry!
   They have broken your doll, I know;
      And your tea-set blue,
      And your play-house, too,
   Are things of the long ago;
      But childish troubles will soon pass by.—
         There! little girl; don't cry!

There! little girl; don't cry!
   They have broken your slate, I know;
      And the glad, wild ways
      Of your schoolgirl days
   Are things of the long ago;
      But life and love will soon come by.—
         There! little girl; don't cry!

There! little girl; don't cry!
   They have broken your heart, I know;
      And the rainbow gleams
      Of your youthful dreams
   Are things of the long ago;
      But Heaven holds all for which you sigh.—
         There! little girl; don't cry!

A WATER-COLOR

LOW hidden in among the forest trees
  An artist's tilted easel, ankle-deep
In tousled ferns and mosses, and in these
  A fluffy water-spaniel, half asleep
    Beside a sketch-book and a fallen hat—
    A little wicker flask tossed into that.

A sense of utter carelessness and grace
  Of pure abandon in the slumb'rous scene,—
As if the June, all hoydenish of face,
  Had romped herself to sleep there on the
                green,
    And brink and sagging bridge and sliding
          stream
    Were just romantic parcels of her dream.

UNKNOWN FRIENDS

O FRIENDS of mine, whose kindly words come
      to me
  Voiced only in lost lisps of ink and pen,
If I had power to tell the good you do me,
And how the blood you warm goes laughing through
      me,
  My tongue would babble baby-talk again.

And I would toddle round the world to meet you—
  Fall at your feet, and clamber to your knees
And with glad, happy hands would reach and greet
      you,
And twine my arms about you, and entreat you
  For leave to weave a thousand rhymes like
      these—

A thousand rhymes enwrought of nought but
      presses
  Of cherry-lip and apple-cheek and chin,
And pats of honeyed palms, and rare caresses,
And all the sweets of which as Fancy guesses
  She folds away her wings and swoons therein.

THE SONG OF YESTERDAY

I

BUT yesterday
I looked away
O'er happy lands, where sunshine lay
    In golden blots,
    Inlaid with spots
Of shade and wild forget-me-nots.

    My head was fair
    With flaxen hair,
And fragrant breezes, faint and rare,
    And, warm with drouth
    From out the south,
Blew all my curls across my mouth.

    And, cool and sweet,
    My naked feet
Found dewy pathways through the wheat;
    And out again
    Where, down the lane,
The dust was dimpled with the rain.

II

But yesterday!—
Adream, astray,
From morning's red to evening's gray,
O'er dales and hills
Of daffodils
And lorn sweet-fluting whippoorwills.

I knew nor cares
Nor tears nor prayers—
A mortal god, crowned unawares
With sunset—and
A scepter-wand
Of apple-blossoms in my hand!

The dewy blue
Of twilight grew
To purple, with a star or two
Whose lisping rays
Failed in the blaze
Of sudden fireflys through the haze.

III

But yesterday
I heard the lay
Of summer birds, when I, as they
With breast and wing,
All quivering
With life and love, could only sing.

My head was leant
Where, with it, blent
A maiden's, o'er her instrument;
While all the night,
From vale to height,
Was filled with echoes of delight.

And all our dreams
Were lit with gleams
Of that lost land of reedy streams,
Along whose brim
Forever swim
Pan's lilies, laughing up at him.

IV

But yesterday! . . .
O blooms of May,
And summer roses—where away?
O stars above;
And lips of love,
And all the honeyed sweets thereof!—

O lad and lass,
And orchard pass,
And briered lane, and daisied grass!
O gleam and gloom,
And woodland bloom,
And breezy breaths of all perfume!—

No more for me
Or mine shall be
Thy raptures—save in memory,—
No more—no more—
Till through the Door
Of Glory gleam the days of yore.

AN END

GO away from me—do! I am tired of you!—
That I loved you last May isn't this season, too;
And, you know, every spring there's a new bird to
sing
In the nest of the old, and a ghost on the wing!

Now, don't you assert that I'm simply a flirt—
And it's babyish for you to say that I hurt,
And my words are a dart, when they're only a part
Of your own fickle nature committed to heart.

It was all a mistake, and I don't want to make
The silly thing over for your silly sake—
Though I really once may have been such a dunce
As to fancy you loved me, some far away months.

So, go away—do! I am tired clean through,
And you can't make me even feel sorry for you—
For, with us, every spring there's a new bird to sing
In the nest of the old, and a ghost on the wing.

HER CHOICE

"MY love or hate—choose which you
　　　will,"
He says; and o'er the window-sill
The rose-bush, jostled by the wind,
Rasps at his hands, close-clenched behind,
As she makes answer, smiling clear
As is the day,—"Your hate, my dear!"

An interval of silence—so
Intensely still, the cattle's low
Across the field's remotest rim
Comes like a near moan up to him,
While o'er the open sill once more
The rose-bush rasps him as before.

Then, with an impulse strange and new
To him, he says: " 'Tis wise of you
To choose thus—for by such a choice
You lose so little, that,"—his voice
Breaks suddenly—the rose-bush stirs—
But ah! his hands are—safe in hers.

OUR OWN

THEY walk here with us, hand in hand;
  We gossip, knee by knee;
They tell us all that they have planned—
  Of all their joys to be,—
And, laughing, leave us: And, to-day,
  All desolate we cry
Across wide waves of voiceless graves—
  Good-by! Good-by! Good-by!

THE DRUM

O THE drum!
      There is some
            Intonation in thy grum
Monotony of utterance that strikes the spirit dumb,
As we hear
      Through the clear
            And unclouded atmosphere,
Thy palpitating syllables roll in upon the ear!

There's a part
      Of the art
            Of thy music-throbbing heart
That thrills a something in us that awakens with a
      start,
And in rhyme
      With the chime
            And exactitude of time,
Goes marching on to glory to thy melody sublime.

And the guest
      Of the breast
            That thy rolling robs of rest
Is a patriotic spirit as a Continental dressed;

241

And he looms
    From the glooms
        Of a century of tombs,
And the blood he spilled at Lexington in living
    beauty blooms.

And his eyes
    Wear the guise
        Of a purpose pure and wise,
As the love of them is lifted to a something in the
    skies
That is bright
    Red and white,
        With a blur of starry light,
As it laughs in silken ripples to the breezes day and
    night.

There are deep
    Hushes creep
        O'er the pulses as they leap,
As thy tumult, fainter growing, on the silence falls
    asleep,
While the prayer
    Rising there
        Wills the sea and earth and air
As a heritage to Freedom's sons and daughters
    everywhere.

Then, with sound
    As profound
        As the thunderings resound,

Come thy wild reverberations in a throe that shakes
      the ground,
And a cry
    Flung on high,
        Like the flag it flutters by,
Wings rapturously upward till it nestles in the sky.

O the drum!
    There is some
        Intonation in thy grum
Monotony of utterance that strikes the spirit dumb,
As we hear,
    Through the clear
        And unclouded atmosphere,
Thy palpitating syllables roll in upon the ear!

A CASE IN PINT

WE don't go much on larnin'
    Here in around the mines?—
Well, now, you're just hurrahin'
    Like the wind amongst the pines!
Of course we allus aim to
    Give "the prisoner" a chance—
Though sometimes a jury's game **to**
    Ring a verdict in advance!

What wuz his name—this feller
    'At stold the Jedge's mare
Last spring?—wuz tryin' to sell her
    Down here at Rip and Tear,
When "Faro Bill" dropped on him,
    And bagged him, sound and good
And biznesslike, dog-gone him,
    As the constable a-could!

Well, anyway, his trial
    Wuz a case in pint:—He pled
"Not guilty"—a denial
    'At his attorney said

Could be substantiated
   On the grounds, 'at when the mare
Wuz "stold," as claimed and stated,
   The defendant wuzn't square,—

But he'd be'n a testifyin',
   Round the raw edge of a spree
At Stutsman's bar, a-tryin'
   To hold one drink in three,
To "Jim-jams"; and he reconed
   'At his client's moral tone
Could not be classed as second
   To the Jedge's—er his own.

"That savin'-clause is timely,"
   Says the Jedge, a-turnin' back
To color as sublimely
   As I've seed him turn a jack.—
"But," says he to the defendant,
   "Ef you didn't 'steal' the mare
I'll ask ef your attendant
   'Pharos William,' didn't swear

"You wuzn't 'full' when captured?"
   Then, a-drawin' of his gun,
The Jedge went on, enraptured
   With the trail 'at he'd begun,—
"I'll tax your re-collection
   To enquire ef you know
That hoss left my protection
   On'y jes' five hours ago?—

"In consequence, it follers,
  No man as drunk as you—
And I'll bet a hundred dollars
  To the opposition two!—
Could sober to the beauty
  Of the standerd you present
This writin'—hence my duty
  Plainly is—to circumvent—"

And afore the jury knowed it,
  Bang! his gun went!—"And I'll ask,"
He went on, as he th'owed it
  Up to finish out his task,
"Ef it's mortal?"—then, betrayin'
  Some emotion, with a bow,
He closed by simply sayin'—
  "You can take the witness now!"

OLE BULL

DEAD; IN BERGEN, NORWAY; AUGUST 18, 1880

THE minstrel's mystic wand
Has fallen from his hand;
  Stilled is the tuneful shell;
The airs he used to play
For us but yesterday
Have failed and died away
  In sad farewell.

Forgive—O noble heart,
Whose pure and gracious art
  Enraptured, all these years,
Sang sweet, and sweeter yet
Above all sounds that fret,
And all sobs of regret—
  Forgive our tears!

Forgive us, weeping thus
That thou art gone from us—
  Because thy song divine,
Too, with the master, gone,
Leaves us to listen on
In silence till the dawn
  That now is thine.

A WRAITH OF SUMMER-TIME

IN its color, shade and shine,
'Twas a summer warm as wine,
With an effervescent flavoring of flowered
bough and vine,
And a fragrance and a taste
Of ripe roses gone to waste,
And a dreamy sense of sun- and moon- and
starlight interlaced.

'Twas a summer such as broods
O'er enchanted solitudes,
Where the hand of Fancy leads us through
voluptuary moods,
And with lavish love outpours
All the wealth of out-of-doors,
And woos our feet o'er velvet paths and
honeysuckle floors.

'Twas a summer-time long dead,—
And its roses, white and red,
And its reeds and water-lilies down along
the river-bed,—
O they all are ghostly things—
For the ripple never sings,
And the rocking lily never even rustles as it
rings!

JACK THE GIANT-KILLER

Bad Boy's Version

TELL you a story—an' it's a fac':—
Wunst wuz a little boy, name wuz Jack,
An' he had sword an' buckle an' strap
Maked of gold, an' a " 'visibul cap";
An' he killed Gi'nts 'at et whole cows—
Th' horns an' all—an' pigs an' sows!
But Jack, his golding sword wuz, oh!
So awful sharp 'at he could go
An' cut th' ole Gi'nts clean in two
'Fore 'ey knowed what he wuz goin' to do!
An' *one* ole Gi'nt, he had four
Heads, an' name wuz "Bumblebore"—
An' he wuz feared o' Jack—'cause he,
Jack, he killed six—five—ten—three,
An' all o' th' uther ole Gi'nts but him:
An' thay wuz a place Jack haf to swim
'Fore he could git t' ole "Bumblebore"—
Nen thay wuz "griffuns" at the door:
But Jack, he thist plunged in an' swum
Clean acrost; an' when he come
To th' uther side, he thist put on

His " 'visibul cap," an' nen, dog-gone!
You couldn't see him at all!—An' so
He slewed the "griffuns"—*boff,* you know!
Nen wuz a horn hunged over his head,
High on th' wall, an' words 'at read,—
"Whoever kin this trumput blow
Shall cause the Gi'nt's overth'ow!"
An' Jack, he thist reached up an' blowed
The stuffin' out of it! an' th'owed
Th' castul gates wide open, an'
Nen tuk his gold sword in his han',
An' thist marched in t' ole "Bumblebore,"
An', 'fore he knowed, he put 'bout four
Heads on him—an' chopped 'em off, too!—
Wisht 'at *I'd* been Jack!—don't you?

REQUIESCAT

BE it life, be it death, there is nearing
   The dawn of a glorious day,
When the murmurs of doubt we are hearing
   In silence shall dwindle away;
And the hush and content that we covet—
   The rest that we need, and the sleep
That abides with the eyelids that love it,
   Shall come as we weep.

We shall listen no more to the sobbing
   Of sorrowing lips, and the sound
In our pillows at night of the throbbing
   Of feverish hearts will have found
The quiet beyond understanding
   The rush and the moan of the rain,
That shall beat on the shingles, demanding
   Admittance in vain.

The hand on the dial shall number
   The hours unmarked; and the bell
Shall waken us not from the slumber
   That knows neither tolling of knell

Nor the peals of glad melody showered
   Like roses of song o'er the pave
Where the bride and the groom walk their
      flowered
   Green way to the grave.

In that dawn, when it breaks, we shall wonder
   No more why the heavens send back
To our prayers but the answer of thunder,
   And the lightning-scrawl, writ on the black
Of the storm in a language no mortal
   May read till his questioning sight
Shall have pierced through the innermost
      portal
   Of death to the light.

AT SEA

YEA, we go down to sea in ships—
  But Hope remains behind,
And Love, with laughter on his lips,
  And Peace, of passive mind;
While out across the deeps of night,
  With lifted sails of prayer,
We voyage off in quest of light,
  Nor find it anywhere.

O Thou who wroughtest earth and sea,
  Yet keepest from our eyes
The shores of an eternity
  In calms of Paradise,
Blow back upon our foolish quest
  With all the driving rain
Of blinding tears and wild unrest,
  And waft us home again!

SOMEP'N COMMON-LIKE

SOMEP'N 'at's common-like, and good
  And plain, and easy understood;
Somep'n 'at folks like me and you
Kin understand, and relish, too,
And find some sermint in 'at hits
The spot, and sticks and benefits.

We don't need nothin' extry fine;
'Cause, take the run o' minds like mine,
And we'll go more on good horse-sense
Than all your flowery eloquence;
And we'll jedge best of honest acts
By Nature's statement of the facts.

So when you're wantin' to express
Your misery, er happiness,
Er anything 'at's wuth the time
O' telling in plain talk er rhyme—
Jes' sort o' let your subject run
As ef the Lord wuz listenun.

BLIND

YOU think it is a sorry thing
    That I am blind. Your pitying
Is welcome to me; yet indeed,
I think I have but little need
Of it. Though you may marvel much
That *we,* who see by sense of touch
And taste and hearing, see things *you*
May never look upon; and true
Is it that even in the scent
Of blossoms *we* find something meant
No eyes have in their faces read,
Or wept to see interpreted.

And you might think it strange if now
I told you you were smiling. How
Do I know that? I hold your hand—
Its language I can understand—
Give both to me, and I will show
You many other things I know.
Listen: We never met before
Till now?—Well, you are something lower
Than five-feet-eight in height; and you
Are slender; and your eyes are blue —
Your mother's eyes—your mother's hair—

Your mother's likeness everywhere
Save in your walk—and that is quite
Your father's; nervous.—Am I right?
I thought so. And you used to sing,
But have neglected everything
Of vocalism—though you may
Still thrum on the guitar, and play
A little on the violin,—
I know that by the callus in
The finger-tips of your left hand—
And, by the by, though nature planned
You as most men, you are, I see,
"*Left*-handed," too,—the mystery
Is clear, though,—your right arm has been
Broken, to "break" the left one in.
And so, you see, though blind of sight,
I still have ways of seeing quite
Too well for you to sympathize
Excessively, with your good eyes.—
Though *once,* perhaps, to be sincere,
Within the whole asylum here,
From cupola to basement hall,
I was the blindest of them all!

Let us move farther down the walk—
The man here waiting hears my talk,
And is disturbed; besides, he may
Not be quite friendly anyway.
In fact—(this will be far enough;
Sit down)—the man just spoken of
Was once a friend of mine. He came

For treatment here from Burlingame—
A rich though brilliant student there,
Who read his eyes out of repair,
And groped his way up here, where we
Became acquainted, and where he
Met one of our girl-teachers, and,
If you'll believe me, asked her hand
In marriage, though the girl was blind
As I am—and the girl *declined*.
Odd, wasn't it? Look, you can see
Him waiting there. Fine, isn't he?
And handsome, eloquently wide
And high of brow, and dignified
With every outward grace, his sight
Restored to him, clear and bright
As day-dawn; waiting, waiting still
For the blind girl that never will
Be wife of his. How do I know?
You will recall a while ago
I told you he and I were friends.
In all that friendship comprehends,
I *was* his friend, I swear! why, now,
Remembering his love, and how
His confidence was all my own,
I hear, in fancy, the low tone
Of his deep voice, so full of pride
And passion, yet so pacified
With his affliction, that it seems
An utterance sent out of dreams
Of saddest melody, withal
So sorrowfully musical

It was, and is, must ever be—
But I'm digressing, pardon me.
I knew not anything of love
In those days, but of that above
All worldly passion,—for my art—
Music,—and that, with all my heart
And soul, blent in a love too great
For words of mine to estimate.
And though among my pupils she
Whose love my friend sought came to me,
I only knew her fingers' touch
Because they loitered overmuch
In simple scales, and needs must be
Untangled almost constantly.
But she was bright in other ways,
And quick of thought; with ready plays
Of wit, and with a voice as sweet
To listen to as one might meet
In any oratorio—
And once I gravely told her so,—
And, at my words, her limpid tone
Of laughter faltered to a moan,
And fell from that into a sigh
That quavered all so wearily,
That I, without the tear that crept
Between the keys, had known she wept;
And yet the hand I reached for then
She caught away, and laughed again.
And when that evening I strolled
With my old friend, I, smiling, told
Him I believed the girl and he

Were matched and mated perfectly:
He was so noble; she, so fair
Of speech, and womanly of air;
He, strong, ambitious; she, as mild
And artless even as a child;
And with a nature, I was sure,
As worshipful as it was pure
And sweet, and brimmed with tender things
Beyond his rarest fancyings.
He stopped me solemnly. He knew,
He said, how good, and just, and true
Was all I said of her; but as
For his own virtues, let them pass,
Since they were nothing to the one
That he had set his heart upon;
For but that morning she had turned
Forever from him. Then I learned
That for a month he had delayed
His going from us, with no aid
Of hope to hold him,—meeting still
Her ever-firm denial, till
Not even in his new-found sight
He found one comfort or delight.
And as his voice broke there, I felt
The brother-heart within me melt
In warm compassion for his own
That throbbed so utterly alone.
And then a sudden fancy hit
Along my brain; and coupling it
With a belief that I, indeed,
Might help my friend in his great need,

I warmly said that I would go
Myself, if he decided so,
And see her for him—that I knew
My pleadings would be listened to
Most seriously, and that she
Should love him, listening to me.
Go; bless me! And that was the last—
The last time his warm hand shut fast
Within my own—so empty since,
That the remembered finger-prints
I've kissed a thousand times, and wet
Them with the tears of all regret!

I know not how to rightly tell
How fared my quest; and what befell
Me, coming in the presence of
That blind girl, and her blinder love.
I know but little else than that
Above the chair in which she sat
I leant—reached for, and found her hand,
And held it for a moment, and
Took up the other—held them both—
As might a friend, I will take oath:
Spoke leisurely, as might a man
Praying for no thing other than
He thinks Heaven's justice:—She was blind,
I said, and yet a noble mind
Most truly loved her; one whose fond
Clear-sighted vision looked beyond
The bounds of her infirmity,
And saw the woman, perfectly

Modeled, and wrought out pure and true
And lovable. She quailed, and drew
Her hands away, but closer still
I caught them. "Rack me as you will!"
She cried out sharply—"Call me 'blind'—
Love ever is—I am resigned!
Blind is your friend; as blind as he
Am I—but blindest of the three—
Yea, blind as death—you will not see
My love for you is killing me!"

There is a memory that may
Not ever wholly fade away
From out my heart, so bright and fair
The light of it still glimmers there.
Why, it did seem as though my sight
Flamed back upon me, dazzling white
And godlike. Not one other word
Of hers I listened for or heard,
But I *saw* songs sung in her eyes
Till they did swoon up drowning-wise,
As my mad lips did strike her own,
And we flashed one, and one alone!
Ah! was it treachery for me
To kneel there, drinking eagerly
That torrent-flow of words that swept
Out laughingly the tears she wept?—
Sweet words! O sweeter far, maybe,
Than light of day to those that see,—
God knows, who did the rapture send
To me, and hold it from my friend.

And we were married half a year
Ago.—And he is—waiting here,
Heedless of that—or anything,
But just that he is lingering
To say good-by to her, and bow—
As you may see him doing now,—
For there's her footstep in the hall;
God bless her!—help him!—save us all!

JUST AS OF OLD

JUST as of old! The world rolls on and on;
   The day dies into night—night into dawn—
Dawn into dusk—through centuries untold.—
      Just as of old.

Time loiters not. The river ever flows,
Its brink or white with blossoms or with snows;
Its tide or warm with spring or winter cold:
      Just as of old.

Lo! where is the beginning, where the end
Of living, loving, longing? *Listen,* friend!—
God answers with a silence of pure gold—
      Just as of old.

THE PRAYER PERFECT

DEAR Lord! kind Lord!
    Gracious Lord! I pray
Thou wilt look on all I love,
    Tenderly to-day!
Weed their hearts of weariness;
    Scatter every care
Down a wake of angel-wings
    Winnowing the air.

Bring unto the sorrowing
    All release from pain;
Let the lips of laughter
    Overflow again;
And with all the needy
    O divide, I pray,
This vast treasure of content
    That is mine to-day!

MONSIEUR LE SECRETAIRE

[JOHN CLARK RIDPATH]

MON cher Monsieur le Secretaire,
  Your song flits with me everywhere;
It lights on Fancy's prow and sings
Me on divinest voyagings:
And when my ruler love would fain
Be laid upon it—high again
It mounts, and hugs itself from me
With rapturous wings—still dwindlingly—
On!—on! till but a *ghost* is there
Of song, Monsieur le Secretaire!

A PHANTOM

LITTLE baby, you have wandered far away,
   And your fairy face comes back to me
      to-day,
  But I can not feel the strands
    Of your tresses, nor the play
  Of the dainty velvet-touches of your hands.

Little baby, you were mine to hug and hold;
Now your arms cling not about me as of old—
  O my dream of rest come true,
    And my richer wealth than gold,
  And the surest hope of Heaven that I know!

O for the lisp long silent, and the tone
Of merriment once mingled with my own—
  For the laughter of your lips,
    And the kisses plucked and thrown
  In the lavish wastings of your finger-tips!

Little baby, O as then, come back to me,
And be again just as you used to be,
  For this phantom of you stands
    All too cold and silently,
  And will not kiss nor touch me with its hands.

In Spring, when the green gits back in the trees,
  And the sun comes out and stays;
And yer boots pulls on with a good tight squeeze,
  And you think o' yer barefoot days;
When you ought to work and you want to not,
  And you and yer wife agrees
It's time to spade up the garden-lot
  When the green gits back in the trees,—
    Well! work is the least o' my idees
    When the green, you know, gits back in the trees!

When the green gits back in the trees, and bees
  Is a=buzzin' around agin
In that kind of a lazy "go=as=you=please"
  Old gait they bum round in;
When the green's all bald where the hay=rick stood;
  And the crick's riz, and the breeze
Coaxes the bloom in the old dogwood—
  And the green gits back in the trees,—
    I like, as I say, in such scenes as these
    The time when the green gits back in the trees!

Neighborly Poems pg. 110.

"When the Green Gits Back in the Trees"

When the whole tail-feathers o' wintertime
   Is all pulled out and gone!
And the sap it thaws and begins to climb,
   And the sweat it starts out on
A feller's forrid, a-gittin' down,
   At the old spring, on his knees —
I kindo' like jes' a-laferin' roun'
   When the green gits back in the trees —
     Jes' a-pottirin' roun' — as I — dunno-please,
   When the green, you know, gits back in the trees!
          —James Whitcomb Riley.

WHAT REDRESS

I PRAY you, do not use this thing
　For vengeance; but if questioning
What wound, when dealt your humankind,
Goes deepest,—surely he will find
Who wrongs *you,* loving *him* no less—
There's nothing hurts like tenderness.

A LOST LOVE

'TWAS a summer ago when he left me here—
A summer of smiles, with never a tear
Till I said to him, with a sob, my dear,—
Good-by, my lover; good-by!

For I loved him, O as the stars love night!
And my cheeks for him flashed red and white
When first he called me his Heart's delight,—
Good-by, my lover; good-by!

The touch of his hand was a thing divine
As he sat with me in the soft moonshine
And drank of my love as men drink wine,—
Good-by, my lover; good-by!

And never a night as I knelt in prayer,
In thought as white as our own souls were,
But in fancy he came and he kissed me there,—
Good-by, my lover; good-by!

But now—ah, *now!* what an empty place
My whole heart is!—Of the old embrace
And the kiss I loved there lives no trace—
Good-by, my lover; good-by!

He sailed not over the stormy sea,
And he went not down in the waves—not he—
But O, he is lost—for he married me—
    Good-by, my lover; good-by!

LET US FORGET

LET us forget. What matters it that we
　　Once reigned o'er happy realms of long ago,
　And talked of love, and let our voices low,
And ruled for some brief sessions royally?
What if we sung, or laughed, or wept maybe?
　　It has availed not anything, and so
　　Let it go by that we may better know
How poor a thing is lost to you and me.
　　But yesterday I kissed your lips, and yet
Did thrill you not enough to shake the dew
　　From your drenched lids—and missed, with no
　　　　regret,
Your kiss shot back, with sharp breaths failing
　　　　you:
　　And so, to-day, while our worn eyes are wet
　　With all this waste of tears, let us forget!

THE SHOEMAKER

THOU Poet, who, like any lark,
   Dost whet thy beak and trill
From misty morn till murky dark,
   Nor ever pipe thy fill:
Hast thou not, in thy cheery note,
   One poor chirp to confer—
One verseful twitter to devote
   Unto the Shoe-ma-ker?

At early dawn he doth peg in
   His noble work and brave;
And eke from cark and worldly sin
   He seeketh soles to save;
And all day long, with quip and song,
   Thus stitcheth he the way
Our feet may know the right from wrong,
   Nor ever go astray.

Soak kip in mind the Shoe-ma-ker,
   Nor slight his lasting fame:
Alway he waxeth tenderer
   In warmth of our acclaim;—

Ay, more than any artisan
　　We glory in his art
Who ne'er, to help the under man,
　　Neglects the upper part.

But toe the mark for him, and heel
　　Respond to thee in kine—
Or kid—or calf, shouldst thou reveal
　　A taste so superfine:
Thus let him jest—join in his laugh—
　　Draw on his stock, and be
A shoer'd there's no rival half-
　　Sole liberal as he.

Then, Poet, hail the Shoe-ma-ker
　　For all his goodly deeds,—
Yea, bless him free for booting thee—
　　The first of all thy needs!
And when at last his eyes grow dim,
　　And nerveless drops his clamp,
In golden shoon pray think of him
　　Upon his latest tramp.

IN THE CORRIDOR

AH! at last alone, love!
    Now the band may play
Till its sweetest tone, love,
    Swoons and dies away!
They who most will miss us
    We're not caring for—
Who of them could kiss us
    In the corridor?

Had we only known, dear,
    Ere this long delay,
Just how all alone, dear,
    We might waltz away,
Then for hours, like this, love,
    We are longing for,
We'd have still to kiss, love,
    In the corridor!

Nestle in my heart, love;
    Hug and hold me close—
Time will come to part, love,
    Ere a fellow knows;
There! the Strauss is ended—
    Whirl across the floor,
Isn't waltzing splendid
    In the corridor?

SUSPENSE

A WOMAN'S figure, on a ground of night
    Inlaid with sallow stars that dimly stare
  Down in the lonesome eyes, uplifted there
As in vague hope some alien lance of light
Might pierce their woe. The tears that blind her
       sight—
    The salt and bitter blood of her despair—
    Her hands toss back through torrents of her
       hair
And grip toward God with anguish infinite.
    And O the carven mouth, with all its great
Intensity of longing frozen fast
    In such a smile as well may designate
The slowly murdered heart, that, to the last,
    Conceals each newer wound, and back at Fate
    Throbs Love's eternal lie—"Lo, I can wait!"

A NONSENSE RHYME

RINGLETY-JING!
   And what will we sing?
Some little crinkety-crankety thing
      That rhymes and chimes,
      And skips, sometimes,
As though wound up with a kink in the spring.

      Grunkety-krung!
      And chunkety-plung!
Sing the song that the bullfrog sung,—
      A song of the soul
      Of a mad tadpole
That met his fate in a leaky bowl:
And it's O for the first false wiggle he made
In a sea of pale pink lemonade!
      And it's O for the thirst
         Within him pent,
      And the hopes that burst
         As his reason went—
When his strong arm failed and his strength was
      spent!

Sing, O sing
Of the things that cling,
And the claws that clutch and the fangs that
sting—
Till the tadpole's tongue
And his tail upflung
Quavered and failed with a song unsung!
O the dank despair in the rank morass,
Where the crawfish crouch in the cring-
ing grass,
And the long limp rune of the loon wails on
For the mad, sad soul
Of a bad tadpole
Forever lost and gone!

Jinglety-jee!
And now we'll see
What the last of the lay shall be,
As the dismal tip of the tune, O friends,
Swoons away and the long tale ends.
And it's O and alack!
For the tangled legs
And the spangled back
Of the green grig's eggs,
And the unstrung strain
Of the strange refrain
That the winds wind up like a strand of rain!

And it's O,
Also,
For the ears wreathed low,

Like a laurel-wreath on the lifted brow
Of the frog that chants of the why and how,
    And the wherefore too, and the thus and so
    Of the wail he weaves in a woof of woe!
Twangle, then, with your wrangling strings,
The tinkling links of a thousand things!
And clang the pang of a maddening moan
Till the Echo, hid in a land unknown,
    Shall leap as he hears, and hoot and hoo
    Like the wretched wraith of a Whoopty-
        Doo!

LOUELLA WAINIE

LOUELLA WAINIE! where are you?
  Do you not hear me as I cry?
Dusk is falling; I feel the dew;
  And the dark will be here by and by,
    I hear no thing but the owl's hoo-hoo!
    Louella Wainie! where are you?

Hand in hand to the pasture bars
  We came loitering, Lou and I,
Long ere the fireflies coaxed the stars
  Out of their hiding-place on high.
    O how sadly the cattle moo!
    Louella Wainie! where are you?

Laughingly we parted here—
  "I will go this way," said she,
"And you will go that way, my dear"—
  Kissing her dainty hand at me—
    And the hazels hid her from my view.
    Louella Wainie! where are you?

Is there ever a sadder thing
  Than to stand on the farther brink
Of twilight, hearing the marsh-frogs sing?

Nothing could sadder be, I think!
  And ah! how the night-fog chills me
      through.
    Louella Wainie! where are you?

Water-lilies and oozy leaves—
  Lazy bubbles that bulge and stare
Up at the moon through the gloom it weaves
  Out of the willows waving there!
    Is it despair I am wading through?
    Louella Wainie! where are you?

Louella Wainie, listen to me,
  Listen, and send me some reply,
For so will I call unceasingly
  Till death shall answer me by and by—
    Answer, and help me to find you too!
    Louella Wainie! where are you?

FOR YOU

FOR you, I could forget the gay
 Delirium of merriment,
And let my laughter die away
 In endless silence of content.
 I could forget, for your dear sake,
 The utter emptiness and ache
 Of every loss I ever knew.—
 What could I not forget for you?

I could forget the just deserts
 Of mine own sins, and so erase
The tear that burns, the smile that hurts,
 And all that mars and masks my face.
 For your fair sake I could forget
 The bonds of life that chafe and fret,
 Nor care if death were false or true.—
 What could I not forget for you?

What could I not forget? Ah me!
 One thing I know would still abide
Forever in my memory,
 Though all of love were lost beside—
 I yet would feel how first the wine
 Of your sweet lips made fools of mine
 Until they sung, all drunken through—
 "What could I not forget for you?"

MY FIRST SPECTACLES

AT first I laughed—for it was quite
    An oddity to see
My reflex looking from the glass
    Through spectacles at me.

But as I gazed I really found
    They so improved my sight
That many wrinkles in my face
    Were mixed with my delight;

And many streaks of silver, too,
    Were gleaming in my hair,
With quite a hint of baldness that
    I never dreamed was there.

And as I readjusted them
    And winked in slow surprise,
A something like a mist had come
    Between them and my eyes.

And, peering vainly still, the old
    Optician said to me,
The while he took them from my nose
    And wiped them hastily:

"Jes' now, of course, your eyes is apt
    To water some—but where
Is any man's on earth that won't
    The first he has to wear?"

THE TEXT

THE text: Love thou thy fellow man!
   He may have sinned. One proof in-
      deed,
He is thy fellow, reach thy hand
  And help him in his need!

Love thou thy fellow man. He may
  Have wronged thee—then, the less excuse
Thou hast for wronging him. Obey
  What he has dared refuse!

Love thou thy fellow man—for, be
  His life a light or heavy load,
No less he needs the love of thee
  To help him on his road.

AN OUT-WORN SAPPHO

HOW tired I am! I sink down all alone
    Here by the wayside of the Present. Lo,
Even as a child I hide my face and moan—
    A little girl that may no farther go:
    The path above me only seems to grow
      More rugged, climbing still, and ever **briered**
    With keener thorns of pain than these below;
    And O the bleeding feet that falter so
      And are so very tired!

Why, I have journeyed from the far-off **Lands**
    Of Babyhood—where baby-lilies blew
Their trumpets in mine ears, and filled my **hands**
    With treasures of perfume and honey-dew,
    And where the orchard shadows ever drew
      Their cool arms round me when my cheeks
          were fired
    With too much joy, and lulled mine eyelids **to**,
    And only let the starshine trickle through
      In sprays, when I was tired!

Yet I remember, when the butterfly
    Went flickering about me like a flame

That quenched itself in roses suddenly,
    How oft I wished that *I* might blaze the same,
    And in some rose-wreath nestle with my name,
        While all the world looked on it and admired.—
    Poor moth!—Along my wavering flight toward
        fame
    The winds drive backward, and my wings are
        lame
        And broken, bruised and tired!

I hardly know the path from those old times;
    I know at first it was a smoother one
Than this that hurries past me now, and climbs
    So high, its far cliffs even hide the sun
    And shroud in gloom my journey scarce begun.
        I could not do quite all the world required—
    I could not do quite all I should have done,
    And in my eagerness I have outrun
        My strength—and I am tired. . . .

Just tired! But when of old I had the stay
    Of mother-hands, O very sweet indeed
It was to dream that all the weary way
    I should but follow where I now must lead—
    For long ago they left me in my need,
        And, groping on alone, I tripped and mired
    Among rank grasses where the serpents breed
    In knotted coils about the feet of speed.—
        There first it was I tired.

And yet I staggered on, and bore my load
  Right gallantly: The sun, in summer-time,
In lazy belts came slipping down the road
  To woo me on, with many a glimmering rhyme
  Rained from the golden rim of some fair clime,
    That, hovering beyond the clouds, inspired
  My failing heart with fancies so sublime
I half forgot my path of dust and grime,
    Though I was growing tired.

And there were many voices cheering me:
  I listened to sweet praises where the wind
Went laughing o'er my shoulders gleefully
  And scattering my love-songs far behind;—
  Until, at last, I thought the world so kind—
    So rich in all my yearning soul desired—
  So generous—so loyally inclined,
I grew to love and trust it. . . . I was blind—
    Yea, blind as I was tired!

And yet one hand held me in creature-touch:
  And O, how fain it was, how true and strong,
How it did hold my heart up like a crutch,
  Till, in my dreams, I joyed to walk along
  The toilsome way, contented with a song—
    'Twas all of earthly things I had acquired,
  And 'twas enough, I feigned, or right or wrong,
Since, binding me to man—a mortal thong—
    It stayed me, growing tired. . . .

Yea, I had e'en resigned me to the strait
   Of earthly rulership—had bowed my head
Acceptant of the master-mind—the great
    One lover—lord of all,—the perfected
     Kiss-comrade of my soul;—had stammering said
      My prayers to him;—all—all that he desired
I rendered sacredly as we were wed.—
Nay—nay!—'twas but a myth I worshipèd.—
    And—God of love!—how tired!

For, O my friends, to lose the latest grasp—
   To feel the last hope slipping from its hold—
To feel the one fond hand within your clasp
    Fall slack, and loosen with a touch so cold
    Its pressure may not warm you as of old
     Before the light of love had thus expired—
To know your tears are worthless, though they
      rolled
Their torrents out in molten drops of gold.—
    God's pity! I am tired!

And I must rest.—Yet do not say "She *died*,"
   In speaking of me, sleeping here alone.
I kiss the grassy grave I sink beside,
    And close mine eyes in slumber all mine own:
    Hereafter I shall neither sob nor moan
     Nor murmur one complaint;—all I desired,
And failed in life to find, will now be known—
So let me dream. Good night! And on the stone
    Say simply: She was tired.

WILLIAM BROWN

"HE bore the name of William Brown"—
   His name, at least, did not go down
With him that day
He went the way
Of certain death where duty lay.

He looked his fate full in the face—
He saw his watery resting-place
   Undaunted, and
   With firmer hand
   Held others' hopes in sure command.—

The hopes of full three hundred lives—
Aye, babes unborn, and promised wives!
   "The odds are dread,"
   He must have said,
   "Here, God, is one poor life instead."

No time for praying overmuch—
No time for tears, or woman's touch
   Of tenderness,
   Or child's caress—
   His last "God bless them!" stopped at
         "bless"—

Thus man and engine, nerved with steel,
Clasped iron hands for woe or weal,
   And so went down
   Where dark waves drown
   All but the name of William Brown.

THE NINE LITTLE GOBLINS

THEY all climbed up on a high board-fence—
    Nine little goblins, with green-glass eyes—
Nine little goblins that had no sense,
    And couldn't tell coppers from cold mince pies;
        And they all climbed up on the fence, and sat—
        And I asked them what they were staring at.

And the first one said, as he scratched his head
    With a queer little arm that reached out of his ear
And rasped its claws in his hair so red—
    "This is what this little arm is fer!"
        And he scratched and stared, and the next one
            said,
        "How on earth do *you* scratch your head?"

And he laughed like the screech of a rusty hinge—
    Laughed and laughed till his face grew black;
And when he choked, with a final twinge
    Of his stifling laughter, he thumped his back
        With a fist that grew on the end of his tail
        Till the breath came back to his lips so pale.

And the third little goblin leered round at me—
    And there were no lids on his eyes at all,—
And he clucked one eye, and he says, says he,
    "What is the style of your socks this fall?"
        And he clapped his heels—and I sighed to see
        That he had hands where his feet should be.

Then a bald-faced goblin, gray and grim,
　　Bowed his head, and I saw him slip
His eyebrows off, as I looked at him,
　　And paste them over his upper lip;
　　　　And then he moaned in remorseful pain—
　　　　"Would—Ah, would I'd me brows again!"

And then the whole of the goblin band
　　Rocked on the fence-top to and fro,
And clung, in a long row, hand in hand,
　　Singing the songs that they used to know—
　　　　Singing the songs that their grandsires sung
　　　　In the goo-goo days of the goblin-tongue.

And ever they kept their green-glass eyes
　　Fixed on me with a stony stare—
Till my own grew glazed with a dread surmise,
　　And my hat whooped up on my lifted hair,
　　　　And I felt the heart in my breast snap to,
　　　　As you've heard the lid of a snuff-box do.

And they sang: "You're asleep! There is no board-
　　　　fence,
　　And never a goblin with green-glass eyes!—
'Tis only a vision the mind invents
　　After a supper of cold mince pies.—
　　　　And you're doomed to dream this way," they
　　　　　　said,—
　　　　*"And you shan't wake up till you're clean
　　　　　　plum dead!"*

WHY

WHY are they written—all these lovers'
      rhymes?
  I catch faint perfumes of the blossoms white
  That maidens drape their tresses with at night,
  And, through dim smiles of beauty and the din
  Of the musicians' harp and violin,
  I hear, enwound and blended with the dance,
  The voice whose echo is this utterance,—
Why are they written—all these lovers' rhymes?

Why are they written—all these lovers' rhymes?
  I see but vacant windows, curtained o'er
  With webs whose architects forevermore
  Race up and down their slender threads to bind
  The buzzing fly's wings whirless, and to wind
  The living victim in his winding sheet.—
  I shudder, and with whispering lips repeat,
Why are they written—all these lovers' rhymes?

Why are they written—all these lovers' rhymes?
  What will you have for answer?—Shall I say
  That he who sings the merriest roundelay
  Hath neither joy nor hope?—and he who sings
  The lightest, sweetest, tenderest of things
  But utters moan on moan of keenest pain,
  So aches his heart to ask and ask in vain,
Why are they written—all these lovers' rhymes?

THE TOUCH OF LOVING HANDS

LIGHT falls the rain-drop on the fallen leaf,
    And light o'er harvest-plain and garnered
        sheaf—
  But lightlier falls the touch of loving hands.

Light falls the dusk of mild midsummer night,
And light the first star's faltering lance of light
  On glimmering lawns,—but lightlier loving
      hands.

And light the feathery flake of early snows,
Or wisp of thistle-down that no wind blows,
  And light the dew,—but lightlier loving hands.

Light-falling dusk, or dew, or summer rain,
Or down of snow or thistle—all are vain,—
  Far lightlier falls the touch of loving hands.

THE OLD SCHOOL-CHUM

HE puts the poem by, to say
   His eyes are not themselves to-day!

A sudden glamour o'er his sight—
A something vague, indefinite—

An oft-recurring blur that blinds
The printed meaning of the lines,

And leaves the mind all dusk and dim
In swimming darkness—strange to him!

It is not childishness, I guess,—
Yet something of the tenderness

That used to wet his lashes when
A boy seems troubling him again;—

The old emotion, sweet and wild,
That drove him truant when a child,

That he might hide the tears that fell
Above the lesson—"Little Nell."

And so it is he puts aside
The poem he has vainly tried

To follow ; and, as one who sighs
In failure, through a poor disguise

Of smiles, he dries his tears, to say
His eyes are not themselves to-day.

A CUP OF TEA

I HAVE sipped, with drooping lashes.
  Dreamy draughts of Verzenay;
I have flourished brandy-smashes
  In the wildest sort of way;
I have joked with "Tom and Jerry"
  Till "wee hours ayont the twal"—
But I've found my tea the very
  Safest tipple of them all!

'Tis a mystical potation
  That exceeds in warmth of glow
And divine exhilaration
  All the drugs of long ago—
All of old magicians' potions—
  Of Medea's philtered spells—
Or of fabled isles and oceans
  Where the Lotos-eater dwells!

Though I've reveled o'er late lunches
  With blasé dramatic stars,
And absorbed their wit and punches
  And the fumes of their cigars—

Drank in the latest story,
  With a cocktail either end,—
I have drained a deeper glory
  In a cup of tea, my friend.

Green, Black, Moyune, Formosa,
  Congou, Amboy, Pingsuey—
No odds the name it knows—ah,
  Fill a cup of it for me!
And, as I clink my china
  Against your goblet's brim,
My tea in steam shall twine a
  Fragrant laurel round its rim.

TO THE SERENADER

TINKLE on, O sweet guitar,
　Let the dancing fingers
Loiter where the low notes are
　Blended with the singer's:
Let the midnight pour the moon's
　Mellow wine of glory
Down upon him through the tune's
　Old romantic story!

I am listening, my love,
　Through the cautious lattice,
Wondering why the stars above
　All are blinking at us;
Wondering if his eyes from there
　Catch the moonbeam's shimmer
As it lights the robe I wear
　With a ghostly glimmer.

Lilt thy song, and lute away
　In the wildest fashion:—
Pour thy rippling roundelay
　O'er the heights of passion!—
Flash it down the fretted strings
　Till thy mad lips, missing
All but smothered whisperings,
　Press this rose I'm kissing.

WHAT A DEAD MAN SAID

HEAR what a dead man said to me.
  His lips moved not, and the eyelids lay
Shut as the leaves of a white rose may
Ere the wan bud blooms out perfectly;
And the lifeless hands they were stiffly crossed
As they always cross them over the breast
When the soul goes nude and the corpse is dressed;
And over the form, in its long sleep lost,
From forehead down to the pointed feet
That peaked the foot of the winding-sheet,
Pallid patience and perfect rest.—
It was the voice of a dream, may be,
But it seemed that the dead man said to me:
"I, indeed, am the man that died
Yesternight—and you weep for this;
But, lo, I am with you, side by side,
As we have walked when the summer sun
Made the smiles of our faces one,
And touched our lips with the same warm kiss.
Do not doubt that I tell you true—
I am the man you once called friend,
And caught my hand when I came to you,
And loosed it only because the end

Of the path I walked of a sudden stopped—
And a dead man's hand must needs be dropped—
And I—though it's strange to think so now—
I have wept, as you weep for me,
And pressed hot palms to my aching brow
And moaned through the long night ceaselessly.

Yet have I lived to forget my pain,
As you will live to be glad again—
Though never so glad as this hour am I,
Tasting a rapture of delight
Vast as the heavens are infinite,
And dear as the hour I came to die.
Living and loving, I dreamed my cup
Brimmed sometimes, and with marvelings
I have lifted and tipped it up
·And drunk to the dregs of all sweet things.
Living, 'twas but a *dream* of bliss—
Now I *realize* all it is;
And now my only shadow of grief
Is that I may not give relief
Unto those living and dreaming on,
And woo them graveward, as I have gone,
And show death's loveliness,—for they
Shudder and shrink as they walk this way,
Never dreaming that all they dread
Is their purest delight when dead."

Thus it was, or it seemed to be,
That the voice of the dead man spoke to me.

A TEST

'TWAS a test I designed, in a quiet conceit
Of myself, and the thoroughly fixed and com-
    plete
Satisfaction I felt in the utter control
Of the guileless young heart of the girl of my soul.

So—we parted. I said it were better we should—
That she could forget me—I knew that she could.
For I never was worthy so tender a heart,
And so for her sake it were better to part.

She averted her gaze, and she sighed and looked sad
As I held out my hand for the ring that she had
With the bitterer speech that I hoped she might be
Resigned to look up and be happy with me.

'Twas a test, as I said—but God pity your grief,
At a moment like this when a smile of relief
Shall leap to the lips of the woman you prize,
And no mist of distress in her glorious eyes.

A SONG FOR CHRISTMAS

CHANT me a rhyme of Christmas—
Sing me a jovial song,—
And though it is filled with laughter,
Let it be pure and strong.

Let it be clear and ringing,
And though it mirthful be,
Let a low, sweet voice of pathos
Run through the melody.

Sing of the hearts brimmed over
With the story of the day—
Of the echo of childish voices
That will not die away.—

Of the blare of the tasseled bugle,
And the timeless clatter and beat
Of the drum that throbs to muster
Squadrons of scampering feet.

But, O, let your voice fall fainter,
Till, blent with a minor tone,
You temper your song with the beauty
Of the pity Christ hath shown.

301

And sing one verse for the voiceless;
　　And yet, ere the song be done,
A verse for the ears that hear not,
　　And a verse for the sightless one:

For though it be time for singing
　　A merry Christmas glee,
Let a low, sweet voice of pathos
　　Run through the melody.

SUN AND RAIN

ALL day the sun and rain have been as friends,
   Each vying with the other which shall be
  Most generous in dowering earth and sea
With their glad wealth, till each, as it descends,
Is mingled with the other, where it blends
   In one warm, glimmering mist that falls on me
   As once God's smile fell over Galilee.
The lily-cup, filled with it, droops and bends
   Like some white saint beside a sylvan shrine
In silent prayer; the roses at my feet,
   Baptized with it as with a crimson wine,
Gleam radiant in grasses grown so sweet;
   The blossoms light, with tenderness divine,
   Their wet eyes heavenward with these of mine.

WITH HER FACE

WITH her face between his hands!
    Was it any wonder she
    Stood atiptoe tremblingly?
As his lips along the strands
Of her hair went lavishing
Tides of kisses, such as swing
Love's arms to like iron bands.—
With her face between his hands!

And the hands—the hands that pressed
    The glad face—Ah! where are they?
    Folded limp, and laid away
Idly over idle breast?
He whose kisses drenched her hair,
As he caught and held her there,
In Love's alien, lost lands,
With her face between his hands?

Was it long and long ago,
    When her face was not as now,
    Dim with tears? nor wan her brow
As a winter-night of snow?
Nay, anointing still the strands
Of her hair, his kisses flow
Flood-wise, as she dreaming stands,
With her face between his hands.

MY NIGHT

HUSH! hush! list, heart of mine, and hearken
         low!
   You do not guess how tender is the Night,
   And in what faintest murmurs of delight
Her deep, dim-throated utterances flow
Across the memories of long-ago!
   Hark! do your senses catch the exquisite
   Staccatos of a bird that dreams he sings?
Nay, then, you hear not rightly,—'tis a blur
   Of misty love-notes, laughs and whisperings
The Night pours o'er the lips that fondle her,
   And that faint breeze, filled with all fragrant
         sighs,—
   That is her breath that quavers lover-wise—
O blessed sweetheart, with thy swart sweet-kiss,
Baptize me, drown me in black swirls of bliss!

THE HOUR BEFORE THE DAWN

THE hour before the dawn!
    O ye who grope therein, with fear and
      dread
  And agony of soul, be comforted,
Knowing, ere long, the darkness will be gone,
    And down its dusky aisles the light be shed;
Therefore, in utter trust, fare on—fare on,
    This hour before the dawn!

THE OLD YEAR AND THE NEW

I

AS one in sorrow looks upon
    The dead face of a loyal friend,
By the dim light of New Year's dawn
    I saw the Old Year end.

Upon the pallid features lay
    The dear old smile—so warm and bright
Ere thus its cheer had died away
    In ashes of delight.

The hands that I had learned to love
    With strength of passion half divine,
Were folded now, all heedless of
    The emptiness of mine.

The eyes that once had shed their bright
    Sweet looks like sunshine, now were dull,
And ever lidded from the light
    That made them beautiful.

II

The chimes of bells were in the air,
    And sounds of mirth in hall and street,
With pealing laughter everywhere
    And throb of dancing feet:

The mirth and the convivial din
  Of revelers in wanton glee,
With tunes of harp and violin
  In tangled harmony.

But with a sense of nameless dread,
  I turned me, from the merry face
Of this newcomer, to my dead;
  And, kneeling there a space,

I sobbed aloud, all tearfully:—
  By this dear face so fixed and cold,
O Lord, let not this New Year be
  As happy as the old!

GOOD-BY, OLD YEAR

GOOD-BY, Old Year!
          Good-by!
We have been happy—you and I;
  We have been glad in many ways;
And now, that you have come to die,
  Remembering our happy days,
'Tis hard to say, "Good-by—
  Good-by, Old Year!
          Good-by!"

Good-by, Old Year!
          Good-by!
We have seen sorrow—you and I;
  Such hopeless sorrow, grief and care,
That now, that you have come to die,
  Remembering our old despair,
'Tis sweet to say, "Good-by—
  Good-by, Old Year!
          Good-by!"

AS CREATED

THERE'S a space for good to bloom in
  Every heart of man or woman,—
And however wild or human,
    Or however brimmed with gall,
Never heart may beat without it;
And the darkest heart to doubt it
Has something good about it
        After all.

SOMEDAY

SOMEDAY:—So many tearful eyes
  Are watching for thy dawning light;
So many faces toward the skies
  Are weary of the night!

So many failing prayers that reel
  And stagger upward through the storm,
And yearning hands that reach and feel
  No pressure true and warm.

So many hearts whose crimson wine
  Is wasted to a purple stain
And blurred and streaked with drops of brine
  Upon the lips of Pain.

Oh, come to them!—these weary ones!
  Or if thou still must bide a while,
Make stronger yet the hope that runs
  Before thy coming smile:

And haste and find them where they wait—
  Let summer-winds blow down that way,
And all they long for, soon or late,
  Bring round to them, Someday.

311

FALSE AND TRUE

ONE said: "Here is my hand to lean upon
       As long as you may need it."   And one said:
"Believe me true to you till I am dead."
And one, whose dainty way it was to fawn
About my face, with mellow fingers drawn
    Most soothingly o'er brow and drooping head,
    Sighed tremulously: "Till my breath is fled
Know I am faithful!" . . . Now, all these are gone
    And many like to them—and yet I make
No bitter moan above their grassy graves—
    Alas! they are not dead for me to take
Such sorry comfort!—but my heart behaves
    Most graciously, since one who never spake
    A vow is true to me for true love's sake.

A BALLAD FROM APRIL

I AM dazed and bewildered with living
   A life but an intricate skein
Of hopes and despairs and thanksgiving
   Wound up and unraveled again—
Till it seems, whether waking or sleeping,
   I am wondering ever the while
At a something that smiles when I'm weeping
   And something that weeps when I smile.

And I walk through the world as one dreaming
   Who knows not the night from the day,
For I look on the stars that are gleaming,
   And lo, they have vanished away:
And I look on the sweet-summer daylight,
   And e'en as I gaze it is fled,
And, veiled in a cold, misty, gray light,
   The winter is there in its stead.

I feel in my palms the warm fingers
   Of numberless friends—and I look,
And lo, not a one of them lingers
   To give back the pleasure he took;

And I lift my sad eyes to the faces
    All tenderly fixed on my own,
But they wither away in grimaces
    That scorn me, and leave me alone.

And I turn to the woman that told me
    Her love would live on until death—
But her arms they no longer enfold me,
    Though barely the dew of her breath
Is dry on the forehead so pallid
    That droops like the weariest thing
O'er this most inharmonious ballad
    That ever a sorrow may sing.

So I'm dazed and bewildered with living
    A life but an intricate skein
Of hopes and despairs and thanksgiving
    Wound up and unraveled again—
Till it seems, whether waking or sleeping,
    I am wondering ever the while
At a something that smiles when I'm weeping
    And a something that weeps when I smile.

WHEN DE FOLKS IS GONE

WHAT dat scratchin' at de kitchen do'?
Done heah'n dat foh an hour er mo'!
Tell you, Mr. Niggah, das sho's you' bo'n,
Hit's mighty lonesome waitin' when de folks is
gone!

Blame my trap! how de wind do blow!
An' dis is das de night foh de witches, sho'!
Dey's trouble gon' to waste when de old slut whine,
An' you heah de cat a-spittin' when de moon don't
shine!

Chune my fiddle, an' de bridge go *"bang!"*
An' I lef' 'er right back whah she allus hang,
An' de tribble snap short an' de apern split
When dey no mortal man wah a-tetchin' hit!

Dah! *Now,* what? How de ole j'ice cracks!
'Spec' dis house, ef hit tell plain fac's,
'Ud talk about de ha'nts wid dey long tails on
What das'n't on'y come when de folks is gone!

What I tuk an' done ef a sho'-'nuff ghos'
Pop right up by de ole bed-pos'?
What dat shinin' fru de front do' crack? . . .
God bress de Lo'd! hit's de folks got back!

315

THE TWINS

ONE'S the pictur' of his Pa,
  And the *other* of her Ma—
Jes' the bossest pair o' babies 'at a mortal
    ever saw!
And we love 'em as the bees
Loves the blossoms on the trees,
A-ridin' and a-rompin' in the breeze!

One's got her Mammy's eyes—
Soft and blue as Apurl-skies—
With the same sort of a *smile,* like—Yes,
    and mouth about her size,—
Dimples, too, in cheek and chin,
'At my lips jes' *wallers* in,
A-goin' to work, er gittin' home ag'in.

And the *other*—Well, they say
That he's got his Daddy's way
O' bein' ruther soberfied, er ruther extry
    gay,—
That he eether cries his best,
Er he laughs his howlin'est—
Like all he lacked was buttons and a vest!

316

Look at *her!*—and look at *him!*—
Talk about yer "Cheru-*bim!*"
Roll 'em up in dreams together, rosy arm
    and chubby limb!
O we love 'em as the bees
Loves the blossoms on the trees,
A-ridin' and a-rompin' in the breeze!

THE ORCHARD LANDS OF LONG AGO

THE orchard lands of Long Ago!
O drowsy winds, awake, and blow
The snowy blossoms back to me,
And all the buds that used to be!
Blow back along the grassy ways
Of truant feet, and lift the haze
Of happy summer from the trees
That trail their tresses in the seas
Of grain that float and overflow
The orchard lands of Long Ago!

Blow back the melody that slips
In lazy laughter from the lips
That marvel much if any kiss
Is sweeter than the apple's is.
Blow back the twitter of the birds—
The lisp, the titter, and the words
Of merriment that found the shine
Of summer-time a glorious wine
That drenched the leaves that loved it so,
In orchard lands of Long Ago!

O memory! alight and sing
Where rosy-bellied pippins cling,
And golden russets glint and gleam,
As, in the old Arabian dream,
The fruits of that enchanted tree
The glad Aladdin robbed for me!
And, drowsy winds, awake and fan
My blood as when it overran
A heart ripe as the apples grow
In orchard lands of Long Ago!

BRUDDER SIMS

DAH'S Brudder Sims! Dast slam yo' Bible shet
   An' lef' dat man alone—kase he's de boss
  Ob all de preachahs ev' I come across!
Day's no twis' in dat gospil book, I bet,
Ut Brudder Sims cain't splanify, an' set
   You' min' at eaze! W'at's Moses an' de Laws?
   W'at's fo'ty days an' nights ut Noey toss
Aroun' de Dil-ooge?—W'at dem Chillen et
   De Lo'd rain down? W'at s'prise ole Joney so
In dat whale's inna'ds?—W'at dat laddah mean
   Ut Jacop see?—an' wha' dat laddah go?—
Who clim dat laddah?—Wha' dat laddah lean?—
   An' wha' dat laddah now? "Dast chalk yo' toe
   Wid Faith," sez Brudder Sims, "an' den you
      know!"

DEFORMED

CROUCHED at the corner of the street
  She sits all day, with face too white
And hands too wasted to be sweet
  In anybody's sight.

Her form is shrunken, and a pair
  Of crutches leaning at her side
Are crossed like homely hands in prayer
  At quiet eventide.

Her eyes—two lustrous, weary things—
  Have learned a look that ever aches,
Despite the ready jinglings
  The passer's penny makes.

And, noting this, I pause and muse
  If any precious promise touch
This heart that has so much to lose
  If dreaming overmuch—

And, in a vision, mistily
  Her future womanhood appears,—
A picture framed with agony
  And drenched with ceaseless tears—

Where never lover comes to claim
 The hand outheld so yearningly—
The laughing babe that lisps her name
 Is but a fantasy!

And, brooding thus, all swift and wild
 A daring fancy, strangely sweet,
Comes o'er me, that the crippled child
 That crouches at my feet—

Has found her head a resting-place
 Upon my shoulder, while my kiss
Across the pallor of her face
 Leaves crimson trails of bliss.

WHILE THE MUSICIAN PLAYED

O IT was but a dream I had
⠀⠀While the musician played!—
And here the sky, and here the glad
⠀⠀Old ocean kissed the glade;
And here the laughing ripples ran,
⠀⠀And here the roses grew
That threw a kiss to every man
⠀⠀That voyaged with the crew.

Our silken sails in lazy folds
⠀⠀Drooped in the breathless breeze:
As o'er a field of marigolds
⠀⠀Our eyes swam o'er the seas;
While here the eddies lisped and purled
⠀⠀Around the island's rim,
And up from out the underworld
⠀⠀We saw the mermen swim.

And it was dawn and middle-day
⠀⠀And midnight—for the moon
On silver rounds across the bay
⠀⠀Had climbed the skies of June,—

And there the glowing, glorious king
    Of day ruled o'er his realm,
With stars of midnight glittering
    About his diadem.

The sea-gull reeled on languid wing
    In circles round the mast,
We heard the songs the sirens sing
    As we went sailing past;
And up and down the golden sands
    A thousand fairy throngs
Flung at us from their flashing hands
    The echoes of their songs.

O it was but a dream I had
    While the musician played!—
For here the sky, and here the glad
    Old ocean kissed the glade;
And here the laughing ripples ran,
    And here the roses grew
That threw a kiss to every man
    That voyaged with the crew.

FAITH

THE sea was breaking at my feet,
  And looking out across the tide,
Where placid waves and heaven meet,
  I thought me of the Other Side.

For on the beach on which I stood
  Were wastes of sands, and wash, and roar,
Low clouds, and gloom, and solitude,
  And wrecks, and ruins—nothing more.

"O, tell me if beyond the sea
  A heavenly port there is!" I cried,
And back the echoes laughingly
  "There is! there is!" replied.

BE OUR FORTUNES AS THEY MAY

BE our fortunes as they may,
  Touched with loss or sorrow,
Saddest eyes that weep to-day
  May be glad to-morrow.

Yesterday the rain was here,
  And the winds were blowing—
Sky and earth and atmosphere
  Brimmed and overflowing.

But to-day the sun is out,
  And the drear November
We were then so vexed about
  Now we scarce remember.

Yesterday you lost a friend—
  Bless your heart and love it!—
For you scarce could comprehend
  All the aching of it;—

But I sing to you and say:
  Let the lost friend sorrow—
Here's another come to-day,
  Others may to-morrow.

A HINT OF SPRING

'TWAS but a hint of Spring—for still
     The atmosphere was sharp and chill,
Save where the genial sunshine smote
The shoulders of my overcoat,
And o'er the snow beneath my feet
Laid spectral fences down the street.

My *shadow,* even, seemed to be
Elate with some new buoyancy,
And bowed and bobbed in my advance
With trippingest extravagance,
And, when the birds chirpt out somewhere,
It seemed to wheel with me and stare.

Above I heard a rasping stir—
And on a roof the carpenter
Was perched, and prodding rusty leaves
From out the choked and dripping eaves—
And some one, hammering about,
Was taking all the windows out.

Old scraps of shingles fell before
The noisy mansion's open door;
And wrangling children raked the yard,
And labored much, and laughed as hard,
And fired the burning trash I smelt
And sniffed again—so good I felt!

LAST NIGHT—AND THIS

LAST night—how deep the darkness was!
And well I knew its depths, because
I waded it from shore to shore,
Thinking to reach the light no more.

She would not even touch my hand.—
The winds rose and the cedars fanned
The moon out, and the stars fled back
In heaven and hid—and all was black!

But ah! To-night a summons came,
Signed with a tear-drop for a name,—
For as I wondering kissed it, lo,
A line beneath it told me so.

And *now*—the moon hangs over me
A disk of dazzling brilliancy,
And every star-tip stabs my sight
With splintered glitterings of light!

LITTLE GIRLY-GIRL

LITTLE Girly-Girl, of you
  Still forever I am dreaming.—
Laughing eyes of limpid blue—
 Tresses glimmering and gleaming
Like glad waters running over
Shelving shallows, rimmed with clover,
  Trembling where the eddies whirl,
  Gurgling, "Little Girly-Girl!"

For your name it came to me
 Down the brink of brooks that brought it
Out of Paradise—and we—
 Love and I—we, leaning, caught it
From the ripples romping nigh us,
And the bubbles bumping by us
  Over shoals of pebbled pearl,
  Lilting, "Little Girly-Girl!"

That was long and long ago,
 But in memory the tender
Winds of summer weather blow,
 And the roses burst in splendor;
And the meadow's grassy billows
Break in blossoms round the willows
  Where the currents curve and curl,
  Calling, "Little Girly-Girl!"

CLOSE THE BOOK

CLOSE the book, and leave the tale
    All unfinished. It is best:
Brighter fancy will not fail
    To relate the rest.

We have read it on and on,
    Till each character, in sooth,
By the master-touches drawn,
    Is a living truth.

Leave it so, and let us sit,
    With the volume laid away—
Cut no other leaf of it,
    But as Fancy may.—

Then the friends that we have met
    In its pages will endure,
And the villain, even yet,
    May be white and pure.

Close the book, and leave the tale
    All unfinished. It is best:
Brighter fancy will not fail
    To relate the rest.

THE MOTHER SAINTED

FAIR girl, fond wife, and dear
Young mother, sleeping here
    So quietly,—
Tell us what dream is thine—
What miracle divine
    Is wrought in thee!

Once—was it yesterday,
Or but one hour away?—
    The folded hands
Were quick to greet our own—
Now—are they God's alone?
    Who understands?

Who, bending low to fold
The fingers as of old
    In pressure warm,
But muses,—"Surely she
Will reach one touch to me,
    And break the charm!"

And yet she does not stir;—
Such silence lies on her
    We hear the drip

Of tear-drops as we press
Our kisses answerless
    On brow and lip.

Not e'en the yearning touch
Of lips she loved so much
    She made their breath
One with her own, will she
Give answer to and be
    Wooed back from death.

And though he kneel and plead
Who was her greatest need,
    And on her cheek
Lay the soft baby-face
In its old resting-place,
    She will not speak.

So brave she was, and good—
In worth of womanhood
    So like the snow—
She, smiling, gave her life
To blend the name of wife
    With mother.—So,

God sees in her a worth
Too great for this dull earth,
    And, beckoning, stands
At Heaven's open gate
Where all His angels wait
    With welcoming hands.

Then, like her, reconciled,
O parent, husband, child,
    And mourning friend,—
Smile out as smiles the light
Of day above the night,
    And—wait the end.

THE LOST THRILL

I GROW so weary, someway, of all things
That love and loving have vouchsafed to
me,
Since now all dreamed-of sweets of ecstacy
Am I possessed of: The caress that clings—
The lips that mix with mine with murmurings
No language may interpret, and the free,
Unfettered brood of kisses, hungrily
Feasting in swarms of honeyed blossomings
Or passion's fullest flower—For yet I miss
The essence that alone makes love divine—
The subtle flavoring no tang of this
Weak wine of melody may here define:—
A something found and lost in the first kiss
A lover ever poured through lips of mine.

REACH YOUR HAND TO ME

REACH your hand to me, my friend,
  With its heartiest caress—
Sometime there will come an end
  To its present faithfulness—
    Sometime I may ask in vain
    For the touch of it again,
    When between us land or sea
    Holds it ever back from me.

Sometime I may need it so,
  Groping somewhere in the night,
It will seem to me as though
  Just a touch, however light,
    Would make all the darkness day,
    And along some sunny way
    Lead me through an April-shower
    Of my tears to this fair hour.

O the present is too sweet
  To go on forever thus!
Round the corner of the street
  Who can say what waits for us?—
    Meeting—greeting, night and day,
    Faring each the selfsame way—
    Still somewhere the path must end—
    Reach your hand to me, my friend!

335

WE MUST GET HOME

WE must get home! How could we stray like
      this?—
So far from home, we know not where it is,—
Only in some fair, apple-blossomy place
Of children's faces—and the mother's face—
We dimly dream it, till the vision clears
Even in the eyes of fancy, glad with tears.

We must get home—for we have been away
So long, it seems forever and a day!
And O so very homesick we have grown,
The laughter of the world is like a moan
In our tired hearing, and its song as vain,—
We must get home—we must get home again!

We must get home! With heart and soul we yearn
To find the long-lost pathway, and return! . . .
The child's shout lifted from the questing band
Of old folk, faring weary, hand in hand,
But faces brightening, as if clouds at last
Were showering sunshine on us as they passed.

We must get home: It hurts so, staying here,
Where fond hearts must be wept out tear by tear,
And where to wear wet lashes means, at best,
When most our lack, the least our hope of rest—
When most our need of joy, the more our pain—
We must get home—we must get home again!

We must get home—home to the simple things—
The morning-glories twirling up the strings
And bugling color, as they blared in blue-
And-white o'er garden-gates we scampered through;
The long grape-arbor, with its under-shade
Blue as the green and purple overlaid.

We must get home: All is so quiet there:
The touch of loving hands on brow and hair—
Dim rooms, wherein the sunshine is made mild—
The lost love of the mother and the child
Restored in restful lullabies of rain,—
We must get home—we must get home again!

The rows of sweetcorn and the China beans
Beyond the lettuce-beds where, towering, leans
The giant sunflower in barbaric pride
Guarding the barn-door and the lane outside;
The honeysuckles, midst the hollyhocks,
That clamber almost to the martin-box.

We must get home, where, as we nod and drowse,
Time humors us and tiptoes through the house,
And loves us best when sleeping baby-wise,
With dreams—not tear-drops—brimming our
    clenched eyes,—
Pure dreams that know nor taint nor earthly
    stain—
We must get home—we must get home again!

We must get home! There only may we find
The little playmates that we left behind,—
Some racing down the road; some by the brook;
Some droning at their desks, with wistful look
Across the fields and orchards—farther still
Where laughs and weeps the old wheel at the mill.

We must get home! The willow-whistle's call
Trills crisp and liquid as the waterfall—
Mocking the trillers in the cherry-trees
And making discord of such rhymes as these,
That know nor lilt nor cadence but the birds
First warbled—then all poets afterwards.

We must get home; and, unremembering there
All gain of all ambition otherwhere,
Rest—from the feverish victory, and the crown
Of conquest whose waste glory weighs us down.—
Fame's fairest gifts we toss back with disdain—
We must get home—we must get home again!

We must get home again—we must—we must!—
(Our rainy faces pelted in the dust)
Creep back from the vain quest through endless
    strife
To find not anywhere in all of life
A happier happiness than blest us then. . . .
We must get home—we must get home again!

MABEL

SWEET little face, so full of slumber now—
 Sweet lips unlifted now with any kiss—
Sweet dimpled cheek and chin, and snowy brow,—
  What quietude is this?

O speak! Have you forgotten, yesterday,
 How gladly you came running to the gate
To meet us in the old familiar way,
  So joyous—so elate—

So filled with wildest glee, yet so serene
 With innocence of song and childish chat,
With all the dear caresses in between—
  Have you forgotten that?

Have you forgotten, knowing gentler charms,
 The boisterous love of one you ran to greet
When you last met, who caught you in his arms
  And kissed you, in the street?

Not very many days have passed since then,
 And yet between that kiss and him there lies
No pathway of return—unless again,
  In streets of Paradise,

Your eager feet come twinkling down the gold
  Of some bright thoroughfare ethereal,
To meet and greet him there just as of old.—
  Till then, farewell—farewell.

AT DUSK

A SOMETHING quiet and subdued
    In all the faces that we meet;
A sense of rest, a solitude
    O'er all the crowded street;
      The very noises seem to be
      Crude utterings of harmony,
      And all we hear, and all we see,
Has in it something sweet.

Thoughts come to us as from a dream
    Of some long-vanished yesterday;
The voices of the children seem
    Like ours, when young as they;
      The hand of Charity extends
      To meet Misfortune's, where it blends,
      Veiled by the dusk—and oh, my friends,
Would it were dusk alway!

ANOTHER RIDE FROM GHENT TO AIX

W̲E̲ sprang for the side-holts—my gripsack
       and I—
It dangled—I dangled—we both dangled by.
"Good speed!" cried mine host, as we landed at
       last—
"Speed?" chuckled the watch we went lumbering
       past;
Behind shut the switch, and out through the rear
       door
I glared while we waited a half hour more.

I had missed the express that went thundering
       down
Ten minutes before to my next lecture town,
And my only hope left was to catch this "wild
       freight,"
Which the landlord remarked was "most luckily
       late—
But the twenty miles distance was easily done,
If they run half as fast as they usually run!"

Not a word to each other—we struck a snail's
       pace—
Conductor and brakeman ne'er changing a place—
Save at the next watering-tank, where they all

Got out—strolled about—cut their names on the
    wall,
Or listlessly loitered on down to the pile
Of sawed wood just beyond us, to doze for a while.

'Twas high noon at starting, but while we drew
    near
"Arcady" I said, "We'll not make it, I fear!
I must strike Aix by eight, and it's three o'clock
    now;
Let me stoke up that engine, and I'll show you
    how!"
At which the conductor, with patience sublime,
Smiled up from his novel with, "Plenty of time!"

At "Trask," as we jolted stock-still as a stone,
I heard a cow bawl in a five o'clock tone;
And the steam from the saw-mill looked misty and
    thin,
And the snarl of the saw had been stifled within:
And a frowzy-haired boy, with a hat full of chips,
Came out and stared up with a smile on his lips.

At "Booneville," I groaned, "Can't I telegraph on?"
No! Why? " 'Cause the telegraph-man had just
    gone
To visit his folks in Almo"—and one heard
The sharp snap of my teeth through the throat of a
    word,
That I dragged for a mile and a half up the track,
And strangled it there, and came skulkingly back.

Again we were off. It was twilight, and more,
As we rolled o'er a bridge where beneath us the
　　roar
Of a river came up with so wooing an air
I mechanic'ly strapped myself fast in my chair
As a brakeman slid open the door for more light,
Saying: "Captain, brace up, for your town is in
　　sight!"

"How they'll greet me!"—and all in a moment—
　　"che-wang!"
And the train stopped again, with a bump and a
　　bang.
What was it? "The section-hands, just in ad-
　　vance."
And I spit on my hands, and I rolled up my pants,
And I clumb like an imp that the fiends had let loose
Up out of the depths of that deadly caboose.

I ran the train's length—I lept safe to the ground—
And the legend still lives that for five miles around
They heard my voice hailing the hand-car that
　　yanked
Me aboard at my bidding, and gallantly cranked,
As I groveled and clung, with my eyes in eclipse,
And a rim of red foam round my rapturous lips.

Then I cast loose my ulster—each ear-tab let fall—
Kicked off both my shoes—let go arctics and all—
Stood up with the boys—leaned—patted each head

As it bobbed up and down with the speed that we
    sped;
Clapped my hands—laughed and sang—any noise,
    bad or good,
Till at length into Aix we rotated and stood.

And all I remember is friends flocking round
As I unsheathed my head from a hole in the
    ground;
And no voice but was praising that hand-car divine,
As I rubbed down its spokes with that lecture of
    mine,
Which (the citizens voted by common consent)
Was no more than its due. 'Twas the lecture they
    meant.

THE RIPEST PEACH

THE ripest peach is highest on the tree—
    And so her love, beyond the reach of me,
Is dearest in my sight. Sweet breezes, bow
Her heart down to me where I worship now!

She looms aloft where every eye may see
The ripest peach is highest on the tree.
Such fruitage as her love I know, alas!
I may not reach here from the orchard grass.

I drink the sunshine showered past her lips
As roses drain the dewdrop as it drips.
The ripest peach is highest on the tree,
And so mine eyes gaze upward eagerly.

Why—why do I not turn away in wrath
And pluck some heart here hanging in my path?—
Love's lower boughs bend with them—but, ah me!
The ripest peach is highest on the tree!

BEDOUIN

O LOVE is like an untamed steed!—
    So hot of heart and wild of speed,
And with fierce freedom so in love,
The desert is not vast enough,
With all its leagues of glimmering sands,
To pasture it! Ah, that my hands
Were more than human in their strength,
That my deft lariat at length
Might safely noose this splendid thing
That so defies all conquering!
Ho! but to see it whirl and reel—
The sands spurt forward—and to feel
The quivering tension of the thong
That throned me high, with shriek and song!
To grapple tufts of tossing mane—
To spurn it to its feet again,
And then, sans saddle, rein or bit,
To lash the mad life out of it!

A DITTY OF NO TONE—

Piped to the Spirit of John Keats

I

WOULD that my lips might pour out in thy
praise
A fitting melody—an air sublime,—
A song sun-washed and draped in dreamy haze—
The floss and velvet of luxurious rhyme:
A lay wrought of warm languors, and o'er-brimmed
With balminess, and fragrance of wild flowers
Such as the droning bee ne'er wearies of—
Such thoughts as might be hymned
To thee from this midsummer land of ours
Through shower and sunshine, blent for very
love.

II

Deep silences in woody aisles wherethrough
Cool paths go loitering, and where the trill
Of best-remembered birds hath something new
In cadence for the hearing—lingering still

Through all the open day that lies beyond;
  Reaches of pasture-lands, vine-wreathen oaks,
    Majestic still in pathos of decay;—
The road—the wayside pond
  Wherein the dragon-fly an instant soaks
    His filmy wing-tips ere he flits away.

III

And I would pluck from out the dank, rich mold,
  Thick-shaded from the sun of noon, the long
Lithe stalks of barley, topped with ruddy gold,
  And braid them in the meshes of my song;
And with them I would tangle wheat and rye,
  And wisps of greenest grass the katydid
    E'er crept beneath the blades of, sulkily,
As harvest-hands went by;
  And weave of all, as wildest fancy bid,
    A crown of mingled song and bloom for thee.

THE SPHINX

I KNOW all about the Sphinx—
I know even what she thinks,
Staring with her stony eyes
Up forever at the skies.

For last night I dreamed that she
Told me all the mystery—
Why for æons mute she sat :—
She was just cut out for that!

MOTHER GOOSE

DEAR Mother Goose! most motherly and
      dear
  Of all good mothers who have laps wherein
  We children nestle safest from all sin,—
I cuddle to thy bosom, with no fear
There to confess that though thy cap be queer,
    And thy curls gimlety, and thy cheeks thin,
    And though the winkered mole upon thy chin
Tickles thy very nose-tip,—still to hear
    The jolly jingles of mine infancy
Crooned by thee, makes mine eager arms, as now,
    To twine about thy neck, full tenderly
Drawing the dear old face down, that thy brow
    May dip into my purest kiss, and be
    Crowned ever with the baby-love of me.

IN THE HEART OF JUNE

IN the heart of June, love,
  You and I together,
On from dawn till noon, love,
  Laughing with the weather;
Blending both our souls, love,
  In the selfsame tune,
Drinking all life holds, love,
  In the heart of June.

In the heart of June, love,
  With its golden weather,
Underneath the moon, love,
  You and I together.
Ah! how sweet to seem, love,
  Drugged and half aswoon
With this luscious dream, love,
  In the heart of June.

MY BOY

YOU smile and you smoke your cigar,
  my boy;
  You walk with a languid swing;
You tinkle and tune your guitar, my boy,
  And lift up your voice and sing;
The midnight moon is a friend of yours,
  And a serenade your joy—
And it's only an age like mine that cures
  A trouble like yours, my boy!

From a photograph taken when twenty-nine years old

THE ASSASSIN

FLING him amongst the cobbles of the street
    Midmost along a mob's most turbid tide;
  Stun him with tumult upon every side—
Wrangling of hoarsened voices that repeat
His awful guilt and howl for vengeance meet;
    Let white-faced women stare, all torrid-eyed,
    With hair blown forward, and with jaws dropped
        wide,
And some face like his mother's glimmer sweet
An instant in the hot core of his eyes.
    Then snatch him with claw hands, and thong his
        head
That he may look no way but toward the skies
    That glower lividly and crackle red,—
There let some knuckled fist of lightning rise—
    Draw backward flickeringly and knock him dead.

BECAUSE

WHY did we meet long years of yore?
　　And why did we strike hands and
　　　say:
"We will be friends, and nothing more";
　Why are we musing thus to-day?
　　Because because was just because,
　　And no one knew just why it was.

Why did I say good-by to you?
　Why did I sail across the main?
Why did I love not heaven's own blue
　Until I touched these shores again?
　　Because because was just because,
　　And you nor I knew why it was.

Why are my arms about you now,
　And happy tears upon your cheek?
And why my kisses on your brow?
　Look up in thankfulness and speak!
　　Because because was just because,
　　And only God knew why it was.

PANSIES

PANSIES! Pansies! How I love you, pansies!
   Jaunty-faced, laughing-lipped and dewy-eyed
      with glee;
Would my song but blossom out in little five-leaf
    stanzas
         As delicate in fancies
         As your beauty is to me!

But my eyes shall smile on you, and my hands
    infold you,
  Pet, caress, and lift you to the lips that love
      you so,
That, shut ever in the years that may mildew or
    mold you,
        My fancy shall behold you
        Fair as in the long ago.

BABY'S DYING

BABY'S dying,
    Do not stir—
    Let her spirit lightly float
Through the sighing
    Lips of her—
        Still the murmur in the throat;
    Let the moan of grief be curbed—
    Baby must not be disturbed!

Baby's dying,
    Do not stir—
    Let her pure life lightly swim
Through the sighing
    Lips of her—
        Out from us and up to HIM—
    Let her leave us with that smile—
    Kiss and miss her after while.

AN EMPTY GLOVE

I

AN empty glove—long withering in the grasp
Of Time's cold palm. I lift it to my lips,—
And lo, once more I thrill beneath its clasp,
In fancy, as with odorous finger-tips
It reaches from the years that used to be
And proffers back love, life and all, to me.

II

Ah! beautiful she was beyond belief:
Her face was fair and lustrous as the moon's;
Her eyes—too large for small delight or grief,—
The smiles of them were Laughter's afternoons;
Their tears were April showers, and their
love—
All sweetest speech swoons ere it speaks
thereof.

III

White-fruited cocoa shown against the shell
Were not so white as was her brow below
The cloven tresses of the hair that fell

Across her neck and shoulders of nude snow;
  Her cheeks—chaste pallor, with a crimson
      stain—
  Her mouth was like a red rose rinsed with rain.

IV

And this was she my fancy held as good—
  As fair and lovable—in every wise
As peerless in pure worth of womanhood
  As was her wondrous beauty in men's eyes.—
    Yet, all alone, I kiss this empty glove—
    The poor husk of the hand I loved—and love.

TO THE CRICKET

THE chiming seas may clang; and Tubal Cain
  May clink his tinkling metals as he may;
 Or Pan may sit and pipe his breath away;
Or Orpheus wake his most entrancing strain
Till not a note of melody remain!—
  But thou, O cricket, with thy roundelay,
  Shalt laugh them all to scorn! So wilt thou,
      pray
Trill me thy glad song o'er and o'er again:
  I shall not weary; there is purest worth
In thy sweet prattle, since it sings the lone
  Heart home again. Thy warbling hath no
      dearth
Of childish memories—no harsher tone
  Than we might listen to in gentlest mirth,
  Thou poor plebeian minstrel of the hearth.

THE OLD-FASHIONED BIBLE

HOW dear to my heart are the scenes of my
    childhood
  That now but in mem'ry I sadly review;
The old meeting-house at the edge of the wildwood,
  The rail fence and horses all tethered thereto;
The low, sloping roof, and the bell in the steeple,
  The doves that came fluttering out overhead
As it solemnly gathered the God-fearing people
  To hear the old Bible my grandfather read.
      The old-fashioned Bible—
        The dust-covered Bible—
The leathern-bound Bible my grandfather read.

The blessed old volume! The face bent above it—
  As now I recall it—is gravely severe,
Though the reverent eye that droops downward to
  love it
  Makes grander the text through the lens of a tear,
And, as down his features it trickles and glistens,
  The cough of the deacon is stilled, and his head
Like a haloéd patriarch's leans as he listens
  To hear the old Bible my grandfather read.
      The old-fashioned Bible—
        The dust-covered Bible—
The leathern-bound Bible my grandfather read.

Ah! who shall look backward with scorn and
     derision
  And scoff the old book though it uselessly lies
In the dust of the past, while this newer revision
  Lisps on of a hope and a home in the skies?
Shall the voice of the Master be stifled and riven?
  Shall we hear but a tithe of the words He has said,
When so long He has, listening, leaned out of
     Heaven
To hear the old Bible my grandfather read?
     The old-fashioned Bible—
      The dust-covered Bible—
The leathern-bound Bible my grandfather read.

THE LAND OF USED-TO-BE

AND where's the Land of Used-to-be, does little
    baby wonder?
  Oh, we will clap a magic saddle over "Poppie's"
    knee
And ride away around the world, and in and out
    and under
  The whole of all the golden sunny Summer-time
    and see.

Leisurely and lazy-like we'll jostle on our journey,
  And let the pony bathe his hooves and cool them
    in the dew,
As he sidles down the shady way, and lags along the
    ferny
  And green, grassy edges of the lane we travel
    through.

And then we'll canter on to catch the bubble of the
    thistle
  As it bumps among the butterflies and glimmers
    down the sun,

To leave us laughing, all content to hear the robin
      whistle
  Or guess what Katydid is saying little Katy's
     done.

And pausing here a minute, where we hear the
      squirrel chuckle
  As he darts from out the underbrush and
     scampers up the tree,
We will gather buds and locust-blossoms, leaves and
     honeysuckle,
  To wreathe around our foreheads, riding into
     Used-to-be ;—

For here's the very rim of it that we go swinging
      over—
  Don't you hear the Fairy bugles, and the tinkle
     of the bells,
And see the baby-bumblebees that tumble in the
     clover
  And dangle from the tilted pinks and tipsy pim-
     pernels ?

And don't you see the merry faces of the daffo-
     dillies,
  And the jolly Johnny-jump-ups, and the butter-
     cups a-glee,
And the low, lolling ripples ring around the water-
     lilies ?—
  All greeting us with laughter, to the Land of
     Used-to-be !

And here among the blossoms of the blooming vines
      and grasses,
  With a haze forever hanging in the sky forever
      blue,
And with a breeze from over seas to kiss us as it
      passes,
  We will romp around forever as the airy Elfins
      do!

For all the elves of earth and air are swarming here
      together—
  The prankish Puck, King Oberon, and Queen
      Titania too;
And dear old Mother Goose herself, as sunny as the
      weather,
  Comes dancing down the dewy walks to welcome
      me and you!

JUST TO BE GOOD

JUST to be good—
      This is enough—enough!
O we who find sin's billows wild and rough,
Do we not feel how more than any gold
Would be the blameless life we led of old
While yet our lips knew but a mother's kiss!
      Ah! though we miss
      All else but this,
         To be good is enough!

It is enough—
      Enough—just to be good!
To lift our hearts where they are understood,
To let the thirst for worldly power and place
Go unappeased; to smile back in God's face
With the glad lips our mothers used to kiss.
      Ah! though we miss
      All else but this,
         To be good is enough!

A LOUNGER

HE leaned against a lamp-post, lost
    In some mysterious reverie:
His head was bowed; his arms were crossed;
    He yawned, and glanced evasively:
Uncrossed his arms, and slowly put
    Them back again, and scratched his side—
Shifted his weight from foot to foot,
    And gazed out no-ward, idle-eyed.

Grotesque of form and face and dress,
    And picturesque in every way—
    A figure that from day to day
Drooped with a limper laziness;
    A figure such as artists lean,
    In pictures where distress is seen,
Against low hovels where we guess
    No happiness has ever been.

MR. WHAT'S-HIS-NAME

THEY called him Mr. What's-his-name:
    From where he was, or why he came,
Or when, or what he found to do,
Nobody in the city knew.

He lived, it seemed, shut up alone
In a low hovel of his own;
There cooked his meals and made his bed,
Careless of all his neighbors said.

His neighbors, too, said many things
Expressive of grave wonderings,
Since none of them had ever been
Within his doors, or peered therein.

In fact, grown watchful, they became
Assured that Mr. What's-his-name
Was up to something wrong—indeed,
Small doubt of it, we all agreed.

At night were heard strange noises there,
When honest people everywhere
Had long retired; and his light
Was often seen to burn all night.

He left his house but seldom—then
Would always hurry back again,
As though he feared some stranger's knock,
Finding him gone, might burst the lock.

Besides, he carried, every day,
At the one hour he went away,
A basket, with the contents hid
Beneath its woven willow lid.

And so we grew to greatly blame
This wary Mr. What's-his-name,
And look on him with such distrust
His actions seemed to sanction just.

But when he died—he died one day—
Dropped in the street while on his way
To that old wretched hut of his—
You'll think it strange—perhaps it is—

But when we lifted him, and past
The threshold of his home at last,
No man of all the crowd but stepped
With reverence,—ay, *quailed* and *wept!*

What was it? Just a shriek of pain
I pray to never hear again—
A withered woman, old and bowed,
That fell and crawled and cried aloud—

And kissed the dead man's matted hair—
Lifted his face and kissed him there—
Called to him, as she clutched his hand,
In words no one could understand.

Insane? Yes.—Well, we, searching, found
An unsigned letter, in a round
Free hand, within the dead man's breast:
" Look to my mother—*I'm* at rest.

"You'll find my money safely hid
Under the lining of the lid
Of my work-basket. It is hers,
And God will bless her ministers!"

And some day—though he died unknown—
If through the City by the Throne
I walk, all cleansed of earthly shame,
I'll ask for Mr. What's-his-name.

UNCOMFORTED

LELLOINE! Lelloine! Don't you hear me
      calling?
  Calling through the night for you, and calling
      through the day;
Calling when the dawn is here, and when the dusk
      is falling—
  Calling for my Lelloine the angels lured away!

Lelloine! I call and listen, starting from my
      pillow—
  In the hush of midnight, Lelloine! I cry,
And o'er the rainy window-pane I hear the weeping
      willow
  Trail its dripping leaves like baby-fingers in reply.

Lelloine, I miss the glimmer of your glossy tresses,
  I miss the dainty velvet palms that nestled in my
      own;
And all my mother-soul went out in answerless
      caresses,
  And a storm of tears and kisses when you left me
      here alone.

I have prayed, O Lelloine, but Heaven will not hear
    me,
  I can not gain one sign from Him who leads you
    by the hand;
And O it seems that ne'er again His mercy will
    come near me—
  That He will never see my need, nor ever
    understand.

Won't you listen, Lelloine?—just a little leaning
  O'er the walls of Paradise—lean and hear my
    prayer,
And interpret death to Him in all its awful meaning,
  And tell Him you are lonely without your mother
    there.

MY WHITE BREAD

DEM good old days done past and gone
In old Ca'line wha I wuz bo'n
W'en my old Misst'ess she fust sayd,
    "Yo's a-eatin' yo' white braid!"
Oh, dem's de times uts done gone by
W'en de nights shine cla, an' de coon clim'
        high,
An' I sop my soul in 'possum-pie,
    Das a-eatin' my white braid!

It's dem's de nights ut I cross my legs
An' pat de flo' ez I twis' de pegs
O' de banjo up twil de gals all sayd,
    "Yo's a-eatin' yo' white braid!"
Oh, dem's de times ut I usen fo' to blow
On de long reeds cut in de old by-o,
An' de frogs jine in like dey glad fo' to know
    I's a-eatin' my white braid.

An' I shet my eyes fo' to conjuh up
Dem good ole days ut fills my cup
Wid de times ut fust ole Misst'ess sayd,
    "Yo's a-eatin' yo' white braid!"

Oh, dem's de dreams ut I fines de best;
An' bald an' gray ez a hornet's nest,
I drap my head on de good Lord's breast,
    Says a-eatin' my white braid!

HE AND I

JUST drifting on together—
    He and I—
As through the balmy weather
    Of July
  Drift two thistle-tufts embedded
  Each in each—by zephyrs wedded—
  Touring upward, giddy-headed,
    For the sky.

And, veering up and onward,
    Do we seem
Forever drifting dawnward
    In a dream,
  Where we meet song-birds that know us,
  And the winds their kisses blow us,
  While the years flow far below us
    Like a stream.

And we are happy—very—
    He and I—
Aye, even glad and merry
    Though on high

The heavens are sometimes shrouded
By the midnight storm, and clouded
Till the pallid moon is crowded
    From the sky.

My spirit ne'er expresses
    Any choice
But to clothe him with caresses
    And rejoice;
  And as he laughs, it is in
  Such a tone the moonbeams glisten
  And the stars come out to listen
    To his voice.

And so, whate'er the weather,
    He and I,—
With our lives linked thus together,
    Float and fly
  As two thistle-tufts embedded
  Each in each—by zephyrs wedded—
  Touring upward, giddy-headed,
    For the sky.

FROM A BALLOON

HO! we are loose.   Hear how they shout,
      And how their clamor dwindles out
Beneath us to the merest hum
Of earthly acclamation.   Come,
Lean with me here and look below—
Why, bless you, man! don't tremble so!
There is no need of fear up here—
Not higher than the buzzard swings
About upon the atmosphere,
With drowsy eyes and open wings!
There, steady, now, and feast your eyes;—
See, we are tranced—we do not rise;
It is the earth that sinks from us:
But when I first beheld it thus,
And felt the breezes downward flow,
And heard all noises fail and die,
Until but silence and the sky
Above, around me, and below,—
Why, like you now, I swooned almost,
With mingled awe and fear and glee—
As giddy as an hour-old ghost
That stares into eternity.

A TWINTORETTE

HO! my little maiden
With the glossy tresses,
Come thou and dance with me
A measure all divine;
Let my breast be laden
With but thy caresses—
Come thou and glancingly
Mate thy face with mine.

Thou shalt trill a rondel,
While my lips are purling
Some dainty twitterings
Sweeter than the birds';
And, with arms that fondle
Each as we go twirling,
We will kiss, with twitterings,
Lisps and loving words.

WHAT THEY SAID

WHISPERING to themselves apart,
   They who knew her said of her,
"Dying of a broken heart—
   Death her only comforter—
      For the man she loved is dead—
      She will follow soon!" they said.

Beautiful? Ah! brush the dust
   From Raphael's fairest face,
And restore it, as it must
   First have smiled back from its place
      On his easel as he leant
      Wrapt in awe and wonderment!

Why, to kiss the very hem
   Of the mourning-weeds she wore,
Like the winds that rustled them,
   I had gone the round world o'er;
      And to touch her hand I swear
      All things dareless I would dare!

But unto themselves apart,
　　Whispering, they said of her,
"Dying of a broken heart—
　　Death her only comforter—
　　　　For the man she loved is dead—
　　　　She will follow soon!" they said.

So I mutely turned away,
　　Turned with sorrow and despair,
Yearning still from day to day
　　For that woman dying there,
　　　　Till at last, by longing led,
　　　　I returned to find her—dead!

"Dead?"—I know that word would tell
　　Rhyming there—but in this case
"Wed" rhymes equally as well
　　In the very selfsame place—
　　　　And, in fact, the latter word
　　　　Is the one she had preferred.

Yet unto themselves apart,
　　Whisp'ring they had said of her—
"Dying of a broken heart—
　　Death her only comforter—
　　　　For the man she loved is dead—
　　　　She will follow soon!" they said.

AFTER THE FROST

AFTER the frost! O the rose is dead,
  And the weeds lie pied in the garden-bed,
And the peach tree's shade in the wan sunshine,
Faint as the veins in these hands of mine,
Streaks the gray of the orchard wall
Where the vine rasps loose, and the last leaves
    fall,
And the bare boughs writhe, and the winds are
    lost—
        After the frost—the frost!

After the frost! O the weary head
And the hands and the heart are quietéd;
And the lips we loved are locked at last,
And kiss not back, though the rain falls fast
And the lashes drip, and the soul makes moan,
And on through the dead leaves walks alone
Where the bare boughs writhe and the winds are
    lost—
        After the frost—the frost!

CHARLES H. PHILIPS

OBIT NOVEMBER 5TH, 1881

O FRIEND! There is no way
　　To bid farewell to thee!
The words that we would say
Above thy grave to-day
Still falter and delay
　　And fail us utterly.

When walking with us here,
　　The hand we loved to press
Was gentle, and sincere
As thy frank eyes were clear
Through every smile and tear
　　Of pleasure and distress.

In years, young; yet in thought
　　Mature; thy spirit, free,
And fired with fervor caught
Of thy proud sire, who fought
His way to fame, and taught
　　Its toilsome way to thee.

383

So even thou hast gained
   The victory God-given—
Yea, as our cheeks are stained
With tears, and our souls pained
And mute, thou hast attained
   Thy high reward in Heaven!

WHEN IT RAINS

WHEN it rains, and with the rain
    Never bird has heart to sing,
And across the window-pane
  Is no sunlight glimmering;
When the pitiless refrain
  Brings a tremor to the lips,
Our tears are like the rain
  As it drips, drips, drips—
    Like the sad, unceasing rain as it drips.

When the light of heaven's blue
  Is blurred and blotted quite,
And the dreary day to you
  Is but a long twilight;
When it seems that ne'er again
  Shall the sun break its eclipse,
Our tears are like the rain
  As it drips, drips, drips—
    Like the endless, friendless rain as it drips.

When it rains! weary heart,
   O be of better cheer!
The leaden clouds will part,
   And the morrow will be clear;
Take up your load again,
   With a prayer upon your lips,
Thanking Heaven for the rain
   As it drips, drips, drips—
   With the golden bow of promise as it
     drips.

AN ASSASSIN

CAT-LIKE he creeps along where ways are
    dim
  From covert into covert's secrecy;
His shadow in the moonlight shrinks from him
    And crouches warily.

He hugs strange envies to his breast, and nurses
  Wild hatreds, till the murderous hand he grips
Falls, quivering with the tension of the curses
    He launches from his lips.

Drenched in his victim's blood he holds high
    revel;
  He mocks at justice, and in all men's eyes
Insults his God—and no one but the devil
    Is sorry when he dies.

BEST OF ALL

OF all good gifts that the Lord lets fall,
Is not silence the best of all?

The deep, sweet hush when the song is closed,
And every sound but a voiceless ghost;

And every sigh, as we listening leant,
A breathless quiet of vast content?

The laughs we laughed have a purer ring
With but their memory echoing;

And the joys we voiced, and the words we said,
Seem so dearer for being dead.

So of all good gifts that the Lord lets fall,
Is not silence the best of all?

MR. SILBERBERG

AND LITTLE JULIUS

I LIKE me yet dot leedle chile
   Vich climb my lap up in to-day,
  Unt took my cheap cigair avay,
Unt laugh unt kiss me, purty-whvile,—
   Possescially I like dose mout'
     Vich taste his moder's like—unt so,
  Eef my cigair it gone glean out
    —Yust let it go!

Vat I caire den for *any*ding?
   Der "HERALDT" schlip out fon my handt
  Unt all my odvairtizement standt
Mitout new changements boddering;
   I only t'ink—I haf me dis
     One leedle boy to pet unt love
  Unt play me vit, unt hug unt kiss—
    Unt dot's enough!

Der plans unt pairposes I vear
   Out in der vorld all fades avay,
   Unt vit der beeznis of der day
I got me den no time to spare;

Der caires of trade vas caires no more—
　　Dem cash accoundts dey dodge me by,
　　Unt vit my chile I roll der floor,
　　　　Unt laugh unt gry!

Ach! frient! dem childens is der ones
　　Dot got some happy times—you bet!—
　　Dot's vy ven I been growed up yet
I visht I schtill been leedle vonce!
　　Unt ven dot leedle roozter tries
　　　　Dem baby-tricks I used to do,
　　My mout' it vater, unt my eyes
　　　　Dey vater too!

Unt all der summer-time unt spring
　　Of childhoodt it come back to me,
　　So dot it vas a dream I see
Ven I yust look at anyding!
　　Unt ven dot leedle boy run' by,
　　　　I t'ink "Dot's *me,*" fon hour to hour
　　Schtill chasing yet dose butterfly
　　　　Fon flower to flower!

Oxpose I vas lots money vairt,
　　Vit blenty schtone-front schtore to rent,
　　Unt mor'gages at twelf-per tcent.,
Unt diamondts in my ruffled shairt,—
　　I make a'signment of all dot,
　　　　Unt tairn it over vit a schmile
　　Aber you please—but, don'd forgot,
　　　　I keep dot chile!

THE HEREAFTER

HEREAFTER! O we need not waste
   Our smiles or tears, whate'er
     befall:
No happiness but holds a taste
   Of something sweeter, after all;—
No depth of agony but feels
   Some fragment of abiding trust,—
Whatever Death unlocks or seals,
   The mute beyond is just.

THE LOVING CUP

TRANCED in the glamour of a dream
  Where banquet-lights and fancies gleam,
And ripest wit and wine abound,
And pledges hale go round and round,—
Lo, dazzled with enchanted rays—
As in the golden olden days
Sir Galahad—my eyes swim up
To greet your splendor, Loving Cup!

What is the secret of your art,
Linking together hand and heart
Your myriad votaries who do
Themselves most honor honoring you?
What gracious service have you done
To win the name that you have won?—
Kissing it back from tuneful lips
That sing your praise between the sips!

Your spicy breath, O Loving Cup,
That, like an incense steaming up,
Full-freighted with a fragrance fine
As ever swooned on sense of mine,

Is rare enough.—But then, ah me!
How rarer every memory
That, rising with it, wreathes and blends
In forms and faces of my friends!

O Loving Cup! in fancy still,
I clasp their hands, and feel the thrill
Of fellowship that still endures
While lips are theirs and wine is yours!
And while my memory journeys down
The years that lead to Boston Town,
Abide where first were rendered up
Our mutual loves, O Loving Cup!

EROS

THE storm of love has burst at last
 Full on me: All the world, before,
Was like an alien, unknown shore
Along whose verge I laughing passed.—
 But now—I laugh not any more,—
Bowed with a silence vast in weight
 As that which falls on one who stands
 For the first time on ocean sands,
Seeing and feeling all the great
 Awe of the waves as they wash the lands
And billow and wallow and undulate.

THE QUIET LODGER

THE man that rooms next door to me:
   Two weeks ago, this very night,
He took possession quietly,
  As any other lodger might—
    But why the room next mine should so
    Attract him I was vexed to know,—
    Because his quietude, in fine,
    Was far superior to mine.

"Now, I like quiet, truth to tell;
   A tranquil life is sweet to me—
But *this*," I sneered, "suits me too well.—
  He shuts his door so noiselessly,
    And glides about so very mute,
    In each mysterious pursuit,
    His silence is oppressive, and
    Too deep for me to understand."

Sometimes, forgetting book or pen,
   I've found my head in breathless poise
Lifted, and dropped in shame again,
   Hearing some alien ghost of noise—

Some smothered sound that seemed to be
A trunk-lid dropped unguardedly,
Or the crisp writhings of some quire
Of manuscript thrust in the fire.

Then I have climbed, and closed in vain
My transom, opening in the hall;
Or close against the window-pane
Have pressed my fevered face,—but all
The day or night without held not
A sight or sound or counter-thought
To set my mind one instant free
Of this man's silent mastery.

And often I have paced the floor
With muttering anger, far at night,
Hearing, and cursing, o'er and o'er,
The muffled noises, and the light
And tireless movements of this guest
Whose silence raged above my rest
Hoarser than howling storms at sea—
The man that rooms next door to me.

But twice or thrice, upon the stair,
I've seen his face—most strangely wan,—
Each time upon me unaware
He came—smooth'd past me, and was
gone.—
So like a whisper he went by,
I listened after, ear and eye,
Nor could my chafing fancy tell
The meaning of one syllable.

Last night I caught him, face to face,—
  He entering his room, and I
Glaring from mine: He paused a space
  And met my scowl all shrinkingly,
    But with full gentleness: The key
    Turned in his door—and I could see
    It tremblingly withdrawn and put
    Inside, and then—the door was shut.

Then silence. *Silence!*—why, last night
  The silence was tumultuous,
And thundered on till broad daylight;—
  O never has it stunned me thus!—
    It rolls, and moans, and mumbles yet.—
    Ah, God! how loud may silence get
    When man mocks at a brother man
    Who answers but as silence can!

The silence grew, and grew, and grew,
  Till at high noon to-day 'twas heard
Throughout the house; and men flocked
     through
  The echoing halls, with faces blurred
    With pallor, gloom, and fear, and awe,
    And shuddering at what they saw,—
    The quiet lodger, as he lay
    Stark of the life he cast away.

   .   .   .   .   .   .

So strange to-night—those voices there,
  Where all so quiet was before:
They say the face has not a care
  Nor sorrow in it any more. . . .

His latest scrawl:—"Forgive me—You
Who prayed, 'They know not what they
 do!'"
My tears will never let me see
This man that rooms next door to me!

THE BROOK-SONG

LITTLE brook! Little brook!
   You have such a happy look—
Such a very merry manner, as you swerve and curve
        and crook—
      And your ripples, one and one,
      Reach each other's hands and run
Like laughing little children in the sun!

      Little brook, sing to me:
      Sing about a bumblebee
That tumbled from a lily-bell and grumbled mumb-
        lingly,
      Because he wet the film
      Of his wings, and had to swim,
While the water-bugs raced round and laughed at
        him!

      Little brook—sing a song
      Of a leaf that sailed along
Down the golden-braided center of your current
        swift and strong,
      And a dragon-fly that lit
      On the tilting rim of it,
And rode away and wasn't scared a bit.

And sing—how oft in glee
Came a truant boy like me,
Who loved to lean and listen to your lilting melody,
Till the gurgle and refrain
Of your music in his brain
Wrought a happiness as keen to him as pain.

Little brook—laugh and leap!
Do not let the dreamer weep:
Sing him all the songs of summer till he sink in
softest sleep;
And then sing soft and low
Through his dreams of long ago—
Sing back to him the rest he used to know!

BIN A-FISHIN'

W'EN de sun's gone down, an' de moon
    is riz,
  Bin a-fishin'! Bin a-fishin'!
It's I's aguine down wha' the by-o is!
  Bin a-fishin' all night long!

CHORUS

  Bin a-fishin'! Bin a-fishin'!
Bin a-fishin' clean fum de dusk of night
Twel away long on in de mornin' light.

Bait my hook, un I plunk her down!
  Bin a-fishin'! Bin a-fishin'!
Un I lay dat catfish weigh five pound!
  Bin a-fishin' all night long!

CHORUS

Folks tells me ut a sucker won't bite,
  Bin a-fishin'! Bin a-fishin'!
Yit I lif' out fo' last Chuesday night,
  Bin a-fishin' all night long!

401

Chorus

Little fish nibble un de big fish come;
  Bin a-fishin'! Bin a-fishin'!
"Go way, little fish! I want some!"
  Bin a-fishin' all night long!

Chorus

Sez de bullfrog, "D-runk!" sez de ole owl
    "Whoo!"
  Bin a-fishin'! Bin a-fishin'!
'Spec, Mr. Nigger, dey's a-meanin' you,
  Bin a-fishin' all night long!

Chorus

UNCLE DAN'L IN TOWN OVER SUNDAY

I CAINT get used to city ways—
   Ner never could, I' bet my hat!
Jevver know jes' whur I was raised?—
Raised on a farm! D' ever tell you that?
Was undoubtedly, I declare!
And now, on Sunday—fun to spare
Around a farm! Why jes' to set
Up on the top three-cornered rail
Of Pap's old place, nigh La Fayette,
I'd swap my soul off, hide and tail!
You fellers in the city here,
You don't know nothin'!—S'pose to-day,
This clatterin' Sunday, you waked up
Without no jinglin'-janglin' bells,
Ner rattlin' of the milkman's cup,
Ner any swarm of screechin' birds
Like these here English swallers—S'pose
Ut you could miss all noise like those,
And git shet o' thinkin' of 'em afterwards,
And then, in the country, wake and hear
Nothin' but silence—wake and see
Nothin' but green woods fur and near?—
What sort o' Sunday would that be? . . .
Wisht I hed you home with me!

Now think! The laziest of all days—
To git up any time—er sleep—
Er jes' lay round and watch the haze
A-dancin' 'cross the wheat, and keep
My pipe a-goern laisurely,
And puff and whiff as pleases me—
And ef I leave a trail of smoke
Clean through the house, no one to say,
"Wah! throw that nasty thing away;
Hev some regyard fer decency!"
To walk round barefoot, if you choose;
Er saw the fiddle—er dig some bait
And go a-fishin'—er pitch hoss shoes
Out in the shade somewhurs, and wait
For dinner-time, with an appetite
Ut folks in town caint equal quite!
To laze around the barn and poke
Fer hens' nests—er git up a match
Betwixt the boys, and watch 'em scratch
And rassle round, and sweat and swear
And quarrel to their hearts' content;
And me a-jes' a-settin' there
A-hatchin' out more devilment!
What sort o' Sunday would that be?
Wisht I hed you home with me!

EMERSON

CONCORD, APRIL 27, 1882

WHAT shall we say? In quietude,
    Within his home, in dreams un-
        guessed,
He lies; the grief a nation would
    Evince must be repressed.

Nor meet is it the loud acclaim
    His countrymen would raise—that he
Has left the riches of his fame
    The whole world's legacy.

Then, prayerful, let us pause until
    We find, as grateful spirits can,
The way most worthy to fulfil
    The tribute due the man.

Think what were best in his regard
    Who voyaged life in such a cause:
Our simplest faith were best reward—
    Our silence, best applause.

YOUR VIOLIN

YOUR violin! Ah me!
　　'Twas fashioned o'er the sea,
In storied Italy—
　　What matter where?
It is its voice that sways
And thrills me as it plays
The airs of other days—
　　The days that were!

Then let your magic bow
Glide lightly to and fro.—
I close my eyes, and so,
　　In vast content,
I kiss my hand to you,
And to the tunes we knew
Of old, as well as to
　　Your instrument!

Poured out of some dim dream
Of lulling sounds that seem
Like ripples of a stream
　　Twanged lightly by

The slender, tender hands
Of weeping-willow wands
That droop where gleaming sands
    And pebbles lie.

A melody that swoons
In all the truant tunes
Long listless afternoons
    Lure from the breeze,
When woodland boughs are stirred,
And moaning doves are heard,
And laughter afterward
    Beneath the trees.

Through all the chorusing,
I hear on leaves of spring
The drip and pattering
    Of April skies,
With echoes faint and sweet
As baby-angel feet
Might wake along a street
    Of Paradise.

SOLDIERS HERE TO-DAY

I

SOLDIERS and saviors of the homes we love;
  Heroes and patriots who marched away,
And who marched back, and who marched on
        above—
    All—all are here to-day!

By the dear cause you fought for—you are here;
  At summons of bugle, and the drum
Whose palpitating syllables were ne'er
    More musical, you come!

Here—by the stars that bloom in fields of blue,
  And by the bird above with shielding wings;
And by the flag that floats out over you,
    With silken beckonings—

Ay, here beneath its folds are gathered all
  Who warred unscathed for blessings that it
        gave—
Still blessed its champion, though it but fall
    A shadow on his grave!

II

We greet you, Victors, as in vast array
    You gather from the scenes of strife and
        death—
From spectral fortress-walls where curls away
    The cannon's latest breath.

We greet you—from the crumbling battlements
    Where once again the old flag feels the breeze
Stroke out its tattered stripes and smooth its rents
    With rippling ecstasies.

From living tombs where every hope seemed
        lost—
    With famine quarantined by bristling guns—
The prison-pens—the guards—the "dead-line"
        crossed
        By—riddled skeletons!

From furrowed plains, soon thick with bursting
        shells—
    From mountain gorge, and toppling crags
        o'erhead—
From wards of pestilential hospitals,
    And trenches of the dead.

III

In fancy all are here. The night is o'er,
    And through dissolving mists the morning
        gleams;

And clustered round their hearts we see once
　　　more
　　The heroes of our dreams.

Strong, tawny faces, some, and some are fair,
　　And some are marked with age's latest prime,
And, seer-like, browed and aureoled with hair
　　As hoar as winter-time.

The faces of fond lovers, glorified—
　　The faces of the husband and the wife—
The babe's face nestled at the mother's side,
　　And smiling back at life;

A bloom of happiness in every cheek—
　　A thrill of tingling joy in every vein—
In every soul a rapture they will seek
　　In Heaven, and find again!

IV

'Tis not a vision only—we who pay
　　But the poor tribute of our praises here
Are equal sharers in the guerdon they
　　Purchased at price so dear.

The angel, Peace, o'er all uplifts her hand,
　　Waving the olive, and with heavenly eyes
Shedding a light of love o'er sea and land
　　As sunshine from the skies.

Her figure pedestaled on Freedom's soil—
    Her sandals kissed with seas of golden grain—
Queen of a realm of joy-requited toil
      That glories in her reign.

O blessed land of labor and reward!
    O gracious Ruler, let Thy reign endure;
In pruning-hook and plough-share beat the sword,
      And reap the harvest sure!

A WINDY DAY

THE dawn was a dawn of splendor,
  And the blue of the morning skies
Was as placid and deep and tender
  As the blue of a baby's eyes;
The sunshine flooded the mountain,
  And flashed over land and sea
Like the spray of a glittering fountain.—
  But the wind—the wind—Ah me!

Like a weird invisible spirit,
  It swooped in its airy flight;
And the earth, as the stress drew near it,
  Quailed as in mute affright;
The grass in the green fields quivered—
  The waves of the smitten brook
Chillily shuddered and shivered,
  And the reeds bowed down and shook.

Like a sorrowful miserere
  It sobbed, and it blew and blew,
Till the leaves on the trees looked weary,
  And my prayers were weary, too;
And then, like the sunshine's glimmer
  That failed in the awful strain,
All the hope of my eyes grew dimmer
  In a spatter of spiteful rain.

SHADOW AND SHINE

STORMS of the winter, and deepening
   snows,
  When will you end? I said,
For the soul within me was numb with woes,
  And my heart uncomforted.
When will you cease, O dismal days?
  When will you set me free?
For the frozen world and its desolate ways
  Are all unloved of me!

I waited long, but the answer came—
  The kiss of the sunshine lay
Warm as a flame on the lips that frame
  The song in my heart to-day.
Blossoms of summer-time waved in the air,
  Glimmers of sun in the sea;
Fair thoughts followed me everywhere,
  And the world was dear to me.

THE OLD SWIMMIN'-HOLE

OH! the old swimmin'-hole! whare the crick so
    still and deep
Looked like a baby-river that was laying half asleep,
And the gurgle of the worter round the drift jest
    below
Sounded like the laugh of something we onc't ust
    to know
Before we could remember anything but the eyes
Of the angels lookin' out as we left Paradise;
But the merry days of youth is beyond our controle,
And it's hard to part ferever with the old swimmin'-
    hole.

Oh! the old swimmin'-hole! In the happy days of
    yore,
When I ust to lean above it on the old sickamore,
Oh! it showed me a face in its warm sunny tide
That gazed back at me so gay and glorified,
It made me love myself, as I leaped to caress
My shadder smilin' up at me with sich tenderness.
But them days is past and gone, and old Time's
    tuck his toll
From the old man come back to the old swimmin'-
    hole.

Oh! the old swimmin'-hole! In the long, lazy days
When the humdrum of school made so many run-
a-ways,
How plesant was the jurney down the old dusty
lane,
Whare the tracks of our bare feet was all printed so
plane
You could tell by the dent of the heel and the sole
They was lots o' fun on hands at the old swimmin'-
hole.
But the lost joys is past! Let your tears in sorrow
roll
Like the rain that ust to dapple up the old swimmin'-
hole.

Thare the bullrushes growed, and the cattails so tall,
And the sunshine and shadder fell over it all;
And it mottled the worter with amber and gold
Tel the glad lilies rocked in the ripples that rolled;
And the snake-feeder's four gauzy wings fluttered
by
Like the ghost of a daisy dropped out of the sky,
Or a wownded apple-blossom in the breeze's
controle
As it cut acrost some orchurd to'rds the old
swimmin'-hole.

Oh! the old swimmin'-hole! When I last saw the
place,
The scenes was all changed, like the change in my
face;

The bridge of the railroad now crosses the spot
Whare the old divin'-log lays sunk and fergot.
And I stray down the banks whare the trees ust to
    be—
But never again will theyr shade shelter me!
And I wish in my sorrow I could strip to the soul,
And dive off in my grave like the old swimmin'-hole.

The Old Swimmin' Hole

"Oh! The old swimmin' hole! where the crick, so still and deep
Looked like a baby-river that was layin' half asleep,
And the gurgle of the worter round the drift jist below
Sounded like the laugh of something we once ust to know
Before we could remember anything but the eyes
Of the angels lookin' out as we left Paradise;—
But the merry days of youth is beyond our controal,
And its hard to part ferever with the old swimmin' hole!"

I clapped my hands in genuine applause. "Read on"
I said,—"Read on! Read all of it!"
The old man's face grew radiant as he continued:

"Oh! the old swimmin' hole! In the happy days of yore,
When I ust to lean above it on the old sycamore!
Oh! it showed me a face in its warm, sunny tide,
That gazed back at me so gay and glorified,
It made me love myself as I leaped to caress
My shadder smilin' up at me with sich tenderness;
But those days is past and gone, and Old Time's tuck his toll
From the old man come back to the old swimmin' hole!"

"Oh! the old Swimmin' Hole! In the long lazy days
When the hum-drum of school made so many "runaways;"
How pleasant was the journey down the old dusty lane,
Whare the tracks of our bare feet was all printed so plain
You could tell by the dent of the heel and the sole
They was lots o' fun on hands at the old Swimmin'-Hole.
But the last joys is past! Let your tears in sorrow roll
Like the rain that ust to dapple up the old Swimmin' Hole.

"Thare the bullrushes growed, and the cat-tails so tall,
And the sunshine and shadder fell over it all;
And it mottled the worter with amber and gold
Tell the glad lilies rocked in the ripples that rolled;
And the snakefeeders four gauzy wings fluttered by
Like the ghost of a daisy dropped out of the sky,
Er a wounded apple-blossom in the breeze's control,
As it cut across some orchard far the old Swimmin' Hole.

"Oh! the Old Swimmin' Hole! When I last saw the place
The scenes was all changed, like the change in my face;—
The bridge of the railroad now crosses the spot
Whare the old divin'-log lays sunk and forgot.
And I stray down the banks whare the trees ust to be—
But never again will their shade shelter me!
And I wisht in my sorrow I could strip to the soul,
And dive off in my grave like the old Swimmin' Hole."

———

THOUGHTS FER THE DISCURAGED
FARMER

THE summer winds is sniffin' round the bloomin'
    locus' trees;
And the clover in the pastur is a big day fer the
    bees,
And they been a-swiggin' honey, above board and
    on the sly,
Tel they stutter in theyr buzzin' and stagger as they
    fly.
The flicker on the fence-rail 'pears to jest spit on
    his wings
And roll up his feathers, by the sassy way he sings;
And the hoss-fly is a-whettin'-up his forelegs fer
    biz,
And the off-mare is a-switchin' all of her tale they
    is.

You can hear the blackbirds jawin' as they foller up
    the plow—
Oh, theyr bound to git theyr brekfast, and theyr not
    a-carin' how;

So they quarrel in the furries, and they quarrel on
    the wing—
But theyr peaceabler in pot-pies than any other
    thing:
And it's when I git my shotgun drawed up in stiddy
    rest,
She's as full of tribbelation as a yeller-jacket's nest;
And a few shots before dinner, when the sun's
    a-shinin' right,
Seems to kindo'-sorto' sharpen up a feller's appe-
    tite!

They's been a heap o' rain, but the sun's out to-day,
And the clouds of the wet spell is all cleared away,
And the woods is all the greener, and the grass is
    greener still;
It may rain again to-morry, but I don't think it will.
Some says the crops is ruined, and the corn's
    drownded out,
And propha-sy the wheat will be a failure, without
    doubt;
But the kind Providence that has never failed us
    yet,
Will be on hands onc't more at the 'leventh hour, I
    bet!

Does the medder-lark complane, as he swims high
    and dry
Through the waves of the wind and the blue of the
    sky?

Does the quail set up and whissel in a disappinted
    way,
Er hang his head in silunce, and sorrow all the day?
Is the chipmuck's health a-failin'?—Does he walk,
    er does he run?
Don't the buzzards ooze around up thare jest like
    they've allus done?
Is they anything the matter with the rooster's lungs
    er voice?
Ort a mortul be complanin' when dumb animals
    rejoice?

Then let us, one and all, be contentud with our lot;
The June is here this morning, and the sun is
    shining hot.
Oh! let us fill our harts up with the glory of the day,
And banish ev'ry doubt and care and sorrow fur
    away!
Whatever be our station, with Providence fer guide,
Sich fine circumstances ort to make us satisfied;
Fer the world is full of roses, and the roses full of
    dew,
And the dew is full of heavenly love that drips fer
    me and you.

A GOOD-BY

"GOOD-BY, my friend!"
　　He takes her hand—
The pressures blend:
　They understand
　　　But vaguely why, with drooping eye,
　　　Each moans—"Good-by!—Good-by!"

"Dear friend, good-by!"
　O she could smile
If she might cry
　A little while!—
　　　She says, "I *ought* to smile—but I—
　　　Forgive me—*There!*—Good-by!"

"'Good-by?' Ah, no:
　I hate," says he,
"These 'good-bys' so!"
　"And *I*," says she,
　　　"Detest them so—why, I should *die*
　　　Were this a *real* 'good-by'!"

A SUMMER'S DAY

THE Summer's put the idy in
   My head that I'm a boy ag'in;
And all around's so bright and gay
I want to put my team away,
And jest git out whare I can lay
And soak my hide full of the day!
But work is work, and must be done—
Yit, as I work, I have my fun,
Jest fancyin' these furries here
Is childhood's paths onc't more so dear:—
And so I walk through medder-lands,
   And country lanes, and swampy trails
Whare long bullrushes bresh my hands;
   And, tilted on the ridered rails
Of deadnin' fences, "Old Bob White"
Whissels his name in high delight,
And whirs away. I wunder still,
Whichever way a boy's feet will—
Whare trees has fell, with tangled tops
   Whare dead leaves shakes, I stop fer breth,
Heerin' the acorn as it drops—
   H'istin' my chin up still as deth,
And watchin' clos't, with upturned eyes,

The tree whare Mr. Squirrel tries
To hide hisse'f above the limb,
But lets his own tale tell on him.
I wunder on in deeper glooms—
   Git hungry, hearin' female cries
From old farmhouses, whare perfumes
   Of harvest dinners seems to rise
And ta'nt a feller, hart and brane,
With memories he can't explane.

I wunder through the underbresh,
   Whare pig-tracks, pintin' to'rds the crick,
Is picked and printed in the fresh
   Black bottom-lands, like wimmern pick
Theyr pie-crusts with a fork, some way,
When bakin' fer camp-meetin' day.

I wunder on and on and on,
Tel my gray hair and beard is gone,
And ev'ry wrinkle on my brow
Is rubbed clean out and shaddered now
With curls as brown and fare and fine
As tenderls of the wild grape-vine
That ust to climb the highest tree
To keep the ripest ones fer me.
I wunder still, and here I am
Wadin' the ford below the dam—
The worter chucklin' round my knee
   At hornet-welt and bramble-scratch,
And me a-slippin' 'crost to see
      Ef Tyner's plums is ripe, and size

The old man's wortermelon-patch,
   With juicy mouth and drouthy eyes.
Then, after sich a day of mirth
And happiness as worlds is wurth—
   So tired that Heaven seems nigh about,—
The sweetest tiredness on earth
   Is to git home and flatten out—
So tired you can't lay flat enugh,
And sorto' wish that you could spred
Out like molasses on the bed,
And jest drip off the aidges in
The dreams that never comes ag'in.

A HYMB OF FAITH

O, THOU that doth all things devise
And fashon fer the best,
He'p us who sees with mortul eyes
To overlook the rest.

They's times, of course, we grope in doubt,
And in afflictions sore;
So knock the louder, Lord, without,
And we'll unlock the door.

Make us to feel, when times looks bad
And tears in pitty melts,
Thou wast the only he'p we had
When they was nothin' else.

Death comes alike to ev'ry man
That ever was borned on earth;
Then let us do the best we can
To live fer all life's wurth.

Ef storms and tempusts dred to see
Makes black the heavens ore,
They done the same in Galilee
Two thousand years before.

But after all, the golden sun
  Poured out its floods on them
That watched and waited fer the One
  Then borned in Bethlyham.

Also, the star of holy writ
  Made noonday of the night,
Whilse other stars that looked at it
  Was envious with delight.

The sages then in wurship bowed,
  From ev'ry clime so fare;
O, sinner, think of that glad crowd
  That congergated thare!

They was content to fall in ranks
  With One that knowed the way
From good old Jurden's stormy banks
  Clean up to Jedgmunt Day.

No matter, then, how all is mixed
  In our near-sighted eyes,
All things is fer the best, and fixed
  Out straight in Paradise.

Then take things as God sends 'em here,
  And, ef we live er die,
Be more and more contenteder,
  Without a-astin' why.

O, Thou that doth all things devise
And fashon fer the best,
He'p us who sees with mortul eyes
To overlook the rest.

AT BROAD RIPPLE

AH, luxury! Beyond the heat
  And dust of town, with dangling feet,
Astride the rock below the dam,
In the cool shadows where the calm
Rests on the stream again, and all
Is silent save the waterfall,—
I bait my hook and cast my line,
And feel the best of life is mine.

No high ambition may I claim—
I angle not for lordly game
Of trout, or bass, or wary bream—
A black perch reaches the extreme
Of my desires; and "goggle-eyes"
Are not a thing that I despise;
A sunfish, or a "chub," or "cat"—
A "silver-side"—yea, even that!

In eloquent tranquillity
The waters lisp and talk to me.
Sometimes, far out, the surface breaks,
As some proud bass an instant shakes

427

His glittering armor in the sun,
And romping ripples, one by one,
Come dallying across the space
Where undulates my smiling face.

The river's story flowing by,
Forever sweet to ear and eye,
Forever tenderly begun—
Forever new and never done.
Thus lulled and sheltered in a shade
Where never feverish cares invade,
I bait my hook and cast my line,
And feel the best of life is mine.

THE COUNTRY EDITOR

A THOUGHTFUL brow and face—of
    sallow hue,
  But warm with welcome, as we find him there,
  Throned in his old misnomered "easy chair,"
Scrawling a "leader," or a book-review;
Or staring through the roof for something new
  With which to lift a wretched rival's hair,
  Or blow some petty clique in empty air
And snap the party-ligaments in two.
  A man he is deserving well of thee,—
So be compassionate—yea, pay thy dues,
  Nor pamper him with thy spring-poetry,
But haul him wood, or something he can use;
  And promptly act, nor tarry long when he
  Gnaweth his pen and glareth rabidly.

WORTERMELON TIME

OLD wortermelon time is a-comin' round ag'in,
    And they ain't no man a-livin' any tickleder'n
      me,
Fer the way I hanker after wortermelons is a sin—
    Which is the why and wharefore, as you can
      plainly see.

Oh! it's in the sandy soil wortermelons does the
      best,
    And it's thare they'll lay and waller in the sun-
      shine and the dew
Tel they wear all the green streaks clean off of theyr
      breast;
    And you bet I ain't a-findin' any fault with them;
      air you?

They ain't no better thing in the vegetable line;
    And they don't need much 'tendin', as ev'ry
      farmer knows;
And when theyr ripe and ready fer to pluck from
      the vine,
    I want to say to you theyr the best fruit that
      grows.

It's some likes the yeller-core, and some likes the
red,
   And it's some says "The Little Californy" is the
   best;
But the sweetest slice of all I ever wedged in my
head,
   Is the old "Edingburg Mounting-sprout," of the
   West.

You don't want no punkins nigh your wortermelon
vines—
   'Cause, some-way-another, they'll spile your
   melons, shore;—
I've seed 'em taste like punkins, from the core to
the rines,
   Which may be a fact you have heerd of before.

But your melons that's raised right and 'tended to
with care,
   You can walk around amongst 'em with a parent's
   pride and joy,
And thump 'em on the heads with as fatherly a air
   As ef each one of them was your little girl er boy.

I joy in my hart jest to hear that rippin' sound
   When you split one down the back and jolt the
   halves in two,
And the friends you love the best is gethered all
around—
   And you says unto your sweethart, "Oh, here's
   the core fer you!"

And I like to slice 'em up in big pieces fer 'em all,
  Espeshally the childern, and watch theyr high
    delight
As one by one the rines with theyr pink notches
    falls,
  And they holler fer some more, with unquenched
    appetite.

Boys takes to it natchurl, and I like to see 'em eat—
  A slice of wortermelon's like a frenchharp in
    theyr hands,
And when they "saw" it through theyr mouth sich
    music can't be beat—
  'Cause it's music both the sperit and the stummick
    understands.

Oh, they's more in wortermelons than the purty-
    colored meat,
  And the overflowin' sweetness of the worter
    squshed betwixt
The up'ard and the down'ard motions of a feller's
    teeth,
  And it's the taste of ripe old age and juicy child-
    hood mixed.

Fer I never taste a melon but my thoughts flies
    away
  To the summer-time of youth; and again I see the
    dawn,
And the fadin' afternoon of the long summer day,
  And the dusk and dew a-fallin', and the night
    a-comin' on.

And thare's the corn around us, and the lispin'
 leaves and trees,
 And the stars a-peekin' down on us as still as
  silver mice,
And us boys in the wortermelons on our hands and
 knees,
 And the new-moon hangin' ore us like a yeller-
  cored slice.

Oh! it's wortermelon time is a-comin' round ag'in,
 And they ain't no man a-livin' any tickelder'n me,
Fer the way I hanker after wortermelons is a sin—
 Which is the why and wharefore, as you can
  plainly see.

A SONG OF THE CRUISE

O THE sun and the rain, and the rain and the
    sun!
There'll be sunshine again when the tempest is
    done;
And the storm will beat back when the shining is
    past;
But in some happy haven we'll anchor at last.
       Then murmur no more,
        In lull or in roar,
But smile and be brave till the voyage is o'er.

O the rain and the sun, and the sun and the rain!
When the tempest is done, then the sunshine again;
And in rapture we'll ride through the stormiest
    gales,
For God's hand's on the helm and His breath in
    the sails.
       Then murmur no more,
        In lull or in roar,
But smile and be brave till the voyage is o'er.

MY PHILOSOFY

I AIN'T, ner don't p'tend to be,
  Much posted on philosofy;
But thare is times, when all alone,
I work out idees of my own.
And of these same thare is a few
I'd like to jest refer to you—
Pervidin' that you don't object
To listen clos't and rickollect.

I allus argy that a man
Who does about the best he can
Is plenty good enugh to suit
This lower mundane institute—
No matter ef his daily walk
Is subject fer his neghbor's talk,
And critic-minds of ev'ry whim
Jest all git up and go fer him!

I knowed a feller onc't that had
The yeller-janders mighty bad,—
And each and ev'ry friend he'd meet
Would stop and give him some receet

435

Fer cuorin' of 'em. But he'd say
He kindo' thought they'd go away
Without no medicin', and boast
That he'd git well without one doste.

He kep' a-yellerin' on—and they
Perdictin' that he'd die some day
Before he knowed it! Tuck his bed,
The feller did, and lost his head,
And wundered in his mind a spell—
Then rallied, and, at last, got well;
But ev'ry friend that said he'd die
Went back on him eternally!

It's natchurl enugh, I guess,
When some gits more and some gits less,
Fer them-uns on the slimmest side
To claim it ain't a fare divide;
And I've knowed some to lay and wait,
And git up soon, and set up late,
To ketch some feller they could hate
Fer goin' at a faster gait.

The signs is bad when folks commence
A-findin' fault with Providence,
And balkin' 'cause the earth don't shake
At ev'ry prancin' step they take.
No man is grate tel he can see
How less than little he would be
Ef stripped to self, and stark and bare
He hung his sign out anywhare.

My doctern is to lay aside
Contensions, and be satisfied:
Jest do your best, and praise er blame
That follers that, counts jest the same.
I've allus noticed grate success
Is mixed with troubles, more er less,
And it's the man who does the best
That gits more kicks than all the rest.

WHEN AGE COMES ON

WHEN Age comes on!—
 The deepening dusk is where the dawn
 Once glittered splendid, and the dew,
In honey-drips from red rose-lips,
 Was kissed away by me and you.—
And now across the frosty lawn
Black footprints trail, and Age comes on—
   And Age comes on!
 And biting wild-winds whistle through
Our tattered hopes—and Age comes on!

   When Age comes on!—
O tide of raptures, long withdrawn,
 Flow back in summer floods, and fling
Here at our feet our childhood sweet,
 And all the songs we used to sing! . . .
Old loves, old friends—all dead and gone—
Our old faith lost—and Age comes on—
   And Age comes on!
 Poor hearts! have we not anything
But longings left when Age comes on?

THE CIRCUS-DAY PARADE

OH! the Circus-Day Parade! How the bugles
    played and played!
And how the glossy horses tossed their flossy manes
    and neighed,
As the rattle and the rhyme of the tenor-drummer's
    time
Filled all the hungry hearts of us with melody sub-
    lime!

How the grand band-wagon shone with a splendor
    all its own,
And glittered with a glory that our dreams had
    never known!
And how the boys behind, high and low of every
    kind,
Marched in unconscious capture, with a rapture un-
    defined!

How the horsemen, two and two, with their plumes
    of white and blue
And crimson, gold and purple, nodding by at me
    and you,

Waved the banners that they bore, as the knights in
    days of yore,
Till our glad eyes gleamed and glistened like the
    spangles that they wore!

How the graceless-graceful stride of the elephant
    was eyed,
And the capers of the little horse that cantered at
    his side!
How the shambling camels, tame to the plaudits of
    their fame,
With listless eyes came silent, masticating as they
    came.

How the cages jolted past, with each wagon bat-
    tened fast,
And the mystery within it only hinted of at last
From the little grated square in the rear, and nos-
    ing there
The snout of some strange animal that sniffed the
    outer air!

And, last of all, The Clown, making mirth for all
    the town,
With his lips curved ever upward and his eyebrows
    ever down,
And his chief attention paid to the little mule that
    played
A tattoo on the dashboard with his heels, in the
    Parade.

Oh! the Circus-Day Parade! How the bugles
    played and played!
And how the glossy horses tossed their flossy manes
    and neighed,
As the rattle and the rhyme of the tenor-drummer's
    time
Filled all the hungry hearts of us with melody sub-
    lime!

WHEN THE FROST IS ON THE PUNKIN

WHEN the frost is on the punkin and the
    fodder's in the shock,
And you hear the kyouck and gobble of the strut-
    tin' turkey-cock,
And the clackin' of the guineys, and the cluckin' of
    the hens,
And the rooster's hallylooer as he tiptoes on the
    fence;
O, it's then's the times a feller is a-feelin' at his
    best,
With the risin' sun to greet him from a night of
    peaceful rest,
As he leaves the house, bareheaded, and goes out
    to feed the stock,
When the frost is on the punkin and the fodder's
    in the shock.

They's something kindo' harty-like about the at-
    musfere
When the heat of summer's over and the coolin' fall
    is here—
Of course we miss the flowers, and the blossums on
    the trees,
And the mumble of the hummin'-birds and buzzin'
    of the bees;

442

But the air's so appetizin'; and the landscape
  through the haze
Of a crisp and sunny morning of the airly autumn
  days
Is a pictur' that no painter has the colorin' to
  mock—
When the frost is on the punkin and the fodder's in
  the shock.

The husky, rusty russel of the tossels of the corn,
And the raspin' of the tangled leaves, as golden as
  the morn;
The stubble in the furries—kindo' lonesome-like,
  but still
A-preachin' sermuns to us of the barns they growed
  to fill;
The strawstack in the medder, and the reaper in the
  shed;
The hosses in theyr stalls below—the clover overhead!—
O, it sets my hart a-clickin' like the tickin' of a
  clock,
When the frost is on the punkin and the fodder's
  in the shock!

Then your apples all is getherd, and the ones a
  feller keeps
Is poured around the celler-floor in red and yeller
  heaps;

And your cider-makin' 's over, and your wimmern-
    folks is through
With their mince and apple-butter, and theyr souse
    and saussage, too! . . .
I don't know how to tell it—but ef sich a thing
    could be
As the Angels wantin' boardin', and they'd call
    around on *me*—
I'd want to 'commodate 'em—all the whole-indurin'
    flock—
When the frost is on the punkin and the fodder's in
    the shock!

THAT NIGHT

YOU and I, and that night, with its perfume
    and glory!—
  The scent of the locusts—the light of the moon;
And the violin weaving the waltzers a story,
    Enmeshing their feet in the weft of the tune,
      Till their shadows uncertain
      Reeled round on the curtain,
    While under the trellis we drank in the June.

Soaked through with the midnight the cedars were
    sleeping,
  Their shadowy tresses outlined in the bright
Crystal, moon-smitten mists, where the fountain's
    heart, leaping
    Forever, forever burst, full with delight;
      And its lisp on my spirit
      Fell faint as that near it
    Whose love like a lily bloomed out in the night.

O your glove was an odorous sachet of blisses!
  The breath of your fan was a breeze from
    Cathay!
And the rose at your throat was a nest of spilled
    kisses!—
    And the music!—in fancy I hear it to-day,
      As I sit here, confessing
      Our secret, and blessing
    My rival who found us, and waltzed you away.

THE BAT

I

THOU dread, uncanny thing,
With fuzzy breast and leathern wing,
In mad, zigzagging flight,
Notching the dusk, and buffeting
The black cheeks of the night,
With grim delight!

II

What witch's hand unhasps
Thy keen claw-cornered wings
From under the barn roof, and flings
Thee forth, with chattering gasps,
To scud the air,
And nip the ladybug, and tear
Her children's hearts out unaware?

III

The glowworm's glimmer, and the bright,
Sad pulsings of the firefly's light,
Are banquet lights to thee.
O less than bird, and worse than beast,
Thou Devil's self, or brat, at least,
Grate not thy teeth at me!

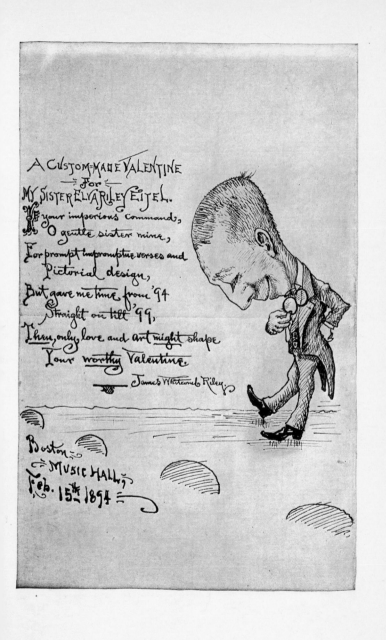

A CUSTOM-MADE VALENTINE
— For —
MY SISTER ELVA RILEY EITEL.

At your imperious command,
O gentle sister mine,
For prompt impromptue verses and
Pictorial design,
But gave me time from '94
Straight on till '99,
Then, only love and art might shape
Your worthy Valentine.

—— James Whitcomb Riley

Boston —
Music Hall,
Feb. 15th 1894

ON THE DEATH OF LITTLE MAHALA
ASHCRAFT

"LITTLE Haly! Little Haly!" cheeps the robin
    in the tree;
"Little Haly!" sighs the clover, "Little Haly!"
    moans the bee;
"Little Haly! Little Haly!" calls the killdeer at
    twilight;
And the katydids and crickets hollers "Haly!" all
    the night.

The sunflowers and the hollyhawks droops over the
    garden fence;
The old path down the garden walks still holds her
    footprints' dents;
And the well-sweep's swingin' bucket seems to wait
    fer her to come
And start it on its wortery errant down the old bee-
    gum.

The beehives all is quiet; and the little Jersey steer,
When any one comes nigh it, acts so lonesome-like
    and queer;

447

And the little Banty chickens kindo' cutters faint
    and low,
Like the hand that now was feedin' 'em was one
    they didn't know.

They's sorrow in the waivin' leaves of all the apple
    trees;
And sorrow in the harvest-sheaves, and sorrow in
    the breeze;
And sorrow in the twitter of the swallers 'round the
    shed;
And all the song her redbird sings is "Little Haly's
    dead!"

The medder 'pears to miss her, and the pathway
    through the grass,
Whare the dewdrops ust to kiss her little bare feet
    as she passed;
And the old pin in the gate-post seems to kindo'-
    sorto' doubt
That Haly's little sunburnt hands'll ever pull it out.

Did her father er her mother ever love her more'n
    me,
Er her sisters er her brother prize her love more
    tendurly?
I question—and what answer?—only tears, and
    tears alone,
And ev'ry neghbor's eyes is full o' tear-drops as my
    own.

"Little Haly! Little Haly!" cheeps the robin in the
    tree;
"Little Haly!" sighs the clover, "Little Haly!"
    moans the bee;
"Little Haly! Little Haly!" calls the killdeer at twi-
    light,
And the katydids and crickets hollers "Haly!" all
    the night.

THE MULBERRY TREE

O, IT'S many's the scenes which is dear to my
mind
As I think of my childhood so long left behind;
The home of my birth, with its old puncheon-floor,
And the bright morning-glorys that growed round
the door;
The warped clabboard roof whare the rain it run off
Into streams of sweet dreams as I laid in the loft,
Countin' all of the joys that was dearest to me,
And a-thinkin' the most of the mulberry tree.

And to-day as I dream, with both eyes wide-awake,
I can see the old tree, and its limbs as they shake,
And the long purple berries that rained on the
ground
Whare the pastur' was bald whare we trommpt it
around.
And again, peekin' up through the thick leafy shade,
I can see the glad smiles of the friends when I
strayed
With my little bare feet from my own mother's knee
To foller them off to the mulberry tree.

Leanin' up in the forks, I can see the old rail,
And the boy climbin' up it, claw, tooth, and toe-
nail,

And in fancy can hear, as he spits on his hands,
The ring of his laugh and the rip of his pants.
But that rail led to glory, as certin and shore
As I'll never climb thare by that rout' any more—
What was all the green lauruls of Fame unto me,
With my brows in the boughs of the mulberry tree!

Then it's who can fergit the old mulberry tree
That he knowed in the days when his thoughts was
       as free
As the flutterin' wings of the birds that flew out
Of the tall wavin' tops as the boys come about?
O, a crowd of my memories, laughin' and gay,
Is a-climbin' the fence of that pastur' to-day,
And a-pantin' with joy, as us boys ust to be,
They go racin' acrost fer the mulberry tree.

AUGUST

O MELLOW month and merry month,
　　Let me make love to you,
And follow you around the world
　　As knights their ladies do.
I thought your sisters beautiful,
　　Both May and April, too,
But April she had rainy eyes,
　　And May had eyes of blue.

And June—I liked the singing
　　Of her lips—and liked her smile—
But all her songs were promises
　　Of something, after while;
And July's face—the lights and shades
　　That may not long beguile
With alternations o'er the wheat
　　The dreamer at the stile.

But you!—ah, you are tropical,
　　Your beauty is so rare;
Your eyes are clearer, deeper eyes
　　Than any, anywhere;
Mysterious, imperious,
　　Deliriously fair,
O listless Andalusian maid,
　　With bangles in your hair!

TO MY OLD FRIEND, WILLIAM LEACH-MAN

FER forty year and better you have been a
　friend to me,
Through days of sore afflictions and dire adversity,
You allus had a kind word of counsul to impart,
Which was like a healin' 'intment to the sorrow of
　my hart.

When I buried my first womern, William Leach-
　man, it was you
Had the only consolation that I could listen to—
Fer I knowed you had gone through it and had
　rallied from the blow,
And when you said I'd do the same, I knowed you'd
　ort to know.

But that time I'll long remember; how I wundered
　here and thare—
Through the settin'-room and kitchen, and out in
　the open air—
And the snowflakes whirlin', whirlin', and the fields
　a frozen glare,
And the neghbors' sleds and wagons congergatin'
　ev'rywhare.

I turned my eyes to'rds heaven, but the sun was hid
    away;
I turned my eyes to'rds earth again, but all was cold
    and gray;
And the clock, like ice a-crackin', clickt the icy
    hours in two—
And my eyes'd never thawed out ef it hadn't been
    fer you!

We set thare by the smoke-house—me and you out
    thare alone—
Me a-thinkin'—you a-talkin' in a soothin' under-
    tone—
You a-talkin'—me a-thinkin' of the summers long
    ago,
And a-writin' "Marthy—Marthy" with my finger in
    the snow!

William Leachman, I can see you jest as plane as
    I could then;
And your hand is on my shoulder, and you rouse
    me up again;
And I see the tears a-drippin' from your own eyes,
    as you say:
"Be rickonciled and bear it—we but linger fer a
    day!"

At the last Old Settlers' Meetin' we went j'intly,
    you and me—
Your hosses and my wagon, as you wanted it to be;

And sence I can remember, from the time we've
    neghbored here,
In all sich friendly actions you have double-done
    your sheer.

It was better than the meetin', too, that nine-mile
    talk we had
Of the times when we first settled here and travel
    was so bad;
When we had to go on hoss-back, and sometimes on
    "Shanks's mare,"
And "blaze" a road fer them behind that had to
    travel thare.

And now we was a-trottin' 'long a level gravel pike,
In a big two-hoss road-wagon, jest as easy as you
    like—
Two of us on the front seat, and our wimmern-folks
    behind,
A-settin' in theyr Winsor-cheers in perfect peace of
    mind!

And we pinted out old landmarks, nearly faded out
    of sight:—
Thare they ust to rob the stage-coach; thare Gash
    Morgan had the fight
With the old stag-deer that pronged him—how he
    battled fer his life,
And lived to prove the story by the handle of his
    knife.

Thare the first griss-mill was put up in the Settle-
    ment, and we
Had tuck our grindin' to it in the Fall of Forty-
    three—
When we tuck our rifles with us, techin' elbows all
    the way,
And a-stickin' right together ev'ry minute, night
    and day.

Thare ust to stand the tavern that they called the
    "Travelers' Rest,"
And thare, beyent the covered bridge, "The Coun-
    terfitters' Nest"—
Whare they claimed the house was ha'nted—that a
    man was murdered thare,
And burried underneath the floor, er 'round the
    place somewhare.

And the old Plank-road they laid along in Fifty-one
    er two—
You know we talked about the times when the old
    road was new:
How "Uncle Sam" put down that road and never
    taxed the State
Was a problum, don't you rickollect, we couldn't
    *dim*onstrate?

Ways was devius, William Leachman, that me and
    you has past;
But as I found you true at first, I find you true at
    last;

And, now the time's a-comin' mighty nigh our jur-
    ney's end,
I want to throw wide open all my soul to you, my
    friend.

With the stren'th of all my bein', and the heat of
    hart and brane,
And ev'ry livin' drop of blood in artery and vane,
I love you and respect you, and I venerate your
    name,
Fer the name of William Leachman and True Man-
    hood's jest the same!

THE GUIDE

WE rode across the level plain—
  We—my sagacious guide and I—
He knew the earth—the air—the sky;
He knew when it would blow or rain,
And when the weather would be dry:
The bended blades of grass spake out
To him when Redskins were about;
The wagon tracks would tell him too,
The very day that they rolled through:
He knew their burden—whence they came—
If any horse along were lame,
And what its owner ought to do;
He knew when it would snow; he knew,
By some strange intuition, when
The buffalo would overflow
The prairies like a flood, and then
Recede in their stampede again.
He knew all things—yea, he did know
The brand of liquor in my flask,
And many times did tilt it up,
Nor halt or hesitate one whit,
Nor pause to slip the silver cup
From off its crystal base, nor ask

Why I preferred to drink from it.
And more and more I plied him, and
Did query of him o'er and o'er,
And seek to lure from him the lore
By which the man did understand
These hidden things of sky and land
And, wrought upon, he sudden drew
His bridle—wheeled, and caught my hand—
Pressed it, as one that loved me true,
And bade me listen . . . . .
. . . . There be few
Like tales as strange to listen to!
He told me all—How, when a child,
The Indians stole him—There he laughed—
"They stole me and I stole their craft!"
Then slowly winked both eyes, and smiled,
And went on ramblingly,—"And they—
They reared me, and I ran away—
'Twas winter, and the weather wild;
And, caught up in the awful snows
That bury wilderness and plain,
I struggled on until I froze
My feet ere human hands again
Were reached to me in my distress,—
And lo, since then not any rain
May fall upon me anywhere,
Nor any cyclone's cussedness
Slip up behind me unaware,—
Nor any change of cold, or heat,
Or blow, or snow, but I do know
It's coming, days and days before;—

I know it by my frozen feet—
I know it by my itching heels,
And by the agony one feels
Who knows that scratching nevermore
Will bring to him the old and sweet
Relief he knew ere thus endowed
With knowledge that a certain cloud
Will burst with storm on such a day,
And when a snow will fall, and—nay,
I speak not falsely when I say
That by my tingling heels and toes
I measure time, and can disclose
The date of month—the week—and lo,
The very day and minute—yea—
Look at your watch!—An hour ago
And twenty minutes I did say
Unto myself with bitter laugh,
'In less than one hour and a half
Will I be drunken!' Is it so?"

SUTTER'S CLAIM

SAY! *you* feller! *You*—
　　With that spade and the pick!—
What do you 'pose to do
　　On this side o' the crick?
Goin' to tackle this claim?　Well, I reckon
　　You'll let up ag'in, purty quick!

No bluff, understand,—
　　But the same has been tried,
And the claim never panned—
　　Or the fellers has lied,—
For they tell of a dozen that tried it,
　　And quit it most onsatisfied.

The luck's dead ag'in' it!—
　　The first man I see
That stuck a pick in it
　　Proved *that* thing to me,—
For he sort o' took down, and got homesick,
　　And went back whar he'd orto be!

Then others they worked it
　　Some—more or less,

461

But finally shirked it,
  In grades of distress,—
With an eye out—a jaw or skull busted,
  Or some sort o' seriousness.

The *last* one was plucky—
  He wasn't afeerd,
And bragged he was "lucky,"
  And said that "he'd heerd
A heap of bluff-talk," and swore awkard
  He'd work any claim that he keered!

Don't you strike nary lick
  With that pick till I'm through;
This-here feller talked slick
  And as peart-like as you!
And he says: "I'll abide here
  As long as I please!"

But he didn't. . . . He died here—
  And I'm his disease!

DOLORES

LITHE-ARMED, and with satin-soft shoulders
   As white as the cream-crested wave;
With a gaze dazing every beholder's,
   She holds every gazer a slave:
Her hair, a fair haze, is outfloated
   And flared in the air like a flame;
Bare-breasted, bare-browed and bare-throated—
   Too smooth for the soothliest name.

She wiles you with wine, and wrings for you
   Ripe juices of citron and grape;
She lifts up her lute and sings for you
   Till the soul of you seeks no escape;
And you revel and reel with mad laughter,
   And fall at her feet, at her beck,
And the scar of her sandal thereafter
   You wear like a gyve round your neck.

MY FIDDLE

MY fiddle?—Well, I kindo' keep her handy,
    don't you know!
Though I ain't so much inclined to tromp the strings
    and switch the bow
As I was before the timber of my elbows got so dry,
And my fingers was more limber-like and caperish
    and spry;
        Yit I can plonk and plunk and plink,
          And tune her up and play,
        And jest lean back and laugh and wink
          At ev'ry rainy day!

My playin' 's only middlin'—tunes I picked up when
    a boy—
The kindo'-sorto' fiddlin' that the folks call "cor-
    daroy";
"The Old Fat Gal," and "Rye-straw," and "My
    Sailyor's on the Sea,"
Is the old cowtillions *I* "saw" when the ch'ice is
    left to me;
        And so I plunk and plonk and plink,
          And rosum-up my bow
        And play the tunes that makes you think
          The devil's in your toe!

I was allus a-romancin', do-less boy, to tell the
 truth,
A-fiddlin' and a-dancin', and a-wastin' of my youth,
And a-actin' and a-cuttin'-up all sorts o' silly pranks
That wasn't worth a button of anybody's thanks!
   But they tell me, when I used to plink
    And plonk and plunk and play,
   My music seemed to have the kink
    O' drivin' cares away!

That's how this here old fiddle's won my hart's
 indurin' love!
From the strings acrost her middle, to the
 schreechin' keys above—
From her "apern," over "bridge," and to the ribbon
 round her throat,
She's a wooin', cooin' pigeon, singin' "Love me"
 ev'ry note!
   And so I pat her neck, and plink
    Her strings with lovin' hands,—
   And, list'nin' clos't, I sometimes think
    She kindo' understands!

NORTH AND SOUTH

OF the North I wove a dream,
  All bespangled with the gleam
  Of the glancing wings of swallows
Dipping ripples in a stream,
That, like a tide of wine,
Wound through lands of shade and shine
Where purple grapes hung bursting on the
    vine.

And where orchard-boughs were bent
Till their tawny fruitage blent
  With the golden wake that marked the
Way the happy reapers went;
Where the dawn died into noon
As the May-mists into June,
And the dusk fell like a sweet face in a
    swoon.

Of the South I dreamed: And there
Came a vision clear and fair
  As the marvelous enchantments
Of the mirage of the air;

And I saw the bayou-trees,
With their lavish draperies,
Hang heavy o'er the moon-washed cypress-
  knees.

Peering from lush fens of rice,
I beheld the Negro's eyes,
 Lit with that old superstition
Death itself can not disguise;
And I saw the palm-tree nod
Like an Oriental god,
And the cotton froth and bubble from the
  pod.

And I dreamed that North and South,
With a sigh of dew and drouth,
 Blew each unto the other
The salute of lip and mouth;
And I wakened, awed and thrilled—
Every doubting murmur stilled
In the silence of the dream I found fulfilled.

THE DAYS GONE BY

O THE days gone by! O the days gone by!
 The apples in the orchard, and the pathway
 through the rye;
The chirrup of the robin, and the whistle of the
 quail
As he piped across the meadows sweet as any nightingale;
When the bloom was on the clover, and the blue
 was in the sky,
And my happy heart brimmed over, in the days
 gone by.

In the days gone by, when my naked feet were
 tripped
By the honeysuckle tangles where the water-lilies
 dipped,
And the ripples of the river lipped the moss along
 the brink
Where the placid-eyed and lazy-footed cattle came
 to drink,
And the tilting snipe stood fearless of the truant's
 wayward cry
And the splashing of the swimmer, in the days gone
 by.

O the days gone by!   O the days gone by!
The music of the laughing lip, the luster of the eye;
The childish faith in fairies, and Aladdin's magic
     ring—
The simple, soul-reposing, glad belief in every
     thing,—
When life was like a story holding neither sob nor
     sigh,
In the golden olden glory of the days gone by.

THE CLOVER

SOME sings of the lilly, and daisy, and rose,
  And the pansies and pinks that the Summer-
    time throws
In the green grassy lap of the medder that lays
Blinkin' up at the skyes through the sunshiny days;
But what is the lilly and all of the rest
Of the flowers, to a man with a hart in his brest
That was dipped brimmin' full of the honey and
    dew
Of the sweet clover-blossoms his babyhood knew?

I never set eyes on a clover-field now,
Er fool round a stable, er climb in the mow,
But my childhood comes back jest as clear and as
    plane
As the smell of the clover I'm sniffin' again;
And I wunder away in a barefooted dream,
Whare I tangle my toes in the blossoms that gleam
With the dew of the dawn of the morning of love
Ere it wept ore the graves that I'm weepin' above.

And so I love clover—it seems like a part
Of the sacerdest sorrows and joys of my hart;
And wharever it blossoms, oh, thare let me bow
And thank the good God as I'm thankin' Him now;
And I pray to Him still fer the stren'th when I die,
To go out in the clover and tell it good-by,
And lovin'ly nestle my face in its bloom
While my soul slips away on a breth of purfume.

NOTES

NOTES

p. 1   WHEN I DO MOCK

Written prior to September, 1878; printed in *The Indianapolis Journal,* August 26, 1882; published in ARMAZINDY—1894, THE LOCKERBIE BOOK—1911. This sonnet, in imitation of Shakespeare, was written while Mr. Riley was "a very young man, when," as he says, he "dared to do such an audacious thing and felt able to accomplish the design."

p. 2   EZRA HOUSE

Printed in *The Indianapolis Saturday Herald,* 1878 (exact date lost); published in NYE AND RILEY'S RAILWAY GUIDE — 1888, NEGHBORLY POEMS—1891. These lines originally bore the subheading, "After the manner of 'the Sweet Singer of Michigan'," a writer of doggerel, famous in her day. Hence the faulty rhymes and other characteristics of the novice. The present subheading in dialect was written for the publication of the lines in NEGHBORLY POEMS, at which time the skit was ascribed to "Benj. F. Johnson of Boone," the feigned author of THE OLD SWIMMIN'-HOLE AND 'LEVEN MORE POEMS.

Stanza 2, l. 2: The boy Riley had a particular aversion for Ray's Arithmetic.

p. 6   THE VISION OF RABBI BEN ISAAC

Dated Greenfield, August 25, 1878, printed in *The Indianapolis Journal,* August 29, 1878; hitherto unpublished in book form.

p. 10   DAN PAINE

Dated Greenfield, September 10, 1878, printed in *The Indianapolis Saturday Herald,* September 14, 1878, with the title, *To My Friend, Dan Paine;* published in GREEN FIELDS AND RUNNING BROOKS— 1892, SONGS O' CHEER—1905, THE LOCKERBIE BOOK —1911.

Dan L. Paine, one of the editors of *The Indianapolis News,* was attracted to Mr. Riley's verse as it appeared in the various country newspapers, and correspondence between the two and a warm personal friendship resulted. Mr. Paine recognized the promise of a new writer, and, after his kindly fashion, showed his appreciation and offered Mr. Riley encouragement and friendly criticism. Mr. Riley, grateful for this recognition and aid, addressed these verses to his friend. Upon the appearance of this poem in GREEN FIELDS AND RUNNING BROOKS, *The Indianapolis News* said:

The hearty verses to Dan L. Paine, who was for many years on the staff of *The News,* and who was and is a kind of local Mæcenas, whom everybody loves, will prove a photograph to those who know the subject.

p. 12   OLD HEC'S IDOLATRY

The portion subtitled *An Idyl of the King,* was first printed in *The Indianapolis Saturday Herald,* September 28, 1878, in the fifth of the *"Respectfully Declined" Papers of the Buzz Club;* published in

ARMAZINDY—1894, though the introductory lines and the present title were first used when the poem was published in HOME-FOLKS (Homestead Edition)—1902; published also in HIS PA'S ROMANCE (Greenfield Edition)—1903, THE LOCKERBIE BOOK —1911.

p. 28 A MOTHER-SONG

Written about October, 1878; published in RHYMES OF CHILDHOOD—1890, THE LOCKERBIE BOOK—1911.

p. 29 THE LOST PATH

Printed in *The Indianapolis Journal,* October 6, 1878; published in PIPES O' PAN AT ZEKESBURY— 1888, LOVE-LYRICS—1899, THE LOCKERBIE BOOK— 1911. The printing of these lines in a newly established Sunday issue, marks Mr. Riley's close connection with *The Indianapolis Journal.*

p. 30 MY BRIDE THAT IS TO BE

Dated October 7, 1878, printed in *The Indianapolis Journal,* October 13, 1878; published in ARMA- ZINDY—1894, LOVE-LYRICS—1899, THE LOCKERBIE BOOK—1911.

p. 33 LULLABY

Printed in *The Indianapolis Journal,* October 20, 1878; published in PIPES O' PAN AT ZEKESBURY— 1888, RHYMES OF CHILDHOOD (first edition only, title, *Cradle Song*)—1890, WHILE THE HEART BEATS YOUNG—1906, SONGS OF SUMMER—1890, THE LOCKERBIE BOOK—1911.

p. 34   THE ROMAUNT OF KING MORDAMEER

Printed in *The Indianapolis Journal,* October 27, 1878, with the title, *The Romaunt of King Valdemere;* published in *Spirk and Wunk Rhymes, Rounds and Catches* in THE FLYING ISLANDS OF THE NIGHT—1900, THE LOCKERBIE BOOK—1911. When the poem was published in THE FLYING ISLANDS OF THE NIGHT many minor changes were made. The name "Valdemere" became "Mordameer." As an example of the thorough revision which many of Mr. Riley's poems have undergone, the early rendering of the parts since altered are given below:—

Stanza 1, ll. 3-4:—
　　A royal crown upon his brow,
　　　And scepter in his hand,
Stanza 7, l. 1:—
　　A thousand shapes in phantom guise.
Stanza 7, l. 6:—
　　That roll from left to right.
Stanza 8, l. 4:—
　　In selfishness denied—
Stanza 9, l. 2:—
　　And from his couch of straw
Stanza 9, l. 5:—
　　And stares with maddened eyes upon
Stanza 10, l. 6:—
　　The gallows at the rear.
Stanza 13, l. 3:—
　　And red-lipped shells that ever mock
Stanza 14, l. 3:—
　　And presses kisses on the cheeks
Stanza 14, l. 5:—
　　And old caresses live again
Stanza 16, l. 1:—
　　He bends above the artist's bed
Stanza 17, l. 3:—
　　And fills the chambers of his soul
Stanza 18, l. 1:—
　　He walks the world in every way,

p. 39

DEARTH

Printed in *The Indianapolis Journal,* November 3, 1878; published in AFTERWHILES—1887, THE LOCKERBIE BOOK—1911. These lines originally read as follows:—

ll. 3-5:—
> Of trust and jealously. When eyes are wet
> I can but think they jewel some regret,
> And then the loving arms that round me twine

l. 9:—
> When crimson clusters of your kisses press

l. 11:—
> Of joy, for foolish fancy needs must guess

l. 14:—
> Than e'en your whispered "yes" may now declare.

p. 40

THE SONG I NEVER SING

Printed in *The Indianapolis Journal,* November 10, 1878; published in ARMAZĪNDY—1894, THE LOCKERBIE BOOK—1911. Cf. *The Romaunt of King Mordameer,* stanza 17, l. 6. Stanza 5, ll. 1-6 originally read:—

> A mystic spray of sound that falls
> As though a wave of heavenly art
> Had flooded all the gleaming halls
> And broken o'er the golden walls
> And showered on my heart;
> Until with open arms, and eyes

Stanza 1: Mr. Riley tells of an experience of dreaming a long poem in which a refrain of exquisite melody occurred and reoccurred. "I read along entranced with the delight of it," he says, "turning the leaves of the book as I went and coming across this splendid refrain repeatedly. Sometimes I turned back to it and drank in its music enraptured. Awake I could not recall a line, and yet

I marveled; for somehow this mysterious song was
of course my own creation, and my brain all un-
consciously had fashioned it."

p. 43   UNSPOKEN

Printed in *The Indianapolis Journal,* November
24, 1878; hitherto unpublished in book form.

p. 45   THANKSGIVING DAY AT HUNCHLEY'S

Printed in *The Indianapolis Journal,* December
1, 1878; hitherto unpublished in book form.

The Indianapolis Journal of November 29, 1879,
contained the following account of one of Mr.
Hunchley's Thanksgiving dinners:—

THE MAN

We had dropped in a chop-house for our Thanksgiving
lunch. Not, perhaps, because we really wished to ignore
the comforts of a boarding-house, but—well, we met Mr.
Hunchley on the street by the merest accident, and—"You'll
dine with me to-day," he announced.

"Can't stand this Thanksgivin' racket round't home, you
know, and you don't like it any better'n I do. Big dinner
waitin', of course, but too much company for a hungry
man! Put it up on me that way every season; consequence
is, I'm never there; more introductions than dinner, you
understand; excuse me! Not less'n three young widows
on the bill o' fare to-day—to say nothing of a United
Brethren preacher, and a twittering pilgrim from Oshkosh.
Take you with me round to Du-Klaig's!" And he did.

"Great place for character here!" observed Mr. Hunchley, after the elaborate compilation of an order that completely dazed the waiter and sent him trembling from the
table. "Great place for character," repeated Mr. Hunchley, glancing keenly round the room. "Remember last
Thanksgivin'—was it? Yes, last Thanksgivin', just a year
ago this very day!" continued Mr. Hunchley with italicized

earnestness. "Yes, sir! Sat at this very table, just as I'm a-settin' this very minute. Disremember what friend I had along with me last year—but no matter. Had venison that day, and—well—first-rate bill throughout, and a ferrel o' wine on the end of it—ain't forgot that! Well, as I was goin'non to say—I was settin' just's am now—friend just opposite—no! hold on! was no friend along with me that day—that's so! No. There's where *the man* sat—this character, you know, I'm a-tellin' you 'bout. Yes; now we got it! Well, I was a-settin' here like this, you understand, waitin' for waiter to fetch along my order, you know, and *the man* he comes in, and sets down just where you're a-settin'. Kind o' apologized like, as he took the chair, 'bout all the other tables bein' full, and they was full— 'full's goose'—as the fellow says, and he ordered dinner. Ice was broke purty well, o' course, and we opened up conversation—ordered wine, too, the fellow did—hit it a time or two together, and—well, I never struck just such another chap in my life! Entertainin'est style 'bout him; and blame me if he didn't 'pear to know all about everything, and glanced and rickashayed around, as you fellers says, to beat the world! till, finally—J'ever read this here what's-name-story o' Bulwer's?—'bout some durn occult sort o' a feller, you know, that run ag'in' this fountain-o'- youth-business—secret, you know, o' livin' always—kind o' snake-eyed sort o' rooster, you understand, and mesmerized folks, and all that tomfoolery? You on? Well, sir, this here man kind o' put me in mind o' that feller, and the more I thought about it the more it struck me. Funny; wasn't it? Kep' the slickest talk a-goin', all the time, and said he knowed a man 'at suited him fur's he could see him. Said he never missed an open-hearted man—spot 'im ever' time; guess he could! Said when he took a notion to a feller, that settled it; he was his friend for all time, and didn't care whether school kep' or not—didn't use them words exactly, but just samey—ordered more wine—talked more, and fresher, and clearer every minit. Wish I could call to mind some o' his 'bon-bons', as you fellers says. 'Cause his language was simply dazzlin'—and tear off more poetry, that feller could, 'n would pat chell a mile! But, like all geniuses, I noticed he was inclined to drink a leetle too much; and at last I says to him; 'You're purty full,' says I, 'and you want to let up on this here wine-racket,' says I. And then he laughed in that glitterin' way o' his, and filled the glasses up again, and tore off a toast to our better acquaintance 'at was mos' bu'ful piece o' word-

paintin' ever laid ear to. And he jes' kep' it up, and kep'
it up, till I reckon I jes' must a dropped off to sleep like;
for when I waked up, *the man* was gone—jes' like a ghost.
And when I went to fix up the expenses of the lay-out
we'd had, I found I'd left ever' cent o' money in some other
pants or other; and I was jes' about tellin' how things
was, when the boss says, 'It's all right,' he says; 'the
gemmen that had charge of you's squared everything, and
give us your address, and left orders, when you got sober
'nough, to put you on a street-car, and pay your fare, and
git you in home safe if it cost him a dollar; said money
was no object, so's you was shielded, on'y shielded from
disgrace.' And I give you my sacred word," concluded
Mr. Hunchley, impressively, wiping the table-knife off on
his nose, and sipping his coffee with his left eye,—"give
you my sacred word'n nonner sugemmen, I was jes' sober's
then as I am this min't!"

p. 51.   APART

Printed in *The Indianapolis Journal,* December
8, 1878; hitherto unpublished in book form.

p. 53   TOIL

Printed in *The Indianapolis Journal,* December
15, 1878; published in His Pa's Romance—1903,
The Lockerbie Book—1911.

p. 56   HIS ROOM

Printed in *The Indianapolis Journal,* January 12,
1879, with the title *My Room;* published in His
Pa's Romance—1903, Songs of Home—1910, The
Lockerbie Book—1911. Since its first appearance
the poem has undergone a thorough revision.

p. 59   TO LEONAINIE

Printed in *The Kokomo Tribune,* February 1,
1879; hitherto unpublished in book form. Leo-

nainie, who was the infant daughter of W. B. and Lotta Titus, was named from Mr. Riley's poem *Leonainie* [Vol. 1, p. 194].

p. 61 THE SHOWER

Printed in *The Indianapolis Journal,* April 19, 1879; published in AFTERWHILES — 1887, OLD-FASHIONED ROSES—1888, SONGS OF SUMMER—1908, THE LOCKERBIE BOOK—1911.

p. 62 YE SCHOLAR

Printed in the prose sketch, *Tale of a Spider,* in *The Indianapolis Journal,* May 13, 1879; published in THE BOSS GIRL—1885, SKETCHES IN PROSE—1891.

p. 63 DEATH IS DEAD

Printed in the prose sketch, *Tale of a Spider,* in *The Indianapolis Journal,* May 13, 1879; published in THE BOSS GIRL—1885, SKETCHES IN PROSE—1891.

p. 64 TOM JOHNSON'S QUIT

Printed in *The Kokomo Tribune,* May 31, 1879; published in PIPES O' PAN AT ZEKESBURY—1888.

This poem's appearance marks the author's definite connection with *The Kokomo Tribune.* When Charles Philips of that paper established *The Home Department,* he solicited Mr. Riley's help. The latter contributed under the pseudonym of "John C. Walker," of whom Mr. Riley says:—

"John C. Walker was a 'corduroy' poet of Greenfield, who wrote a rough sort of doggerel, though occasionally rising to an excellent plane of humor. He composed these lines about a boy who, upon quitting the farm, asserted himself in this manner:—

> 'I will not be a farmer,
>   Nor longer till the sod;
> I will not hitch another team
>   Nor hop another clod!' "

Tom Johnson's Quit was copied at the time of its appearance by the press East and West and there was much speculation as to its authorship. Mr. Riley was then writing under various pseudonyms. At least one editor soon penetrated these disguises, as the following article from *The Mishawaka Enterprise* of July, 1879, shows:—

Kokomo Tribune, we'll wager a year's subscription to the *Enterprise* that your "John C. Walker," whose charming little poems have been such a brilliant feature of your paper, is none other than J. W. Riley, Indiana's rising young poet, in disguise. We can't prove it, but if Riley didn't write *Tom Johnson's Quit* and *Romancin'*, he ought to have done so. Moreover, the poet who is cutting up the *Poetical Gymnastics* in *The Indianapolis Saturday Herald,* has a very Riley-ish rhythm, and if he, too, isn't our friend J. W., we should like mightily to know who it is. We call upon both papers to rise and confess and quiet the growing curiosity that prevails throughout the state.

p. 67   THE LITTLE DEAD MAN

Printed in *The Indianapolis Saturday Herald,* June 7, 1879; hitherto unpublished in book form.

p. 70   OLD-FASHIONED ROSES

Printed in *The Indianapolis Saturday Herald,* June 14, 1879; published in THE BOSS GIRL—1885, OLD-FASHIONED ROSES—1888, SKETCHES IN PROSE (first edition only)—1891, AFTERWHILES (not in first edition)—1898, FARM-RHYMES—1901, SONGS OF SUMMER—1908, RILEY ROSES—1909. This poem "was conceived in an affection for the old dooryard flowers that mother used to love," says Mr. Riley. In introducing it in early lectures he said:

While it would seem that the very choicest specimens of our modern dialectic verse, such as produced by Bret Harte, John Hay, Carleton, and others, are destined scarcely to survive the fleeting recognition of the daily press, it becomes something of a problem to the student why the dialectic poetry of Burns should yet be living on, as fresh and sweet to-day as when an age ago it cropped above the heather-bells of Scotland in a bloom of song that filled the whole world with its fragrance. And while it remains a truth that the "Cantie blether o' the Hielands" affords a singularly musical and rich vernacular, I am inclined to think that our own native dialect, with the exception, perhaps, of ungrammatical abandon, is scarcely the inferior of the Scotch, if we but pause to contemplate it with more seriousness, for in our hurried notice of it we catch nothing of its deeper worth; only its lighter attributes are visible. Its quaintness is always apparent, but its variety of tone and color so dazzles on the surface that we rarely look beyond. With such fickle knowledge, then, of all its deeper worth and purity, it is little wonder that its mission is so often debased to serve the ends of the rhyming punsters and poetical thugs of our "Comic Weeklies," until at last its standing in the literary field may be likened more to the character of a lawless intruder than a dear old-fashioned friend who comes to shake a hearty hand with us, and gossip of the good old days "when you and I were young." It has grown to be the popular idea that the dialectic poem must necessarily embrace the slangiest phraseology, with copious suggestions of vulgarity, and "milky-ways" of asterisks, which the reader is left to pepper out with his own choice of expletives. This is all wrong. The field of dialect is flowered over with the rarest growth of poesy, and its bloom is no less fragrant because it springs from loam, and flourishes among the weeds. And I would offer a defense of it in the language of an "old-timer," who once took the trouble to explain to me his love for the "Old-Fashioned Roses" which grew about his doorway, in language substantially as follows.

p. 72 THE EMPTY SONG

Printed in *The Indianapolis Saturday Herald,* June 21, 1879; hitherto unpublished in book form.

These lines mark Mr. Riley's close connection with *The Herald,* for which he wrote an unsigned column called *Poetical Gymnastics.*

This poem had the following introduction:—

DIRECTIONS—To get absolute meat out of this little poem, it is simply necessary for the reader to imagine it a translation from Goethe, Murger, or some poet he knows *is* good —if he could only read his language.

—THE AUTHOR.

p. 73 A ROSE IN OCTOBER

Printed in *The Indianapolis Saturday Herald,* June 21, 1879; hitherto unpublished in book form. The lines had this subheading:—

IMITATED FROM THE MAGAZINE

NOTE—The author of this literary curiosity has been chased over two consecutive continents by admiring publishers in their efforts to secure the only successful imitation of magazine poetry yet produced; but fearing that the little gem might be foisted on the public as genuine, the poet's sense of both personal and poetic justice has overcome all pecuniary blandishments, and only permits him thus to present it to the world draped in the chastity of its own simple worth—as an imitation; nothing more.

p. 75 ROMANCIN'

Printed in *The Kokomo Tribune,* June 21, 1879; signed "John C. Walker;" published in PIPES O' PAN AT ZEKESBURY—1888, NEGHBORLY POEMS— 1891, FARM-RHYMES—1901.

Stanzas 7-8: The author said in an early lecture:—

Poetry is about us everywhere. Its influence has a hold on every heart. He who claims that poetry to him is simply so much nothingness, may be honest enough in his belief, but he is in error none the less. If his tired eyelids have ever drooped beneath the touches of a mother's hand; if he has ever nestled in her lap, his troubled fancies smoothed and lovingly blent into slumber with her lullaby, and if, in memory, he can recall this now, with one emotion of either pleasurable longing or sorrowful regret, he *does* like poetry, however he maintains that he does not.

p. 79
THE LITTLE OLD POEM THAT NOBODY READS

Printed in *The Indianapolis Saturday Herald,* June 28, 1879; hitherto unpublished in book form.

p. 80   A SLEEPING BEAUTY

Printed in *The Indianapolis Saturday Herald,* June 28, 1879, with the title, *Mirage;* published in RHYMES OF CHILDHOOD—1890, THE LOCKERBIE BOOK—1911.

p. 82   LEEDLE DUTCH BABY

Printed in *The Indianapolis Saturday Herald,* June 28, 1879, with the title, *Lullaby,* and subheading, *From the German;* published in AFTERWHILES —1887.

p. 83   LINES ON HEARING A COW BAWL

Dated July 3, 1879, and printed in *The Indianapolis Saturday Herald,* July 5, 1879; published in NYE AND RILEY'S RAILWAY GUIDE—1888.

p. 84   FRIEND OF A WAYWARD HOUR

Printed in *The Indianapolis Saturday Herald,*
July 12, 1879; hitherto unpublished in book form.
The verses were originally inscribed "To H. S. T.,"
who was the Rev. H. S. Taylor, a lifelong friend of
the author.   Beneath the inscription stood the subheading "The Morgue, Midnight, July 3, 1879,"
which referred to the date of his visit to Mr. Riley's
room, called by them "The Morgue."

p. 85   LINES ON RECEIVING A PRESENT

Printed in *The Indianapolis Saturday Herald,*
July 5, 1879; hitherto unpublished in book form.
The friend never divulged his identity.

p. 86   PAN

Printed in *The Indianapolis Saturday Herald,*
July 5, 1879; published in AFTERWHILES—1887,
OLD-FASHIONED ROSES—1888, THE LOCKERBIE
BOOK—1911.   When first printed this quotation
from *A Musical Instrument,* by Elizabeth Barrett
Browning, preceded the poem:—

> What was he doing, the great god Pan,
> Down in the reeds by the river?

p. 87   WHEN OUR BABY DIED

Printed in *The Indianapolis Saturday Herald,*
July 12, 1879; published in RHYMES OF CHILDHOOD
—1890.

p. 88   A FULL HARVEST

Printed in *The Kokomo Tribune,* July 12, 1879;

signed "John C. Walker"; published in GREEN
FIELDS AND RUNNING BROOKS—1892, SONGS O'
CHEER—1905, SONGS O' SUMMER—1908, A SUM-
MER'S DAY AND OTHER POEMS—1911.

p. 89 MY BACHELOR CHUM

Printed in *The Indianapolis Saturday Herald,*
July 19, 1879; published in NYE AND RILEY'S RAIL-
WAY GUIDE—1888, HIS PA'S ROMANCE—1903, THE
LOCKERBIE BOOK—1911.

p. 91 TOMMY SMITH

Printed in *The Indianapolis Saturday Herald,*
July 19, 1879, with the title, *Little Tommy Smith;*
published in THE BOSS GIRL—1885, OLD-FASHIONED
ROSES—1888, RHYMES OF CHILDHOOD (not in first
edition)—1898, SKETCHES IN PROSE (first edition
only)—1891, THE LOCKERBIE BOOK—1911. Stanza
4 was not included in the early vision. The subject
is purely imaginary.

p. 93 THE LAUGHTER OF THE RAIN

Printed in *The Indianapolis Saturday Herald,*
with the title, *The Rain,* July 19, 1879; published in
Spirk and Wunk Rhymes, Rounds and Catches in
THE FLYING ISLANDS OF THE NIGHT—1900.

p. 94 ETERNITY

Printed in *The Indianapolis Saturday Herald,*
July 19, 1879; published in *Spirk and Wunk
Rhymes, Rounds and Catches* in THE FLYING
ISLANDS OF THE NIGHT—1900, THE LOCKERBIE
BOOK—1911.

p. 95   LAST WORDS

Printed in *The Indianapolis Saturday Herald*,
July 26, 1879; hitherto unpublished in book form.

p. 96   AT BAY

Printed in *The Indianapolis Saturday Herald*,
July 26, 1879; hitherto unpublished in book form.

p. 98   A WORN-OUT PENCIL

Printed in *The Indianapolis Saturday Herald*,
July 26, 1879; published in PIPES O' PAN AT ZEKES-
BURY—1888, THE LOCKERBIE BOOK—1911.

p. 100   GOD BLESS US EVERY ONE

Printed in *The Indianapolis Saturday Herald*,
July 26, 1879; published in THE BOSS GIRL—1885,
OLD-FASHIONED ROSES—1888, SKETCHES IN PROSE
—1891, SONGS O' CHEER—1905, THE LOCKERBIE
BOOK—1911. These are the words of little Tim
Cratchit in *A Christmas Carol*. The expression has
long been a favorite with Mr. Riley, and ends many
of his letters.

p. 101   THE TREE-TOAD

Printed in *The Indianapolis Saturday Herald*,
August 2, 1879, with the title, *Only Wanted—A
Chance;* published in NYE AND RILEY'S RAILWAY
GUIDE—1888, with the title, *A Treat Ode,* PIPES O'
PAN AT ZEKESBURY—1888, NEGHBORLY POEMS (not
first edition)—1897, FARM-RHYMES—1901, SONGS
OF SUMMER—1908, DOWN AROUND THE RIVER AND
OTHER POEMS—1911. Mr. Riley used these lines,

with the title, *A Treat Ode,* together with *Babyhood,*
on stationery advertising his lectures in 1882. At-
tached to the verses was the following:—

The little tree-toad of the Hoosier state is variable in hue
according to the color of the tree it inhabits. Its voice is
like the rattle of a cricket, though louder. It is heard most
as night approaches, and always before a rain; and among
many there is a ridiculous belief that its cry not only por-
tends rain, but positively commands and controls it.

In introducing the reading of the verses Mr. Riley
often gave this "rambling dissertation on the tree-
toad":

I hev give—I hev give the tree-toad a heap o' thought.
Fer thirty year and better, boy and man, I hev allus looked
on the tree-toad with the deepest feelin's of respect, 'cause
of all cur'ous things 'at Nature ever laid her hands to gittin' up, I railly think the tree-toad is the boss. Thum the
hypotomus down to the chiggar there're no mortal beast
'at I jest naturally warm to like the tree-toad. 'Ll now I
cain't account fer it, ner I don't p'tend there're any livin'
reason that has prejudust me in favor of the tree-toad, but
of all animals 'at wears wings or hair, give me the tree-
toad; 'cause the tree-toad is my *favorite!*
'Chu fergit it! Time and time ag'in I've heerd it argied,
and you've heerd it argied, 'at the hoss is the intelligentest
animal 'at lives; but now I contend 'at the hoss cain't hold
a candle to the tree-toad—that is—understand me—a
growed-up tree-toad, a tree-toad 'at's got the kink o' draw-
in' rain ever time he's a mind to holler fer it, don't you
understand. Now you cain't tell me 'at the hoss, jest 'cause
he kin grasp the idee o' "gee" and "haw" and "hen over"
orto be set up as a example of—of—set up as a example
alongside of the tree-toad.—Ner I don't keer how long you
figger on the tree-toad, there're allus pints 'at you cain't
git no satisfaction on the tree-toad. Now you kin git at the
hoss. You kin tell when the hoss wants warter, er feed,
er when he's makin' up his mind to run, er kick, er balk,
er anything; but you can't tell nothin' 'bout the tree-toad—
'cause the tree-toad, I reckon, is the closest-mouthed thing
'at walks on legs. There're nobody knows nothin' 'bout the
tree-toad. I'll undertake to say 'at you never heerd no

sermint on the tree-toad. The Bible hain't got nuthin' to say 'bout the tree-toad (even the revised edition), and I'll defy you to perduce any pints in history 'at'll shed any light on the personal habits or the private character of the tree-toad. You cain't do it. Why? 'Cause there're no livin' man 'at's ever got the hang of the tree-toad, 'cept the tree-toad hisself, and you kin bet high 'at old Mr. Tree-toad don't give nothin' away. That hain't his style. Now ever sence I was big enough to climb a cherry-tree—and the fust cherry-tree I ever clumb had a tree-toad roostin' right on the fust limb I laid my hand over—and you couldn't tell him thum the bark of the tree till you felt how cold and gaumy-like he was, and saw his yeller legs mashed out thum in under him. Ever sence I was big enough to climb a cherry-tree I hev done more solid, ser'ous thinkin' on the tree-toad than any other animal 'at lives. And as fur back as when I fust learned to read and write at school, my folks, ef they was a-livin' to-day, my folks ud tell you 'at I was allus a-gittin' off sumpin er nuther on frogs and tree-toads and the like. Got some scraps of 'em saved up yit somers about the place, and ony tuther day I come acrost one 'at started out like this—boy-like, you understand, and yit it goes to show 'at even then I was a-noticin' things more'n boys in gineral. It starts off, as nigh as I kin ricollect, somepin like this :—

"Frogs is the peoples' friend, but they cain't fly. Wunst they was tadpoles 'bout as big as lickrish drops, and after while legs growed out on 'em. O, let us love the frog! He looks so sorry! Frogs kin swim better'n little boys, and they don't hev to hold their nose when they dive neither. Wunst I had a pet frog, and the cars runned over him. It thist squshed him! He never knowed what hurt him. Wunst they was a rich lady swallered one, when he was little, you know, and he growed up in her, and it didn't kill him at all. And you could hear him holler clean through her sealskin sack. It was a tree-toad, and when he'd go 'p-r-r-r-r-r' w'y nen the grand lady she would know it was goin' to rain, and make her little boy run and put the tub out under the spout. Wasn't that a beautiful frog indeed?

'O bless the frogs, the purty frogs,
That plays about our door.'"

Now them was my idees afore I could spell my own name, and o' course it goes to show 'at I orto know somepin 'bout what I'm talkin' on now. And I hev saw—I hev saw many and many of a cur'ous thing, but as I said afore, the tree-toad is my favorite. 'Chur life on that!

Tuther day I heerd one somers in the back lot a-hollerin' fer rain so long and vigers-like, the notion struck me 'at I'd jest watch the little chap, and see, ef he railly could bring it. Needed rain the wust way, but it jest 'peared like it never would rain agin. And there set the little cuss a coaxin' fer it now like a good un. And onct-an-a-while it ud sort o' haze up, and a little skift o' clouds ud mebbe shet the sun off fer a minit er so. But jest about the time old Mr. Tree-toad ud begin to kind o' ease up on his hollerin', don't you understand, out the sun ud pop, hotter'n ever, and the little feller ud hev all his work over agin. And then law! how he would buckle into hit! 'Ll I jest got to thinkin', at last, wonder what must be the feelin's of the tree-toad hisself, after hollerin' that-away, day in and day out, and then not a bringin' no rain nuther. And it worked on me so, and I'm that devilish sympathizin', I could 'a' jest set down and cried—'at finally—finally the idy struck me, 'at ef I could only jest kind o' pictur' the feelin's of the toad hisself—that is, to kind o' write off some poetry, or somepin er nuther, like as ef the toad was a tellin' of it, 'at sich a subject ud be mighty interestin'. And so at last I jest set down to it, and you can jedge fer yourself now ef I hain't got in purty work. Now listen.

p. 103   LAUGHING SONG

Printed in *The Indianapolis Saturday Herald,* August 2, 1879, with the title, *Song;* published in MORNING—1907, SONGS OF SUMMER—1908, THE LOCKERBIE BOOK—1911.

p. 104   THE WITCH OF ERKMURDEN

Printed in *The Indianapolis Saturday Herald,* August 2, 1879; published in *Spirk and Wunk Rhymes, Rounds and Catches* in THE FLYING IS-LANDS OF THE NIGHT—1900, THE LOCKERBIE BOOK—1911.

p. 107 THE BALLAD OF SMILES AND TEARS

Printed in *The Kokomo Tribune,* August 2, 1879; hitherto unpublished in book form. The poem, in its early form, had the subtitle, *After Dobson.* Mr. Riley wrote the first four lines of each stanza and Lee O. Harris the last four.

p. 109 THIS MAN JONES

Printed in *The Kokomo Tribune,* August 2, 1879, signed "John C. Walker"; published in PIPES O' PAN AT ZEKESBURY—1888. This poem was widely copied in the press.

p. 112 WAIT

Printed in *The Indianapolis Saturday Herald,* August 9, 1879; hitherto unpublished in book form. The following stanza, which ends the early version, is not included in the present:—

> The "Open Sesame"
>   Will soon or late
> Ring out like some triumphant melody,
> And you will say, "Lo, now at last I see
>   How even Christ did wait."

p. 113 LELLOINE

Printed in *The Indianapolis Saturday Herald,* August 9, 1879; hitherto unpublished in book form.

p. 115 A DREAM OF AUTUMN

Printed in *The Indianapolis Saturday Herald,* August 9, 1879; published in GREEN FIELDS AND

RUNNING BROOKS—1892, THE LOCKERBIE BOOK—1911.

p. 117   SINCE MY MOTHER DIED

Printed in *The Indianapolis Saturday Herald,* August 16, 1879; hitherto unpublished in book form.

p. 119   BELLS JANGLED

Printed in *The Indianapolis Saturday Herald,* August 16, 1879, with the title, *The Serenade;* published in THE BOSS GIRL—1885, SKETCHES IN PROSE (first edition)—1891, PIPES O' PAN AT ZEKESBURY (Homestead Edition)—1898, THE LOCKERBIE BOOK—1911.

p. 121   DUSK SONG—THE BEETLE

Printed in *The Kokomo Tribune,* August 16, 1879, with the title, *The Beetle;* published in THE BOSS GIRL—1885, OLD-FASHIONED ROSES—1888, RHYMES OF CHILDHOOD—1890, SKETCHES IN PROSE (first edition only)—1891, THE LOCKERBIE BOOK—1911.

p. 123   SLEEP

Printed in *The Indianapolis Saturday Herald,* August 23, 1879; published in AFTERWHILES—1887, OLD-FASHIONED ROSES—1888, THE LOCKERBIE BOOK—1911.

p. 124   MARTHY ELLEN

Printed in *The Kokomo Tribune,* September 6, 1879; published in PIPES O' PAN AT ZEKESBURY—

1888. These verses were originally signed "John
C. Walker" and were claimed by a man in
Tuscola, Illinois. This incident is an example of
a strange experience which Mr. Riley's *nom de
plumes* made possible on more than one occasion.
The Benj. F. Johnson poems in 1882 were likewise
claimed by several persons.

p. 126   THE LITTLE TOWN O' TAILHOLT

Printed in *The Indianapolis Saturday Herald,*
September 13, 1879; published in AFTERWHILES—
1887, OLD-FASHIONED ROSES—1888. This town is
seven miles south of the author's birthplace,
Greenfield. "The plain and expressive title of
Tailholt," says Mr. Riley, "was changed years ago
to Carleton. Then it was found that for post-office
purposes, Carleton, euphonious though it was, would
not do. It conflicted with the name of another
town—Carrollton. The name was finally changed
to Reedville."

The name was changed after the poem was written,—it is said not without a little pique on the
part of the inhabitants.

p. 128   WHERE SHALL WE LAND

Printed in *The Indianapolis News* just prior to
September 13, 1879; published in PIPES O' PAN AT
ZEKESBURY—1888, LOVE-LYRICS—1899, THE LOCK-
ERBIE BOOK—1911.

p. 130   HOPE

Written September 21, 1879, printed in *The Indianapolis Saturday Herald,* September 27, 1879;
hitherto unpublished in book form.

p. 131   THE LITTLE TINY KICKSHAW

Enclosed in a letter, September 22, 1879, to Dr. John N. Taylor; printed in *The Indianapolis Journal,* September 16, 1881; published in PIPES O' PAN AT ZEKESBURY—1888, RHYMES OF CHILDHOOD—1890.

p. 132   DEATH

Printed in *The Indianapolis Journal,* November 1, 1879; published in *Spirk and Wunk Rhymes, Rounds and Catches* in THE FLYING ISLANDS OF THE NIGHT—1900, THE LOCKERBIE BOOK—1911.

p. 133   TO THE WINE-GOD MERLUS

Written on the evening of November 5, 1879, printed in *The Indianapolis Journal,* November 8, 1879, with the title, *To Gambrinus;* published in *Spirk and Wunk Rhymes, Rounds and Catches* in THE FLYING ISLANDS OF THE NIGHT—1900, THE LOCKERBIE BOOK—1911. Jucklet, to whom the toast is ascribed in the subtitle, is a character in the poem, *The Flying Islands of the Night* [Vol. I, p. 275].

p. 134   THE GINOINE AR-TICKLE

Printed in *The Kokomo Tribune,* November 8, 1879, signed "John C. Walker"; hitherto unpublished in book form.

p. 135   A BRIDE

Printed in *The Kokomo Tribune,* November 15, 1879, with the title, *Tired,* signed "John C. Walker"; published in AFTERWHILES—1887, OLD-FASHIONED ROSES—1888, THE LOCKERBIE BOOK—1911.

p. 136   STANZAS FOR A NEW SONG

Printed in *The Indianapolis Journal,* November 24, 1879; hitherto unpublished in book form.

p. 137 LINES TO A ONSETTLED YOUNG MAN

Printed in *The Indianapolis Journal,* November 24, 1879; hitherto unpublished in book form.

p. 138   PLANTATION HYMN

Printed in *The Indianapolis Journal,* November 29, 1879; hitherto unpublished in book form.

p. 140   LAWYER AND CHILD

Printed in *The Indianapolis Journal,* November 29, 1879; published in RHYMES OF CHILDHOOD— 1890. These lines are reminiscent of the old school poem, *How Big Was Alexander, Pa?* found in the McGuffey reader formerly extensively used. The author's name can not be ascertained.

p. 141   THE LOST KISS

Printed in *The Indianapolis Journal,* December 2, 1879; published in AFTERWHILES—1887, OLD-FASHIONED ROSES—1888, RHYMES OF CHILDHOOD (first edition only)—1890, THE LOCKERBIE BOOK— 1911.

BUD'S FAIRY TALE

This was the next skit to appear, printed in *The Indianapolis Herald,* December 2, 1879. It appears in *A Child-World* in Vol. IV.

p. 143   MICHAEL FLYNN AND THE BABY

Printed in *The Indianapolis Journal,* December 15, 1879; hitherto unpublished in book form.

p. 144   ON A SPLENDUD MATCH

These lines were part of a larger poem entitled *John Golliher's Third Womern,* printed in *The Kokomo Tribune,* December 27, 1879, signed "John C. Walker." The verses were published as here given in NEGHBORLY POEMS—1891. The subheading is in the words and orthography of "Benj. F. Johnson of Boone."

p. 145   THE SINGER

The earliest date on this poem is found in Elva Riley Eitel's early note-book, December 27, 1879; published in GREEN FIELDS AND RUNNING BROOKS —1892, THE LOCKERBIE BOOK—1911.

p. 146   GUINEVERE

Printed in *The Indianapolis Journal,* January 4, 1880; hitherto unpublished in book form.

p. 147   THE WEREWIFE

Printed in *The Indianapolis Journal,* January 6, 1880, with the title, *My Ghoul;* published in *Spirk and Wunk Rhymes, Rounds and Catches* in THE FLYING ISLANDS OF THE NIGHT—1900, THE LOCKERBIE BOOK—1911.

p. 149   THE BAN

Printed in *The Indianapolis Journal,* January 8,

1880, with the title, *Opium;* published in THE BOSS GIRL—1885, SKETCHES IN PROSE (first edition)—1891, HOME-FOLKS (Homestead Edition)—1902, THE LOCKERBIE BOOK—1911.

p. 151 AN IDIOT

Printed in *The Indianapolis Journal,* January 9, 1880; published in HOME-FOLKS—1900.

Stanza 2: John A. Riley told that the author's first teacher, "old Mrs. Niel, had a silver dollar with a hole through it and strung on a ribbon, and the favored scholar was allowed to wear it by the week for any special excellence."

p. 153 AN ORDER FOR A SONG

Printed in *The Indianapolis Journal,* January 18, 1880; published in HIS PA'S ROMANCE—1903, THE LOCKERBIE BOOK—1911.

p. 154 THE CONQUEROR

Printed in *The Indianapolis Journal,* January 21, 1880; hitherto unpublished in book form.

p. 155 AFTER DEATH

Printed in *The Indianapolis Journal,* January 23, 1880; published in *Spirk and Wunk Rhymes, Rounds and Catches* in THE FLYING ISLANDS OF THE NIGHT—1900, THE LOCKERBIE BOOK—1911. The early version was subtitled, *A Fancy.*

p. 156 THE MAD LOVER

Printed in *The Indianapolis Journal,* January 25, 1880; hitherto unpublished in book form.

p. 158 · TO ROBERT BURNS

Read by Mr. Riley at the celebration of Burns 121st birthday by the Caledonian Society, Indianapolis, January 26, 1880; printed in *The Indianapolis Journal,* January 27, 1880; published in AFTERWHILES—1887, OLD-FASHIONED ROSES—1888.

The circumstances surrounding the writing of these verses are not without a spice of humor. The Rev. Myron Reed, a thoughtful friend, gave Mr. Riley warning that he would be requested to read a poem at the Burns celebration, and that the committee, as is usual, would doubtless be dilatory in informing him, supposing that a poem can be "dashed off" at will. Mr. Riley set to work immediately and had the poem completed by the time the committee appeared, just one week before the event.

"Gentlemen," said Mr. Riley with an inward twinkle in his eye, "how can I ever get a poem ready in such a short time?"

"Why,—you have a whole *week,*" some one rejoined.

"That is very meager time, very meager time!" he replied. "And yet, I'll do my very best. I *think* I'll have something for you."

p. 161 HER VALENTINE

Written about February 14, 1880, printed in *The Indianapolis Saturday Herald* (exact date lost); hitherto unpublished in book form.

p. 162 SONGS TUNELESS

Printed in *The Indianapolis Journal,* March 7, 1880; published in *Spirk and Wunk Rhymes,*

Rounds and Catches in THE FLYING ISLANDS OF THE NIGHT—1900, THE LOCKERBIE BOOK—1911.

p. 165   SISTER JONES'S CONFESSION

Printed in *The Indianapolis Journal,* March 10, 1880; published in GREEN FIELDS AND RUNNING BROOKS—1892.

p. 166
THE DEAD JOKE AND THE FUNNY MAN

Printed in *The Indianapolis Journal,* March 19, 1880; hitherto unpublished in book form.

p. 167   SLEEP

Printed in *The Indianapolis Journal,* March 21, 1880; published in GREEN FIELDS AND RUNNING BROOKS—1892, THE LOCKERBIE BOOK—1911.

p. 168   ONE ANGEL

Printed in *The Indianapolis Journal,* March 24, 1880; hitherto unpublished in book form.

p. 170   LAUGHTER

Printed in *The Indianapolis Journal,* April 3, 1880; published in *Spirk and Wunk Rhymes, Rounds and Catches* in THE FLYING ISLANDS OF THE NIGHT—1900, SONGS O' CHEER—1905, THE LOCKERBIE BOOK—1911.

p. 171   AN INVOCATION

Printed in *The Indianapolis Journal,* April 4, 1880; hitherto unpublished in book form.

p. 172   FROM BELOW

Printed in *The Indianapolis Journal,* April 5,
1880; hitherto unpublished in book form. The
poem also appeared in *The New York Sun,* April
11, 1880, with the title, *Alas! She Refused Him.*

p. 173   GLAMOUR

Printed in *The Indianapolis Journal,* April 11,
1880; hitherto unpublished in book form.

p. 175   SILENCE

Printed in *The New York Sun,* April 11, 1880;
published in Afterwhiles—1887, Old-Fashioned
Roses—1888, The Lockerbie Book—1911.

p. 176   PUCK

Printed in *The New York Sun,* April 18, 1880;
published in Old-Fashioned Roses—1888.

p. 177   A MORTUL PRAYER

Printed in *The New York Sun,* April 25, 1880,
with the title, *A Skeptic's Prayer;* published in
Neghborly Poems—1891. The original version
has been completely revised in the character and
spelling of "Benj. F. Johnson of Boone" and five
lines have been added at the end of the poem.

p. 179   A ROUGH SKETCH

Printed in *The Indianapolis Journal,* April 30,
1880; published in Afterwhiles—1887.

p. 180 · GRANDFATHER SQUEERS

This poem was printed in sections in *The Kokomo Tribune* as follows: p. 183, l. 17, to p. 184, l. 6, May 1, 1880, with the title, *My Grandfather Squeers;* p. 182, ll. 5-12, May 15, 1880, with the title, *His Grandpa;* p. 180, l. 11, to p. 181, l. 6, May 22, 1880, with the title, *The Elderly Squeers;* p. 181, l. 15, to p. 182, l. 4, May 29, 1880, with the title, *Squeers—The Ancient;* p. 183, ll. 9-16, June 12, 1880, with the title, *The Antique Squeers.* Published in RHYMES OF CHILDHOOD—1890, CHILD-RHYMES—1898. When the skit was put into book form the first and other lines were changed so as to ascribe it to The Raggedy Man.

p. 185 MY LADDIE WI' THE BASHFU' GRACE

Printed in *The Indianapolis Journal,* May 2, 1880, with the subtitle, *Imitated;* hitherto unpublished in book form.

p. 186 A TRESS OF HAIR

Printed in *The Indianapolis Journal,* May 9, 1880; hitherto unpublished in book form.

p. 188 IN A BOX

Printed in *The Indianapolis Journal,* May 14, 1880; published in NYE AND RILEY'S RAILWAY GUIDE—1888, PIPES O' PAN AT ZEKESBURY (Homestead Edition)—1898, THE LOCKERBIE BOOK—1911.

p. 189 THE PASSING OF A HEART

Printed in *The Kokomo Tribune,* May 15, 1880,

with the title, *Just With Your Hands;* published in
GREEN FIELDS AND RUNNING BROOKS—1892, LOVE-
LYRICS—1899, THE LOCKERBIE BOOK—1911.

p. 190   AN OLD-TIMER

Printed in *The Indianapolis Journal,* May 16,
1880; published in ARMAZINDY—1894, THE LOCK-
ERBIE BOOK—1911. The poem was "suggested by
a painting from the brush of Walter Seis," a Craw-
fordsville, Indiana, artist.

p. 192   ERE I WENT MAD

Printed in *The Indianapolis Journal,* May 18,
1880, with the title, *Yrsule;* published in *Spirk and
Wunk Rhymes, Rounds and Catches* in THE FLY-
ING ISLANDS OF THE NIGHT—1900, THE LOCKER-
BIE BOOK—1911.

p. 194   O HER BEAUTY

Printed in *The Indianapolis Journal,* May 20,
1880; hitherto unpublished in book form.

p. 195   THE SUMMER-TIME

Printed in *The Kokomo Tribune,* May 22, 1880,
signed "John C. Walker"; published in SONGS OF
SUMMER—1908. The ecstasy of this poem portrays
Mr. Riley's delight in the summer, his favorite season.

p. 197   SONG OF PARTING

Printed in *The Indianapolis Journal,* May 23,
1880; published in *Spirk and Wunk Rhymes,*

Rounds and Catches in THE FLYING ISLANDS OF THE NIGHT—1900, SONGS OF HOME—1910, THE LOCKERBIE BOOK—1911.

p. 198 THE WANDERING JEW

Printed in *The Indianapolis Journal,* May 28, 1880; published in AFTERWHILES—1887, GREEN FIELDS AND RUNNING BROOKS—1892, THE LOCKERBIE BOOK—1911.

p. 200 THE USED-TO-BE

Printed in *The Indianapolis Journal,* June 3, 1880; published in POEMS HERE AT HOME—1893, THE LOCKERBIE BOOK—1911.

p. 202 AT UTTER LOAF

Printed in *The Indianapolis Journal,* June 13, 1880, with the title, *Sans Souci;* published in GREEN FIELDS AND RUNNING BROOKS—1892, SONGS O' CHEER—1905, THE LOCKERBIE BOOK—1911.

p. 204 MY OLD FRIEND

Printed in *The New York Sun,* June 13, 1880; hitherto unpublished in book form.

p. 206 KISSING THE ROD

Printed in *The Indianapolis Journal,* June 17, 1880; published in PIPES O' PAN AT ZEKESBURY—1888, SONGS O' CHEER—1905, THE LOCKERBIE BOOK—1911. In harmony with the message of this poem were Mr. Riley's words to a friend in adversity: "No mortal condition is better than the one He seems to weigh you down with. In my *own* case I am coming every day to see clearer the gracious uses of adversity.—Simply, it is not adversity.—It is the very kindest—tenderest—most loving and most helpful touch of the hand Divine."

p. 207   THE RIVAL

Printed in *The Kokomo Tribune,* June 19, 1880; published in GREEN FIELDS AND RUNNING BROOKS —1892, LOVE-LYRICS—1899, THE LOCKERBIE BOOK —1911. The title of the poem originally was *The Rivals* and the first two stanzas formerly read:—

> I loved once, and when Death came by I hid
>   Away my face,
> And all my sweetheart's tresses I undid
>   To make my hiding-place.
>
> And so the dread shade passed unheeding; and
>   I hastened then
> To smooth the lifted brow and shielding hand,
>   And kiss my love again.

p. 208   THE LIGHT OF LOVE

Printed in *The Indianapolis Journal,* June 20, 1880, with the title, *Song;* published in *Spirk and Wunk Rhymes, Rounds and Catches* in THE FLYING ISLANDS OF THE NIGHT—1900, SONGS O' CHEER —1905, THE LOCKERBIE BOOK—1911.

p. 209   LET SOMETHING GOOD BE SAID

Printed in *The New York Sun,* June 20, 1880, with the title, *Something Good;* published in HOME-FOLKS—1900, SONGS O' CHEER—1905, THE LOCKERBIE BOOK—1911. The poem was written in abiding affection for one of the author's friends.

p. 210   THE OLD HAND-ORGAN

Printed in *The Indianapolis Journal,* June 23, 1880; hitherto unpublished in book form.

p. 211   HOME AT NIGHT

Printed in *The Indianapolis Journal,* June 26, 1880; published in GREEN FIELDS AND RUNNING BROOKS—1892, LOVE-LYRICS—1899, THE LOCKERBIE BOOK—1911. Originally the poem was entitled *Kate* and began with the following stanza, since discarded:—

> When languid cattle low, and all
> The land is dim with evenfall,
> I know my Kate is waiting me
> Expectantly—Expectantly.

p. 212   A DREAM OF INSPIRATION

Printed in *The Indianapolis Journal,* June 27, 1880; published without a title in *Spirk and Wunk Rhymes, Rounds and Catches* in THE FLYING ISLANDS OF THE NIGHT—1900, SONGS OF SUMMER—1908, A SUMMER'S DAY AND OTHER POEMS—1911. The title now given is the one under which the verse originally appeared. The first line was later used as the title.

p. 213   THE PIPER'S SON

Printed in *The Indianapolis Journal,* July 1, 1880, with the heading, *Mother Goose Classically Rendered;* hitherto unpublished in book form.

p. 214   HIS LAST PICTURE

Printed in *The Indianapolis Saturday Herald,*

July 3, 1880, with the title, *In Memoriam—John W. Love;* published in MORNING—1907, THE LOCKER-BIE BOOK—1911. These lines were written in memoriam of John W. Love, an Indianapolis artist who was a friend of the author.

p. 216   A VARIATION

Printed in *The Indianapolis Journal,* July 4, 1880; published in LOVE-LYRICS—1899, in *Spirk and Wunk Rhymes, Rounds and Catches* in THE FLYING ISLANDS OF THE NIGHT—1900, THE LOCKERBIE BOOK—1911.

p. 218   THERE IS A NEED

Printed in *The Indianapolis Journal,* July 5, 1880; hitherto unpublished in book form.

p. 219   TO A SKULL

Printed in *The Indianapolis Journal,* July 7, 1880; published in POEMS HERE AT HOME—1893, THE LOCKERBIE BOOK—1911.

p. 221   THE VOICES

Printed in *The Indianapolis Journal,* July 9, 1880, with the title, *Voices;* published in ARMA-ZINDY—1894, THE LOCKERBIE BOOK—1911. Stanza 1 read in the early version:—

> Down in the night I hear them—
> The voices of things unknown;
> That murmur, and mumble, and chuckle,
> And whisper, and sob, and moan.

Stanzas 2, 3 and 4 are not found in the early version. Line 1, stanza 8 was:—

To the strange, mysterious murmur

Line 2, stanza 9 was:—

Of a vision once beheld.

p. 223   MY HENRY

Printed in *The Kokomo Tribune,* July 10, 1880, signed "John C. Walker"; published in ARMAZINDY —1894.

p. 225   LOVE'S AS BROAD AS LONG

Printed in *The Indianapolis Journal,* July 11, 1880; hitherto unpublished in book form.

p. 227   LOCKERBIE STREET

Printed in *The Indianapolis Journal* July 12, 1880; published in AFTERWHILES—1887, OLD-FASHIONED ROSES—1888, THE LOCKERBIE BOOK—1911. On the evening prior to the appearance of these verses in *The Indianapolis Journal,* Mr. Riley took a rambling walk about town, during the course of which he came upon a corner marked with the quaint words, "Lockerbie Street." The name fascinated him at once, and the "cool shady" street itself, with its brick walks and quiet dirt roadway and old-fashioned homes, had a peculiar charm. He walked through the street with lingering steps, and saw the people sitting on the porches or on the lawns, children playing about, and flowers in the yards. To a bachelor "who had no home and no children and no flowers," it stood for all that was homelike and lovely. "As I walked back to the office, I repeated every time my feet went down, 'Lockerbie Street — Lockerbie Street — Lockerbie Street'—and I couldn't get the words out of my head. That night I wrote the poem and it appeared in the morning paper. When I reached my desk that day I found it covered with flowers sent me by the people of Lockerbie Street, who had read the verses that morning."

Twelve years later he came to live in this charming sequestered spot, which has ever since been his home.

p. 229 THE OLD, OLD WISH

Printed in *The Indianapolis Journal,* with the title, *The Old Wish,* July 14, 1880; published in RHYMES OF CHILDHOOD—1890, THE LOCKERBIE BOOK—1911.

p. 231 A LIFE-LESSON

Printed in *The Indianapolis Journal,* July 25, 1880; published in AFTERWHILES—1887, OLD-FASHIONED ROSES—1888, RHYMES OF CHILDHOOD—1890, CHILD-RHYMES—1898, THE LOCKERBIE BOOK—1911.

p. 232 A WATER-COLOR

Printed in *The Indianapolis Journal,* with the title, *A Bit of Nature,* July 30, 1880; published in GREEN FIELDS AND RUNNING BROOKS—1892, THE LOCKERBIE BOOK—1911.

p. 233 UNKNOWN FRIENDS

Printed in *The Indianapolis Journal,* July 31, 1880; hitherto unpublished in book form.

p. 234   THE SONG OF YESTERDAY

Printed in *The Indianapolis Journal,* with the
title, *Yesterday,* August 1, 1880; published in the
prose sketch, *At Zekesbury,* in PIPES O' PAN AT
ZEKESBURY—1888, RHYMES OF CHILDHOOD—1890,
SONGS OF HOME—1910, THE LOCKERBIE BOOK—
1911. Part II was added when the poem was incorporated into RHYMES OF CHILDHOOD. Part IV
originally read as follows:—

> But yesterday!
> O, Blooms of May,
> And summer-roses, where away?
> O, lips of red,
> On kisses fed,
> Where have thy lisps and laughter fled?
>
> My head is bowed
> As in a cloud
> Of snow—"O, Age!" I cry aloud.
> "Take back your tears
> And doubts and fears,
> And render up my youthful years!"
>
> And Yesterday,—
> I kneel and pray
> That He who gives and takes away,
> Will hold for me
> Some part of thee
> To gladden all eternity.

p. 238   AN END

Printed in *The Indianapolis Journal,* August 6,
1880; hitherto unpublished in book form.

p. 239   HER CHOICE

Printed in *The Indianapolis Journal,* August 9,
1880; hitherto unpublished in book form.

p. 240   OUR OWN

Printed in *The Indianapolis Journal,* August 13,
1880; published in ARMAZINDY—1894, SONGS OF
HOME—1910, THE LOCKERBIE BOOK—1911.

p. 241   THE DRUM

Printed in *The New York Sun,* August 15, 1880;
published in PIPES O' PAN AT ZEKESBURY—1888,
THE LOCKERBIE BOOK—1911.

p. 244   A CASE IN PINT

Printed in *The Indianapolis Journal,* August 16,
1880; hitherto unpublished in book form.

p. 247   OLE BULL

Printed in *The Indianapolis Journal,* August 19,
1880, with the subtitle, *Dead in Bergen, Norway,
August 18, 1880;* hitherto unpublished in book form.
Mr. Riley heard the famous violinist during his
tour through America just prior to his death.

p. 248   A WRAITH OF SUMMER-TIME

Printed in *The Indianapolis Journal,* August 22,
1880; published in GREEN FIELDS AND RUNNING
BROOKS—1892, SONGS OF SUMMER—1910, THE
LOCKERBIE BOOK—1911.

p. 249   JACK THE GIANT-KILLER

Printed in *The Indianapolis Journal,* with the
title, *A Bad Boy's Version of "Jack the Giant-*

Killer," August 27, 1880; published in Green
Fields and Running Brooks—1892.

p. 251 REQUIESCAT

Printed in *The Indianapolis Journal,* August 28,
1880; hitherto unpublished in book form.

p. 253 AT SEA

Printed in *The Indianapolis Journal,* August 29,
1880; published in Home-Folks—1900, Songs of
Home—1910, The Lockerbie Book—1911.

p. 254 SOMEP'N COMMON-LIKE

Printed in *The New York Sun,* August 29, 1880;
hitherto unpublished in book form.

p. 255 BLIND

Printed in *The Indianapolis Journal,* September
12, 1880; published in Green Fields and Running
Brooks—1892, The Lockerbie Book—1911.

p. 263 JUST AS OF OLD

Printed in *The Indianapolis Journal,* September
19, 1880; published in Green Fields and Running
Brooks—1892, The Lockerbie Book—1911.

p. 264 THE PRAYER PERFECT

Printed in *The Indianapolis Journal,* with the
title, *Amen,* September 20, 1880; published in
Rhymes of Childhood—1890, Songs o' Cheer—

1905, The Lockerbie Book—1911, The Prayer Perfect and Other Poems—1912.

p. 265 MONSIEUR LE SECRETAIRE

Printed in *The Indianapolis Journal,* September 21, 1880; hitherto unpublished in book form. These lines to John Clark Ridpath were published without a title, under his poem, *Madame La Secretaire.* Cf. *Lines to Perfesser John Clark Ridpath,* Vol. IV, and *John Clark Ridpath,* Vol. V.

p. 266 A PHANTOM

Printed in *The Indianapolis Journal,* September 26, 1880; hitherto unpublished in book form.

p. 267 WHAT REDRESS

Printed in *The Indianapolis Journal,* with the title, *Redress,* September 29, 1880; published in Armazindy—1894, The Lockerbie Book—1911.

p. 268 A LOST LOVE

Printed in *The Kokomo Tribune,* October 2, 1880; published in His Pa's Romance—1903, The Lockerbie Book—1911.

p. 270 LET US FORGET

Printed in *The Indianapolis Journal,* October 17, 1880; published in Green Fields and Running Brooks—1892, Love-Lyrics—1899, The Lockerbie Book—1911.

p. 271 THE SHOEMAKER

Printed in *The Indianapolis Journal*, October 18, 1880; published in GREEN FIELDS AND RUNNING BROOKS—1892. The original version contained a stanza between 1 and 2 which has since been omitted :—

> We love to praise the shoemaker,
>   And not alone because
> Alway he waxeth tenderer
>   In warmth of our applause;
> But, more than any artisan,
>   We glory in his art
> Who ne'er, to help the under man
>   Neglects the upper part.

p. 273 IN THE CORRIDOR

Printed in *The Indianapolis Journal*, October 29, 1880; hitherto unpublished in book form.

p. 274 SUSPENSE

Printed in *The Indianapolis Journal*, October 31, 1880; published in GREEN FIELDS AND RUNNING BROOKS—1892, LOVE-LYRICS—1899, THE LOCKERBIE BOOK—1911.

p. 275 A NONSENSE RHYME

Printed in *St. Nicholas*, November, 1880; published in RHYMES OF CHILDHOOD—1890, THE LOCKERBIE BOOK—1911.

p. 278 LOUELLA WAINIE

Printed in *The Indianapolis Journal*, November 1, 1880; hitherto unpublished in book form.

p. 280   FOR YOU

Printed in *The Indianapolis Journal,* November 7, 1880; published in *Spirk and Wunk Rhymes, Rounds and Catches* in THE FLYING ISLANDS OF THE NIGHT—1900, SONGS OF HOME—1910, THE LOCK-ERBIE BOOK—1911.

p. 281   MY FIRST SPECTACLES

Printed in *The Indianapolis Journal,* November 8, 1880; published in POEMS HERE AT HOME—1893.

p. 282   THE TEXT

Printed in *The Indianapolis Journal,* November 15, 1880; hitherto unpublished in book form.

p. 283   AN OUT-WORN SAPPHO

Printed in *The Indianapolis Journal,* with the title, *Tired,* November 21, 1880; published in LOVE-LYRICS—1899, THE FLYING ISLANDS OF THE NIGHT—1900, THE LOCKERBIE BOOK—1911. The poem has been revised throughout; lines 6-9, stanza 3, page 285, were

> 'Twas all of earthly things I had acquired,
> And 'twas enough, since it had snapped the thong
> That bound its passion to the pulse of wrong
> Whose throbbings made me tired.

Stanza 1, page 286, was not in the early version.

p. 287   WILLIAM BROWN

Printed in *The Indianapolis Journal,* November 28, 1880; hitherto unpublished in book form. The heroic invariably moved Mr. Riley. *The Journal* printed the following "Exchange" as an introduction to the poem:

Another of those occasions which show the stuff locomotive engineers are made of occurred in California last month. A special train from Sacramento, with a regiment of soldiers on board, was turned from the track by an open switch at Oakland Point, and sent off the wharf into the bay. Rather, the whole train would have made the plunge, but for the self-sacrificing pluck of the engineer, who stood at his post, reversed and applied the air-brakes so effectually that only the engine and tender went into the water. He lost his life, of course, being imprisoned in the cab with no chance of escape after leaving the wharf. He might have jumped and saved himself but thought only of the 308 lives behind him. The decision of the moment saved them and sealed his fate. He bore the plain name of William Brown.

p. 289   THE NINE LITTLE GOBLINS

Printed in *The Indianapolis Journal*, December 5, 1880, with the title, *Nightmare,* under the general heading, *A Fact, A Fancy, and An Imitation;* published in RHYMES OF CHILDHOOD—1890, CHILD-RHYMES—1898. In the original version lines 5 and 6, stanza 4, page 290, were

Yet still you are doomed to dream this way,
Till along towards dusk of the Judgment Day—

p. 291   WHY

Printed in *The Indianapolis Journal*, December 5, 1880, as No. 2 under the general heading, A *Fact, A Fancy, and An Imitation;* hitherto unpublished in book form.

p. 292   THE TOUCH OF LOVING HANDS

Printed in *The Indianapolis Journal*, December

5, 1880, as No. 3, under the general heading *A Fact, A Fancy, and An Imitation;* hitherto unpublished in book form. An imitation of Tennyson.

p. 293   THE OLD SCHOOL-CHUM

Printed in *The Indianapolis Journal,* December 6, 1880, with the title, *Tears;* published in ARMA-ZINDY—1894, THE LOCKERBIE BOOK—1911. The poem was originally written in the first instead of the third person.

p. 295   A CUP OF TEA

Printed in *The Indianapolis Journal,* December 12, 1880; published in GREEN FIELDS AND RUNNING BROOKS—1892.

p. 297   TO THE SERENADER

Printed in *The Indianapolis Journal,* December 13, 1880, with the title, *The Serenade;* published in GREEN FIELDS AND RUNNING BROOKS—1892, THE LOCKERBIE BOOK—1911.

p. 298   WHAT A DEAD MAN SAID

Printed in *The Indianapolis Journal,* December 18, 1880; published in POEMS HERE AT HOME—1893, THE LOCKERBIE BOOK—1911.

p. 300   A TEST

Printed in *The Indianapolis Journal,* December 18, 1880; hitherto unpublished in book form.

p. 301   A SONG FOR CHRISTMAS

Printed in *The Indianapolis Journal,* December

25, 1880; hitherto unpublished in book form. This
poem was written in affectionate imitation of Longfellow. The following stanzas have been omitted :—

Between stanzas 4 and 5 :—

> Of the wide-eyed look of wonder,
>   And the gurgle of baby-glee,
> As the infant hero wrestles
>   From the smiling father's knee,—
>
> Sing the delights unbounded
>   Of the home unknown of care,
> Where wealth as a guest abideth,
>   And want is a stranger there.

Between stanzas 6 and 7 :—

> And one for the outcast mother,
>   And one for the sin-defiled
> And hopeless sick man dying,
>   And one for his starving child.

p. 303   SUN AND RAIN

This poem is taken from an old undated manuscript. It has been impossible to determine when it
was written, except that it belongs to this general
period.

p. 304   WITH HER FACE

This poem is taken from an old undated manuscript. It has been impossible to determine when it
was written, except that it belongs to this general
period.

p. 305   MY NIGHT

From an undated newspaper clipping. Though
no definite date can be found for this poem, Mr.
Riley says it belongs to this general period.

p. 306   THE HOUR BEFORE THE DAWN

From an old manuscript evidently written about this time.

p. 307   THE OLD YEAR AND THE NEW

Printed in *The Indianapolis Journal,* January 1, 1881; published in GREEN FIELDS AND RUNNING BROOKS—1892, LOVE-LYRICS—1899, THE LOCKERBIE BOOK—1911.

p. 309   GOOD-BY, OLD YEAR

Printed in *The Indianapolis Journal,* January 3, 1881; hitherto unpublished in book form.

p. 310   AS CREATED

Printed in *The Indianapolis Journal,* January 14, 1881, under the title, *The Human Heart;* published in HOME-FOLKS—1900, SONGS OF HOME—1910, THE LOCKERBIE BOOK—1911. A most typical expression of Mr. Riley's creed.

p. 311   SOMEDAY

Printed in *The Indianapolis Journal,* January 20, 1881; published in POEMS HERE AT HOME—1893, THE LOCKERBIE BOOK—1911.

p. 312   FALSE AND TRUE

Printed in *The Indianapolis Journal,* January 22, 1881; hitherto unpublished in book form.

p. 313 A BALLAD FROM APRIL

Printed in *The Indianapolis Journal,* January 23, 1881; hitherto unpublished in book form.

p. 315 WHEN DE FOLKS IS GONE

Printed in *The Indianapolis Journal,* January 23, 1881, signed "John C. Walker"; published in AFTER-WHILES—1887.

p. 316 THE TWINS

Printed in *The Indianapolis Journal,* January 26, 1881; published in GREEN FIELDS AND RUNNING BROOKS—1892, SONGS O' CHEER—1905.

p. 318 THE ORCHARD LANDS OF LONG AGO

Printed in *The Indianapolis Journal,* January 30, 1881; published in THE BOSS GIRL—1885, OLD-FASHIONED ROSES—1888, RHYMES OF CHILDHOOD —1890, SKETCHES IN PROSE—1891, FARM-RHYMES —1901, THE LOCKERBIE BOOK—1911, KNEE DEEP IN JUNE AND OTHER POEMS—1912.

p. 320 BRUDDER SIMS

Printed in *The Indianapolis Journal,* January 30, 1881; signed "John C. Walker"; hitherto unpublished in book form.

p. 321 DEFORMED

Printed in *The Indianapolis Journal,* February 4, 1881; hitherto unpublished in book form.

p. 323   WHILE THE MUSICIAN PLAYED

Printed in *The Indianapolis Journal,* February 6,
1881; published in GREEN FIELDS AND RUNNING
BROOKS—1892, SONGS OF SUMMER—1908, THE
LOCKERBIE BOOK—1911.

p. 325   FAITH

Printed in *The Indianapolis Journal,* February
15, 1881; hitherto unpublished in book form. These
verses appeared under the general heading, *There's
Something in the Way You Put the Question,* and
were preceded by the following lines by an unknown
author copied from *The New York Sun:*—

DOUBT

The waves are breaking on the beach,
    And on the soft, wet sand I stand;
Far out as human sight can reach
    The ocean stretches from the land.

What is it that ye seek to reach?
    Cold, curling, crested waves, that rear
An uninterpretable speech
    Along the endless, wreck-strewn shore?

"Oh, tell me that beyond the sea
    A peaceful harbor lies!" I wail.
A mocking echo answers me,
    "Lies! lies!" and I can see no sail.

p. 326   BE OUR FORTUNES AS THEY MAY

Printed in *The Indianapolis Journal,* February
16, 1881, with the title, *The New Friend;* published,
under the title, *Envoy,* in HIS PA'S ROMANCE—1903,
THE LOCKERBIE BOOK—1911.

p. 327 A HINT OF SPRING

Printed in *The Indianapolis Journal,* February 23, 1881; published in NYE AND RILEY'S RAILWAY GUIDE—1888, HIS PA'S ROMANCE—1903.

p. 328 LAST NIGHT—AND THIS

Printed in *The Indianapolis Journal,* February 27, 1881; published in GREEN FIELDS AND RUNNING BROOKS—1892, AFTERWHILES (not in first edition) —1898, LOVE-LYRICS—1899, THE LOCKERBIE BOOK —1911.

p. 329 LITTLE GIRLY-GIRL

Printed in *The Indianapolis Journal,* March 2, 1881; published in RHYMES OF CHILDHOOD—1890, THE LOCKERBIE BOOK—1911. The following two stanzas completed the original version:—

> O to see you ere the ghost
>   Of the golden past grows dimmer!
> But my lips are hushed almost,
>   And my eyes hold but the glimmer
> Of a fairy face another
> Kisses—till his kisses smother
>   All my hopes in one wild swirl!—
>   Good-by! little Girly-Girl!
>
> But if ever any time,—
>   When the summer birds are singing,
> And the honeysuckles climb
>   Up the weeping willows, flinging
> Down their fragrance in the shadow
> Where I'm sleeping in the meadow—
>   You will come, the waves will purl
>   Gladly, "Little Girly-Girl!"

p. 330 **CLOSE** THE BOOK

Printed in *The Indianapolis Journal,* March 6, 1881; published in Poems Here at Home—1893, The Lockerbie Book—1911.

p. 331 THE MOTHER SAINTED

Printed in *The Kokomo Tribune,* March 19, 1881; the poem entire, with the title, *Kate Kennedy Philips,* not hitherto published in book form; stanzas 4, 5 and 6, under the title, *The Mother Sainted,* published in Home-Folks—1900, The Lockerbie Book—1911. Kate Kennedy Philips was the wife of Mr. Riley's beloved friend, Charles H. Philips, editor of *The Kokomo Tribune.* She was a noble woman of distinguished cultivation, and had been from childhood the playmate and sweetheart of the man she married.

p. 334 THE LOST THRILL

Printed in *The Indianapolis Journal,* March 20, 1881; hitherto unpublished in book form.

p. 335 REACH YOUR HAND TO ME

Printed in *The Indianapolis Journal,* March 20, 1881; published in Green Fields and Running Brooks—1892, Songs of Home—1910, The Lockerbie Book—1911.

p. 336 WE MUST GET HOME

The original version, consisting of four stanzas (2, 4, 6 and 8) was printed in *The Indianapolis*

Journal, March 27, 1881, with the title, *Der Heim-gang;* a fifth stanza (stanza 11) was added and the poem with the title, *Home,* contributed to a booklet published by the Indianapolis Flower Mission, a charitable institution, in November, 1890; published in GREEN FIELDS AND RUNNING BROOKS—1892, with the title, *The Home-Going.* Stanzas 1, 3, 5, 7, 9, 10 and 12 were published under the present title in MORNING—1907, SONGS OF HOME—1910. In THE LOCKERBIE BOOK—1911, the two poems were combined to form the present version.

p.340   MABEL

Printed in *The Indianapolis Journal,* April 8, 1881; published in RHYMES OF CHILDHOOD—1890, THE LOCKERBIE BOOK—1911. Mary Mabel Hough, the author's little cousin, was the daughter of Judge William Rufus and Matilda C. Hough, of Green-field. She was born February 18, 1874, and died April 6, 1881.

p. 342   AT DUSK

Printed in *The Indianapolis Journal,* April 10, 1881; hitherto unpublished in book form.

p. 343 ANOTHER RIDE FROM GHENT TO AIX

Printed in *The Indianapolis Journal,* April 16, 1881; hitherto unpublished in book form. The sub-title read *Respectfully Dedicated to Robert J. Bur-dette,* a fellow lecturer at the time. The difficulties Mr. Riley had in making trains was always a sub-ject for jest between him and his friends. See *The Train Misser,* Vol. III.

Cf. Robert Browning's *How They Brought the Good News from Ghent to Aix*.

p. 347 THE RIPEST PEACH

Printed in *The Indianapolis Journal*, April 17, 1881; published in AFTERWHILES—1887, OLD-FASHIONED ROSES—1888, THE LOCKERBIE BOOK—1911. This is the first poem to which the poet signed his full name,—James Whitcomb Riley. The earlier form of signature, J. W. or James W. Riley, had caused no end of confusion with "that host of Rileys named in good old-fashioned manner after the justly celebrated John Wesley."

p. 348 BEDOUIN

Printed in *The Indianapolis Journal*, April 24, 1881; published in GREEN FIELDS AND RUNNING BROOKS—1892, THE LOCKERBIE BOOK—1911.

p. 349 A DITTY OF NO TONE

Printed in *The Indianapolis Journal*, April 30, 1881, with the title, *Summertime;* published in GREEN FIELDS AND RUNNING BROOKS—1892, THE LOCKERBIE BOOK—1911. The title of this poem was suggested by a passage in Keats's *Ode on a Grecian Urn:*—

> Heard melodies are sweet, but those unheard
> Are sweeter; therefore, ye soft pipes, play on;
> Not to the sensual ear, but, more endeared,
> Pipe to the spirit ditties of no tone:

Mr. Riley wrote this poem on a fly-leaf of his own volume of Keats.

p. 351   THE SPHINX

Printed in *The Indianapolis Sentinel,* May 8,
1881; published in AFTERWHIES—1887, THE LOCK-
ERBIE BOOK—1911.

p. 352   MOTHER GOOSE

Printed in *Wide-Awake,* June, 1881; published
in RHYMES OF CHILDHOOD—1890, THE LOCKERBIE
BOOK—1911.

p. 353   IN THE HEART OF JUNE

Printed in *The Indianapolis Journal,* June 25,
1881; hitherto unpublished in book form.

p. 354   MY BOY

Printed in *The Indianapolis Journal,* July 2,
1881; hitherto unpublished in book form.

p. 355   THE ASSASSIN

Written in July, 1881; first printed in *The Indianapolis Journal,* June 23, 1883; published in *Spirk
and Wunk Rhymes, Rounds and Catches* in THE
FLYING ISLANDS OF THE NIGHT—1900. On July 2,
1881, Charles Guiteau shot President Garfield. This
poem, though not printed until long afterward, was
inspired by the horror and revolt caused by the
assassination.

p. 356   BECAUSE

Printed in *The Indianapolis Journal,* July 9, 1881;
hitherto unpublished in book form.

p. 357 PANSIES

Printed in *The Indianapolis Journal,* July 12, 1881; published in RHYMES OF CHILDHOOD—1890, SONGS OF SUMMER—1908, THE LOCKERBIE BOOK—1911.

p. 358 BABY'S DYING

Printed in *The Indianapolis Journal,* July 16, 1881; published in RHYMES OF CHILDHOOD—1890, THE LOCKERBIE BOOK—1911.

p. 359 AN EMPTY GLOVE

Printed in *The Indianapolis Journal,* July 19, 1881; published in ARMAZINDY—1884, THE LOCKERBIE BOOK—1911.

p. 361 TO THE CRICKET

Printed in *The Indianapolis Journal,* July 21, 1881; published in OLD-FASHIONED ROSES—1888.

p. 362 THE OLD-FASHIONED BIBLE

Printed in *The Indianapolis Journal,* July 26, 1881; hitherto unpublished in book form. The form is that of Samuel Woodworth's *The Bucket.* It may be observed that Mr. Riley's grandfather, John Marine, was a Methodist minister and that the bulky, leather-bound family Bible, with the latter's many entries of birth, death and marriage, is still preserved.

p. 364 THE LAND OF USED-TO-BE

Printed in *Wide-Awake,* August, 1881; published

in RHYMES OF CHILDHOOD—1890, WHILE THE
HEART BEATS YOUNG—1906, THE RUNAWAY BOY—
1908, THE LOCKERBIE BOOK—1911.

p. 367   JUST TO BE GOOD

Printed in *The Indianapolis Journal,* August 8,
1881, with the title, *Enough;* published in GREEN
FIELDS AND RUNNING BROOKS—1892, SONGS OF
HOME—1911, THE LOCKERBIE BOOK—1911, THE
PRAYER PERFECT AND OTHER POEMS—1912.

p. 368   A LOUNGER

Printed in *The Indianapolis Journal,* August 13,
1881; published in GREEN FIELDS AND RUNNING
BROOKS—1892, THE LOCKERBIE BOOK—1911.

p. 369   MR. WHAT'S-HIS-NAME

Printed in *The Indianapolis Journal,* August 20,
1881; published in GREEN FIELDS AND RUNNING
BROOKS—1892.

p. 372   UNCOMFORTED

Printed in *The Indianapolis Journal,* August 23,
1881; hitherto unpublished in book form. Cf. *Lelloine:* p. 113.

p. 374   MY WHITE BREAD

Printed in *The Indianapolis Journal,* September
10, 1881; published in POEMS HERE AT HOME—
1893.

p. 376 HE AND I

Printed in *The Indianapolis Journal,* September 10, 1881; published in ARMAZINDY—1894, LOVE-LYRICS—1899, SONGS OF SUMMER—1908, THE LOCKERBIE BOOK—1911.

p. 378 FROM A BALLOON

Printed in *The Indianapolis Journal,* September 12, 1881; published in POEMS HERE AT HOME—1893, THE LOCKERBIE BOOK—1911. When these lines were written the balloon was under popular discussion. A balloonist, known as "Professor King," advertised a passage from Minneapolis to New York, but later abandoned his journey because of a gale that weakened the mechanism.

p. 379 A TWINTORETTE

Printed in *The Indianapolis Journal,* September 17, 1881, with the title, *A Rondel;* published in ARMAZINDY—1894, THE LOCKERBIE BOOK—1911.

p. 380 WHAT THEY SAID

Printed in *The Indianapolis Journal,* October 22, 1881; hitherto unpublished in book form.

p. 382 AFTER THE FROST

Printed in *The Indianapolis Journal,* October 22, 1881; hitherto unpublished in book form.

p. 383 CHARLES H. PHILIPS

Printed in *The Indianapolis Journal,* November 7,

1881, with the title, *C. H. P.;* hitherto unpublished in book form. Charles H. Philips, editor of *The Kokomo Tribune,* was Mr. Riley's friend and ally through the trying strenuous years of 1878-1881. When the former established *The Home Department* of his paper, he was ambitious to make it distinguished throughout the state for literary excellence. Mr. Riley did his utmost to help him attain his purpose and under the pseudonym of "John C. Walker" contributed some of his best verse.

Philips had a generous likable personality, distinguished for high spirit and ambition. The fate of his last year was distressingly pathetic. His wife died in March and his first and only baby a few months later, leaving him in a broken-hearted solitude to which he soon succumbed. Cf. poems in memory of the father and wife, *T. C. Philips,* Vol. I, p. 263; *The Mother Sainted,* Vol. II, p. 331.

p. 385   WHEN IT RAINS

Printed in *The Indianapolis Journal,* November 19, 1881; hitherto unpublished in book form.

p. 387   AN ASSASSIN

Printed in *The Indianapolis Journal,* November 23, 1881; hitherto unpublished in book form. This poem portrays the intense feeling aroused through the recent assassination of President Garfield by Charles Guiteau.

p. 388   BEST OF ALL

Printed in *The Indianapolis Journal,* December 3, 1881; hitherto unpublished in book form.

p. 389 MR. SILBERBERG

Printed in *The Indianapolis Journal,* December 17, 1881, with the title, *The Jew Father;* published in NYE AND RILEY'S RAILWAY GUIDE—1888, HIS PA'S ROMANCE—1903.

p. 391 THE HEREAFTER

Printed in *The Indianapolis Journal,* December 24, 1881, with the title, *Our Fortunes;* published in GREEN FIELDS AND RUNNING BROOKS—1892, SONGS O' CHEER—1905, THE LOCKERBIE BOOK—1911.

p. 392 THE LOVING CUP

Written in January, 1882; published in HOME-FOLKS—1900, THE LOCKERBIE BOOK—1911. These lines refer to the occasion of Mr. Riley's entertainment by the Papyrus Club of Boston, where in January, 1882, he was the joint guest of John Boyle O'Reilly and Dr. Franc A. Harris.

p. 394 EROS

Published in *The Indianapolis Journal,* January 21, 1882; published in ARMAZINDY—1894.

p. 395 THE QUIET LODGER

Printed in *The Indianapolis Journal,* January 28, 1882; published in GREEN FIELDS AND RUNNING BROOKS—1892, THE LOCKERBIE BOOK—1911.

p. 399 THE BROOK-SONG

Printed in *The Indianapolis Journal,* February 4,

1882, with the title, *The Brook;* published in THE
BOSS GIRL—1885, OLD-FASHIONED ROSES—1888,
RHYMES OF CHILDHOOD—1890, SKETCHES IN PROSE
—1891, FARM-RHYMES—1901, THE LOCKERBIE
BOOK—1911, THE PRAYER PERFECT AND OTHER
POEMS—1912.

p. 401   BIN A-FISHIN'

Printed in *The Indianapolis Journal,* April 22,
1882; hitherto unpublished in book form.

p. 403 UNCLE DAN'L IN TOWN OVER SUNDAY

Printed in *The Indianapolis Journal,* April 22,
1882; hitherto unpublished in book form.

p. 405   EMERSON

Printed in *The Indianapolis Journal,* April 29,
1882; published in HOME-FOLKS—1900, THE LOCK-
ERBIE BOOK—1911.

p. 406   YOUR VIOLIN

Printed in *The Indianapolis Journal,* May 20,
1882; published in POEMS HERE AT HOME—1893,
THE LOCKERBIE BOOK—1911. The author played
his favorite instrument, the violin, intuitively.

p. 408   SOLDIERS HERE TO-DAY

Printed in *The Indianapolis Journal,* May 24,
1882; hitherto unpublished in book form. Mr. Riley
read the poem at an entertainment for the benefit of
a Decoration Day fund.

p. 412   A WINDY DAY

Printed in *The Indianapolis Journal,* June 3,
1882; published in ARMAZINDY—1894, THE LOCK-
ERBIE BOOK—1911.

p. 413   SHADOW AND SHINE

Printed in *The Indianapolis Journal,* June 10,
1882; hitherto unpublished in book form. The title
is a favorite phrase. Cf. *In the Dark:*

> For the thoughts that come in the shadows
> Never come in the shine.

p. 414   THE OLD SWIMMIN'-HOLE

Printed in *The Indianapolis Journal,* June 17,
1882; signed "Benj. F. Johnson of Boone"; published in THE OLD SWIMMIN'-HOLE AND 'LEVEN
MORE POEMS—1883, OLD-FASHIONED ROSES—1888,
NEGHBORLY POEMS—1891, SONGS OF SUMMER—
1908, THE OLD SWIMMIN'-HOLE AND OTHER
POEMS—1912.

This poem was the first to appear with the pseudonym, "Benj. F. Johnson of Boone." With its
successors of the same signature, it came to form
the author's earliest volume, entitled THE OLD
SWIMMIN'-HOLE AND 'LEVEN MORE POEMS, which
was later incorporated into NEGHBORLY POEMS. The
introduction of the former consisted of the first
two paragraphs of the following preface, which appeared as here given in NEGHBORLY POEMS:—

As far back into boyhood as the writer's memory may
intelligently go, the "country poet" is most pleasantly re-
called. He was, and is, as common as the "country fiddler,"
and as full of good old-fashioned music. Not a master of
melody, indeed, but a poet, certainly—

> "Who, through long days of labor,
>   And nights devoid of ease,
> Still heard in his soul the music
>   Of wonderful melodies."

And it is simply the purpose of this series of dialetic studies to reflect the real worth of this homely child of nature, and to echo faithfully, if possible, the faltering music of his song.

In adding to this series, as the writer has, for many years, been urged to do, and answering as steadfast a demand of Benj. F. Johnson's first and oldest friends, it has been decided that this further work of his be introduced to the reader of the volume as was the old man's first work to the reader of the newspaper of nearly ten years ago.

Directly, then, referring to the Indianapolis "Daily Journal,"—under whose management the writer had for some time been employed,—from issue of date June 17, 1882, under editorial caption of "A Boone County Pastoral," this article is herewith quoted:

Benj. F. Johnson, of Boone county, who considers the Journal a "very valubul" newspaper, writes to inclose us an original poem, desiring that we kindly accept it for publication, as "many neghbors and friends is astin' him to have the same struck off."

Mr. Johnson thoughtfully informs us that he is "no edjucated man," but that he has, "from childhood up tel old enugh to vote, allus wrote more er less poetry, as many of an albun in the neghborhood can testify." Again, he says that he writes "from the hart out"; and there is a touch of genuine pathos in the frank avowal, "Thare is times when I write the tears rolls down my cheeks."

In all sincerity, Mr. Johnson, we are glad to publish the poem you send, and just as you have written it. That is its greatest charm. Its very defects compose its excellence. You need no better education than the one from which emanates "The Old Swimmin'-Hole." It is real poetry, and all the more tender and lovable for the unquestionable evidence it bears of having been written "from the hart out." The only thing we find to—but hold! Let us first lay the poem before the reader:

Here followed the poem, "The Old Swimmin'-Hole," entire—the editorial comment ending as follows:

The only thing now, Mr. Johnson—as we were about to observe—the only thing we find to criticise, at all rela-

tive to the poem, is your closing statement to the effect
that "It was wrote to the tune of 'The Captin with his
Whiskers!'" You should not have told us that. O Rare
Ben. Johnson!

A week later, in the "Journal" of date June 24th, followed this additional mention of "Benj. F. Johnson, of
Boone":

It is a pleasure for us to note that the publication of the
poem of "The Old Swimmin'-Hole," to which the Journal,
with just pride, referred last week, has proved almost
as great a pleasure to its author as to the hosts of delighted
readers who have written in its praise, or called to per-
sonally indorse our high opinion of its poetic value. We
have just received a letter from Mr. Johnson, the author,
inclosing us another lyrical performance, which in many
features even surpasses the originality and spirit of the
former effort. Certainly the least that can be said of it is
that it stands a thorough proof of our first assertion, that
the author, though by no means a man of learning and
profound literary attainments, is none the less a true poet
and an artist. The letter, accompanying this later am-
aranth of blooming wildwood verse, we publish in its en-
tirety, assured that Mr. Johnson's many admirers will be
charmed, as we have been, at the delicious glimpse he gives
us of his inspiration, modes of study, home-life, and sur-
roundings.

"To the Editer of the Indianoplus Jurnal:

"Respected Sir—The paper is here, markin' the old
swimmin'-hole, my poetry which you seem to like so well.
I joy to see it in print, and I thank you, hart and voice, fer
speakin' of its merrits in the way in which you do. I am
glad you thought it was real poetry, as you said in your
artikle. But I make bold to ast you what was your idy in
sayin' I had ortent of told you it went to the tune I spoke
of in my last. I felt highly flatered tel I got that fur. Was
it because you don't know the tune referred to in the letter? Er wasent some words spelt right er not? Still ef
you hadent of said somepin' aginst it Ide of thought you
was makin' fun. As I said before I well know my own un-
edjucation, but I don't think that is any reason the feelin's
of the soul is stunted in theyr growth however. 'Juge not
less ye be juged,' says The Good Book, and so say I, ef I
thought you was makin' fun of the lines that you
done me the onner to have printed off in sich fine
style that I have read it over and over again in the paper
you sent, and I would like to have about three more ef

you can spare the same and state by mail what they will
come at. All nature was in tune day before yisterday when
your paper come to hand. It had ben a-raining hard fer
some days, but that morning opened up as clear as a whissel. No clouds was in the sky, and the air was bammy
with the warm sunshine and the wet smell of the earth
and the locus blossoms and the flowrs and pennyroil and
boneset. I got up, the first one about the place, and went
forth to the plesant fields. I fed the stock with lavish
hand and wortered them in merry glee, they was no bird
in all the land no happier than me. I have jest wrote a
verse of poetry in this letter; see ef you can find it. I
also send you a whole poem which was wrote off the very
day your paper come. I started it in the morning I have
so feebly tride to pictur' to you and wound her up by sup-
pertime, besides doin' a fare day's work around the place.

"Ef you print this one I think you will like it better than
the other. This ain't a sad poem like the other was, but
you will find it full of careful thought. I pride myself
on that. I also send you 30 cents in stamps fer you to take
your pay out of fer the other papers I said, and also fer
three more with this in it ef you have it printed and oblige.
Ef you don't print this poem, keep the stamps and send me
three more papers with *the other one* in—makin' the sum
totul of six (6) papers altogether in full. Ever your true
friend,   BENJ. F. JOHNSON.

"N. B.—The tune of this one is 'The Bold Privateer.'"

Here followed the poem, "Thoughts Fer The Discur-
aged Farmer";—and here, too, fittingly ends any comment but that which would appear trivial and gratuitous.

Simply, in briefest conclusion, the hale, sound, artless,
lovable character of Benj. F. Johnson remains, in the
writer's mind, as from the first, far less a fiction than a
living, breathing, vigorous reality.—So strong, indeed, has
his personality been made manifest, that many times, in
visionary argument with the sturdy old myth over certain
changes from the original forms of his productions, he has
so incontinently beaten down all suggestions as to a less
incongruous association of thoughts and words, together
with protests against his many violations of poetic method,
harmony, and grace, that nothing was left the writer but
to submit to what has always seemed—and in truth still
seems—a superior wisdom of dictation.   J. W. R.

Indianapolis, July, 1891.

Cf. *A Caller from Boone,* and the bibliographical notes, Vol. VI.

"The old swimmin'-hole" at Greenfield, where the boy Riley and his chums went swimming, lies a short walk to the east of the town. The actual spot used in the old days is now high and dry meadow-land, but the diverted current near by forms a new though shallow swimming place still enjoyed by the children of Greenfield.

p. 417

THOUGHTS FER THE DISCURAGED FARMER

Printed in *The Indianapolis Journal,* June 24, 1882, signed "Benj. F. Johnson of Boone"; published in THE OLD SWIMMIN'-HOLE AND 'LEVEN MORE POEMS—1883, OLD-FASHIONED ROSES—1888, NEGHBORLY POEMS—1891, FARM-RHYMES—1901, SONGS OF SUMMER—1908, WHEN THE FROST IS ON THE PUNKIN AND OTHER POEMS—1911. Cf. previous note.

It should be observed that the dialect of the Benj. F. Johnson poems reproduces the old farmer's spelling as well as his speech, as for instance where he writes the word "heart" as he supposes it to be spelled,—"hart." In this connection a paragraph from the author's preface to the Homestead Edition of his works, referring to NEGHBORLY POEMS, may be read with interest:—

No further word seems due or pertinent, at this new beginning and first volume, unless it be to emphasize the strictly conscientious intent of the real writer to be lost wholly in the personality of this book's supposed old Hoosier author, Benj. F. Johnson. Therefore the generous reader is fervently invoked to regard the verse-product herein not only as the work of the old man's mind, but as the patient labor of his unskilled hand and pen as well—and the whole of it thus reverently held unedited, save in simplest essential marks of punctuation,—these conditions only changing in his prose sketch, *An Old Settler's Story,* which primitive chronicle is, for apparent reasons, retold as by a pleased listener to the originally impromptu narration.

The series of poems signed "Benj. F. Johnson" was claimed by three different persons before the author revealed his identity.

p. 420   A GOOD-BY

Printed in *The Indianapolis Journal,* June 24, 1882; published in Armazindy—1894, The Lockerbie Book—1911.

p. 421   A SUMMER'S DAY

Printed in *The Indianapolis Journal,* July 1, 1882, with the subtitle, *And Its Effects on Benj. F. Johnson of Boone;* published in The Old Swimmin'-Hole and 'Leven More Poems — 1883, Old-Fashioned Roses—1888, Neghborly Poems— 1891, Songs o' Cheer—1905, Songs of Summer —1908, A Summer's Day and Other Poems— 1911.

p. 424   A HYMB OF FAITH

Printed in *The Indianapolis Journal,* July 8, 1882, under the editorial caption, *Mr. Johnson of Boone Is Inspired to Write a Hymn;* published in The Old Swimmin'-Hole and 'Leven More Poems— 1883, Neghborly Poems—1891, Songs o' Cheer— 1905. In the early print the following lines are used as a subtitle :—

So ran the honest, earnest prayer
Of old Ben Johnson pleading there.

The following editorial comment appeared with the poem:—

In a letter now lying before us, Mr. Johnson of Boone says: "It will be an undoubtabel surprise to you to git the poem I now send to you herein enclosed; but I was a-readin' one which starts out 'God moves in a mysterious way His wunders to purform,' and the idy struck me that I could write off somepin in that style which would express a man's views that still ain't no perfesser of religion, ner a member of no church, as I take fer granted Watts was when he wrote that and the rest of all his hymb-book full of the same kind," etc., etc.

Briefly, we would acknowledge, in reply to Mr. Johnson, that the poem sent is something of a surprise to us, but none the less a pleasant one. But while we place it with pride before Mr. Johnson's admirers, we beg to inform the author that while Mr. Watts has given to hymnal literature a numberless array of very creditable verses, the poem referred to by Mr. Johnson is by no means a Watts production. *God Moves in a Mysterious Way* was written by William Cowper, the English poet, who was as little a pretender of religion, perhaps, as Mr. Johnson himself, since that famous poem was written immediately upon returning from an unsuccessful attempt at suicide—an idea which seems never to have occurred to Mr. Watts.

p. 427   AT BROAD RIPPLE

Printed in *The Indianapolis Journal,* July 20, 1882; published in Pipes o' Pan at Zekesbury—1888, Songs o' Cheer—1905, The Lockerbie Book —1911. When the poem was written Broad Ripple was a very small town on the banks of White River north of Indianapolis.

p. 429   THE COUNTRY EDITOR

Printed in *The Indianapolis Journal,* July 21,

1882, with the title, *The Editor;* published in Morning—1907, The Lockerbie Book—1911. Mr.
Riley's own experiences on county papers in Greenfield, Anderson and Kokomo furnished the spice
for these lines.

p. 430   WORTERMELON TIME

Printed in *The Indianapolis Journal,* July 22,
1882, signed "Benj. F. Johnson of Boone"; published in The Old Swimmin'-Hole and 'Leven
More Poems—1883, Neghborly Poems—1891,
Farm-Rhymes—1901, The Prayer Perfect and
Other Poems—1912. The boy Riley's delight in
the watermelon dates back to that early time when
he first saw a mischievous little barefoot comrade
of his slip behind an unsuspecting farmer on his
heaping wagon-load of melons and topple a choice
fruit into the street, where it broke with a great
hearty bump. The farmer did not see the culprit
still hiding behind the wagon and so generously
gave the melon to the crowd of little fellows "op-
portunely" gathered about. Such incidents, it is
not amiss to add, became a common occurrence in
the poet's boyhood.

p. 434   A SONG OF THE CRUISE

Printed in *The Indianapolis Journal,* July 22,
1882; published in Poems Here at Home—1893,
The Lockerbie Book—1911.

p. 435   MY PHILOSOFY

Printed in *The Indianapolis Journal,* July 29,
1882, with the title, *Mr. Johnson of Boone Philoso-*

phizes; signed "Benj. F. Johnson"; published in THE OLD SWIMMIN'-HOLE AND 'LEVEN MORE POEMS — 1883. OLD-FASHIONED ROSES — 1888, NEGHBORLY POEMS—1891, SONGS O' CHEER—1905. In introducing the reading of a poem in dialect, Mr. Riley once drew the character of "Benj. F. Johnson" in a very striking manner when he asked the audience to "listen to the philosophy of an old Hoosier farmer. Many of you have known him. He was not a man of books. His library was small. First, there was the Book of Books, then probably *The Prince of the House of David,* or the *The Pillar of Fire,* then, if any history at all, a dog's-eared history of a true American like himself—Daniel Boone; then we might find *The Scottish Chiefs,* and, if any poetry, it would likely be a hymnal or Watts' hymns."

p. 438   WHEN AGE COMES ON

Printed in *The Indianapolis Journal,* July 29, 1882; published in GREEN FIELDS AND RUNNING BROOKS—1892, LOVE-LYRICS—1899, THE LOCKERBIE BOOK—1911.

p. 439   THE CIRCUS-DAY PARADE

Printed in *Wide-Awake,* August, 1882; published in RHYMES OF CHILDHOOD—1890, CHILD-RHYMES —1898, THE LOCKERBIE BOOK—1911. The following sketch by Mr. Riley is from an old newspaper clipping [undated]:

THE CIRCUS SEASON

We all know all about the day and date of the circus, however little we may know of the date our next month's rent is due. The flaming circus posters have for long weeks been looming up between us and forgetfulness. Their *"mene, mene!"* blazoned on the wall has been too dazzlingly legible for our weak vision to escape. "The Greatest Show on Earth" is not to be ignored, and so it does not hesitate to speak its great white truths in letters taller than a man.

The first "stand of bills" that met our eyes we passed by carelessly, perhaps, for it was twilight, haply, and we were weary with a long day's work, and knew that supper would be waiting; besides, there was a crowd of wrangling boys about the men in crusted overalls that slashed the boards with spattering paste, and balanced on their long slim brushes the big blank sheets that by their dexterous touches were unfurled, reversed, and flattened out and fastened down in great square segments into such glowing scenes as made the boy-heart thrill with rapture through and through—yes, and our own old hearts were stirred, perchance, as for a moment's pause we mechanically peered to catch the name of this "Colossal Aggregation of Unprecedented—" something that had abruptly turned the corner of the fence and gone prospecting down another street. And then we turned and went our separate way, musing, doubtless, on the opulence of license peculiarly the circus and menagerie-artist's own, and we could still recall from farthest youth how bigger, wilder, redder-mouthed and yellower the lions were on paper than they were in dens; how streaked the zebras, and how grinnier the hyenas; how fat and plump and smooth were all the elephants as pictured on the bills, and yet how poor and flabby in real life, when the show got round—and even yet do we recall a striking observation regarding this peculiar fact, made by the village shoemaker, who, as the street procession slowly passed his shop, scornfully remarked that there was "enough extra hide on that elephant to cover two elephants, if it was only properly 'lasted'."

But this is circus season, and now as in the long ago, the old anticipations are revived. We shall studiously refrain from any outward demonstrations of interest or expectancy, and yet we can but feel and know that, however craftily we may disguise the fact from all the prying world, the still small voice secreted on the person of our inner self will cry up through our grave and dignified exterior: I want to see the band-wagon come in; I want to hear the music and the drums; I want to catch the gleam and glare and glamour of it all; I want the glittering pageant

to go by with clash and clang and din of jubilee, and flourish of glad trumpets, and the palpitating throb and roll of
reverberating drums; I want proud-prancing horses, silk-
en-tailed and silver-maned, and mottled glossily with
blended brown and white, and so caparisoned and richly
trapped and prankt, the plumed knights and ladies that
come riding two and two seem spilled out of some
old fairy tale before my dreamy eyes. And then the van
of the menagerie! My fancy shall unlock each lidded
cage as it goes jostling past. Oh, this day is a dream from
which I never want to wake! I want to be the same fool-
boy I used to be. I want to run away from school again,
and carry water for the animals. I want to see 'em lay
the old ring out, and plow it up, and smooth and level it,
and pat the old ridge round it like an endless grave wherein
are buried all my truant fears of the sure punishment
awaiting me at home. I want to just don't care for anything, only the clean, white, naked glory of the day!—to
be again the bold bad boy that no one but my mother ever
loved—the same neglected, wayward little boy that runs at
large to-day, with ragged knees, torn coat and unkempt
hair—but such a boy as Keats—had he but lived in this
delightful age—might have embalmed in lines like these:—

Season of myths and monster circuses,
  Close bosom friend of the maturing son!—
Suggesting he had better study less,
  And lie more to his folks and have more fun!—
To play ingeniously all sorts of pranks
  To gain his wanton ends on circus day—
Run off from school, and in the street parade
  March, envying the drummers as they play,
High-toned and charioted, with dangling shanks,
Until he thinks the whole world should give thanks
For Adam Forepaugh's gorgeous cavalcade.

Who hath not seen him oft amid the throng
  About the side-show entrance, warily
Watching a chance to slip in, right or wrong,
  To envy the "fat boy's" obesity,
Or wish himself a "living skeleton,"
  Or, "armless," to fire pistols with his toes—
Or had white hair, pink eyes, and purple tights,
  With lots of silver spangles on his clothes?
Could "swallow" swords as there he sees it done
In the "ten mammoth shows combined in one"—
Delight of all conceivable delights!

p. 442 WHEN THE FROST IS ON THE PUNKIN

Printed in *The Indianapolis Journal*, August 5,
1882, signed "Benj. F. Johnson"; published in THE
OLD SWIMMIN'-HOLE AND 'LEVEN MORE POEMS—
1883, OLD-FASHIONED ROSES—1888, NEGHBORLY
POEMS—1891, FARM-RHYMES—1901, WHEN THE
FROST IS ON THE PUNKIN AND OTHER POEMS—
1911. The last stanza was not added until the pub-
lication of OLD-FASHIONED ROSES—1888. See Vol.
I, p. 382; see preceding note on *The Old Swimmin'-
Hole*, p. 535.

p. 445 THAT NIGHT

Printed in *The Indianapolis Journal*, August 5,
1882; published in NYE AND RILEY'S RAILWAY
GUIDE—1888.

p. 446 THE BAT

Printed in *The Indianapolis Journal*, August 12,
1882; published in PIPES O' PAN AT ZEKESBURY—
1888, THE LOCKERBIE BOOK—1911.

p. 447
ON THE DEATH OF LITTLE MAHALA ASHCRAFT

Printed in *The Indianapolis Journal*, August 16,
1882, with the title, *Lines on the Death of Little
Mahala Ashcraft*, signed "Benj. F. Johnson"; published in THE OLD SWIMMIN'-HOLE AND 'LEVEN
MORE POEMS—1883, OLD-FASHIONED ROSES—1888,
RHYMES OF CHILDHOOD—1890, NEGHBORLY POEMS
—1911.

p. 450 THE MULBERRY TREE

Printed in *The Indianapolis Journal*, August 19,

1882, signed "Benj. F. Johnson"; published in THE OLD SWIMMIN'-HOLE AND 'LEVEN MORE POEMS—1883, NEGHBORLY POEMS—1891, SONGS OF HOME—1910. Mr. Riley says: "This poem is a childhood memory. A mulberry tree, if fruit-bearing, was left standing when the field was cleared, and so it invariably stood alone in a meadow or pasture. Its branches hung low and a rail was placed in the fork of the tree to give help to the boys climbing up. I recall vividly how we used to scramble across the meadow for such a tree. Not until we were directly beneath it did the birds, voraciously feeding on the berries, notice us, and then they flew away with a great whir and confusion. And oh, the fruit of that tree! It had a strange deliciousness. —Simply,—it was to all other fruits as maple syrup is to all other syrups."

p. 452   AUGUST

Printed in *The Indianapolis Journal,* August 19, 1882; published in NYE AND RILEY'S RAILWAY GUIDE—1888.

p. 453
TO MY OLD FRIEND, WILLIAM LEACHMAN

Printed in *The Indianapolis Journal,* August 26, 1882, signed "Benj. F. Johnson"; published in THE OLD SWIMMIN'-HOLE AND 'LEVEN MORE POEMS—1883, OLD-FASHIONED ROSES—1888, NEGHBORLY POEMS—1891, SONGS OF HOME—1910. Squire William Leachman lived a few miles west of Greenfield, near Philadelphia, Indiana. The author "knew of him as a loved and very much respected man."

Stanzas 10 and 12 refer to real occurrences of the early days near Greenfield.

p. 458   THE GUIDE

Printed in *The Indianapolis Journal*, August 26, 1882; hitherto unpublished in book form. These lines are in imitation of Joaquin Miller.

At the time of his death, February 17, 1913, Mr. Riley said: "The poetical voice of Joaquin Miller always made me think of the gallant blare of a trumpet from the very battlements of inspiration."

In his study of poetry Mr. Riley has often followed the course approved by Stevenson and played what the latter termed "the sedulous ape" to a great number of writers, though never so continuously as to jeopardize his own individuality. When reading inspired the mood he wrote in imitation of Longfellow, Keats and others of the masters, nor did he hesitate to reiterate the beauties and powers of the poets of his own day whom he loved, such as Lee O. Harris, Mr. Bliss Carman and Mr. Madison Cawein. Compare the two following poems and their notes; also *Old Hec's Idolatry*, p. 12, *Some Imitations*, Vol. VI.

p. 461   SUTTER'S CLAIM

Printed in *The Indianapolis Journal*, August 26, 1882; published in NYE AND RILEY'S RAILWAY GUIDE—1888. An imitation of Bret Harte.

p. 463   DOLORES

Printed in *The Indianapolis Journal*, August 26, 1882; published in ARMAZINDY—1894, THE LOCKERBIE BOOK—1911. An imitation of Swinburne.

p. 464   MY FIDDLE

Printed in *The Indianapolis Journal,* September

2, 1882, signed "Benj. F. Johnson"; published in THE OLD SWIMMIN'-HOLE AND 'LEVEN MORE POEMS—1888, NEGHBORLY POEMS—1891, SONGS O' CHEER—1905. At one time Mr. Riley played the violin with zest and talent. One of his brother's letters to him thus mentioned the "fiddle" which he played: "I can not recall just when you got the old violin you learned on, but, if I am not mistaken, it was greatly improved by being smashed to smithereens and afterwards mended."

In connection with Mr. Riley's love for the violin, these lines on a piano player are of interest. They were sent to his friend, Melville Clark.

> You've wrought a miracle—you've made
>   A pianist of me—
> Indeed no master ever played
>   Beyond the mastery
> Of this device—And twice and thrice
>   The price in ready tin
> I'll pay you for some like device
>   That plays the violin.

The printing of these lines brought an eager letter from a violin-player company, which had actually contrived a reclining mechanism to manipulate the violin!

Mr. Riley gave other evidence of his fondness for the violin in the following sketch [an undated newspaper clipping] written about this time:—

THE OLD FIDDLER

The old fiddler! What has become of him? The dear old-fashioned fiddler of our boyhood, who occupied the one chair in the kitchen, and beat such hearty time to his music on the bare oak floor! Ah! what a whole-soled thing his foot was! No dainty and inaudible pulsation of the toe, but a genuine flat-footed "stomp" whose boisterous palpitations, heard high above the rhythmic patter of the

dancers' feet, jarred and jingled the little eight-by-ten
window-panes at his back, and thrilled the very china on
the "cubbard" shelves. There were no affectations about
the old fiddler. His instrument was just a fiddle; he a fiddler, and for this homely reason alone, perhaps, it was
the youthful listener felt the vibrant current of the tune
in every vein, with such ecstatic spurts of inward mirth-
fulness at times he felt his very breath sucked up in swirls
of the intoxication, as one may feel it lost and caught up,
swooping down the breezy atmosphere in a long pendulat-
ing grape-vine swing. And what quaint old tunes he
played; *Guilderoy* was the name of one of them; *The Gray
Eagle* was another, and *The Forked Deer,* and *Old Fat
Gal*—all favorites. Telling the names over again, in fancy
they all come whisking back—the bottom of the present is
knocked out, and peering through a long maelstromic vista,

> "We see the fiddler, through the dusk,
>   Twanging the ghost of 'Money Musk';"

we see the dancers skurrying to their places—we feel once
more encased in our "best" clothes—and all mechanically
our hand goes up again to stroke the bear-greased roach
upon our forehead ere we salute our blushing "pardner,"
who, for all her shining face and chaste and rustling toilet,
has still an odor of dish-water clinging to the mellow
hands we love to clasp no less. We pause impatiently as
the fiddler slowly "rosums up" again; we hear the long pre-
monitory rasping of the bow; we see the old man cross
his legs with the old-time abandon, and with a bewildering
flourish of wrist and elbow the frolicsome old tune comes
cantering over the strings like a gamesome colt down a
corduroy road, and then, "Salute your pardners! corners!
All hands round!" and away we go, too happy, happy,
happy, to recall the half of the long-vanished delight from
this old, hopeless and bald-headed standpoint of to-day, and
the magician—the maestro—the old fiddler whose deft
touches either lulled or fired our blood in those old days—
ah! where is he? We wander wearily in quest of him.
We do not find him at the banquet, the crowded concert
hall, the theater. They do not want him in the opera.
The orchestra would blush to have him there. In all the
wide, wide world he had not where to lay his head, and so
the old musician journeyed on, simply because—

"His instrument, perhaps, was made
Afar from classic Italy.

*   *   *   *   *   *

And yet we sadly, sadly fear
Such tunes we nevermore may hear;
Some were so sad, and some so gay—
The tunes Dan Harrison used to play."

p. 466   NORTH AND SOUTH

Printed in *The Indianapolis Journal,* September
2, 1882; published in GREEN FIELDS AND RUNNING
BROOKS—1892, THE LOCKERBIE BOOK—1911.

p. 468   THE DAYS GONE BY

Printed in *The Indianapolis Journal,* September
9, 1882; published in PIPES O' PAN AT ZEKESBURY—
1888. OLD-FASHIONED ROSES—1888, RHYMES OF
CHILDHOOD — 1890, CHILD-RHYMES — 1898, THE
LOCKERBIE BOOK—1911.

Stanza 3: In an interview, printed in *The Indianapolis Sentinel,* June 28, 1903, Mr. Riley said to
Charles Virgil Tevis:—

I can never efface from my memory the scenes of my
youth. They furnish both theme and inspiration for my
efforts. Without them I would be lost, for they are re-
sponsible for my being and are an integral part of my
existence. And they are vivid, ah, so vivid! Why, take,
for instance, the time long ago when I read the *Arabian
Nights.* Coal-oil had just been introduced in our town and
father had purchased a lamp, filled and ready for the
burning. I was reading the story of *Aladdin and the Won-
derful Lamp,* and had come to that part where the dis-
guised magician was shouting on the streets, "New lamps
for old! New lamps for old." I remember that I remarked the coincidence then. To this day, when I sniff
coal-oil, why, it's sweet as violets, for I think of Aladdin,
the first original IT. I see a huge iron door at my feet.

I see it raised, descend the narrow steps, hug my clothes tightly about me to avoid the awful death which will be my portion should they touch either wall, and then I pass through the caves of riches and find the jewels on the trees, and "the slave of the lamp." I can see his misty awfulness distinctly; I can hear his mighty voice as he bellows, "What would-st thou?"

p. 470   THE CLOVER

Printed in *The Indianapolis Journal,* September 16, 1882; signed "Benj. F. Johnson"; published in THE OLD SWIMMIN'-HOLE AND 'LEVEN MORE POEMS—1883, OLD-FASHIONED ROSES—1888, NEGH-BORLY POEMS—1891, FARM-RHYMES—1901, SONGS OF SUMMER—1908, WHEN THE FROST IS ON THE PUNKIN AND OTHER POEMS—1911. With this, the last of Benj. F. Johnson's poems, *The Journal* said editorially:

The Journal prints this morning the twelfth and last of the poems purporting to be by "Benj. F. Johnson of Boone county." This author is Mr. James Whitcomb Riley, whose original purpose was to write a series of twelve, giving them the nominal authorship he did in order the better to carry out his dialectic idea. How well the assumption has succeeded the country knows. Mr. Riley has written nothing among all his productions that has had so generous reception and wide reading as these poems. Those who have looked to *The Saturday Journal* for Benj. F. Johnson's quaint but truly poetic contributions, full of homely pictures and contented philosophy, will miss them from our columns, but they will be repaid with other literary work from Mr. Riley's muse.

Date Due

NOV 14 1988			